ABOUT ISLAND PRESS

Island Press, a nonprofit organization, publishes, markets, and distributes the most advanced thinking on the conservation of our natural resources—books about soil, land, water, forests, wildlife, and hazardous and toxic wastes. These books are practical tools used by public officials, business and industry leaders, natural resource managers, and concerned citizens working to solve both local and global resource problems.

Founded in 1978, Island Press reorganized in 1984 to meet the increasing demand for substantive books on all resource-related issues. Island Press publishes and distributes under its own imprint and offers these services to other nonprofit organizations.

Support for Island Press is provided by Apple Computers, Inc., Mary Reynolds Babcock Foundation, The Geraldine R. Dodge Foundation, The Educational Foundation of America, The Charles Engelhard Foundation, The Ford Foundation, The Glen Eagles Foundation, The George Gund Foundation, The William and Flora Hewlett Foundation, The Joyce Foundation, The J. M. Kaplan Fund, The John D. and Catherine T. MacArthur Foundation, The Andrew W. Mellon Foundation, The Joyce Mertz-Gilmore Foundation, The New-Land Foundation, The Jessie Smith Noyes Foundation, The J. N. Pew, Jr., Charitable Trust, Alida Rockefeller, The Rockefeller Brothers Fund, The Florence and John Schumann Foundation, The Tides Foundation, and individual donors.

ABOUT EAST-WEST CENTER

The East-West Center is a public, nonprofit educational institution with an international board of governors. Some two thousand research fellows, graduate students, and professionals in business and government each year work with the center's international staff in cooperative study, training, and research. They examine major issues related to population, resources and development, the environment, culture, and communication in Asia, the Pacific, and the United States. The center was established in 1960 by the U.S. Congress, which provides principal funding. Support also comes from more than twenty Asian and Pacific governments, as well as private agencies and corporations.

ECONOMICS OF PROTECTED AREAS

ECONOMICS OF PROTECTED AREAS

A NEW LOOK AT BENEFITS AND COSTS

JOHN A. DIXON
PAUL B. SHERMAN

EAST-WEST CENTER

WASHINGTON, D.C. □ COVELO, CALIFORNIA

The authors are grateful for permission to include the following previously copyrighted materials:

Table 13, on pp. 170–71, is from *Social Cost-Benefit Analysis of the Korup Project, Cameroon*, by H. J. Ruitenbeek. London: World Wide Fund for Nature, 1989.
Table 14, on pp. 180–81, is from *Inventory of Caribbean Marine and Coastal Protected Areas*. Washington, D.C.: Organization of American States/Natural Park Service, 1988.
Figure 1, on page 10, is from *UN List of National Parks and Protected Areas*. Gland, Switzerland: International Union for the Conservation of Nature (IUCN), 1985.
Figure 6, on page 87, is from *Thailand Natural Resources Profile*. Bangkok: Thailand Development Research Institute, 1987.

Library of Congress Cataloging-in-Publication Data

Dixon, John A., 1946–
    Economics of protected areas : approaches and applications / John A. Dixon and Paul B. Sherman.
        p.   cm.
    ISBN 1-55963-033-7 (alk. paper). — ISBN 1-55963-032-9 (pbk. : alk. paper)
    1. Natural areas—Developing countries—Management. 2. Natural areas—Economic aspects—Developing countries. 3. Natural areas—Government policy—Developing countries. 4. Conservation of natural resources—Developing countries. I. Sherman, Paul B. II. Title.
    QH77.D44D59   1990
    333.7'2'091724—dc20   90-33702
                                                                   CIP

Printed on recycled, acid-free paper

Manufactured in the United States of America

10 9 8 7 6 5 4 3 2 1

For Frani, David, and Peter
J.A.D.

For my parents
P.B.S.

Contents

PART II: APPLICATIONS

List of Figures

List of Tables

Foreword

The establishment and management of parks and protected areas are receiving increasing attention worldwide. Whether spurred by the realization that protected areas play a valuable role in maintaining our inheritance of biological diversity or by a desire to reap economic benefits from tourism and other direct uses, national governments are analyzing the various alternative ways of establishing and managing these areas.

Many different groups are supporting these efforts. In some cases national or international nongovernmental bodies have taken a leading role. Bilateral and multilateral aid agencies, including the U.S. Agency for International Development (U.S.A.I.D.), have also become actively involved. A.I.D.'s environmental and natural resource policy is based on the premise that environmental protection and conservation of natural resources are essential for sustained economic development. Maintenance of ecosystems, habitats, and species of animals and plants is one component of this policy. Such resources are important not only for their current and potential economic value but also for their role in maintaining ecological processes, such as soil and water regulation, within and beyond their boundaries.

While there are many reasons to conserve biological resources, economic arguments carry the greatest weight with development planners in multilateral and bilateral aid agencies and host country governments. As the true economic value of protected areas is difficult to measure, the short-term economic gains from exploiting biological resources frequently appear more attractive than the long-term benefits of conservation.

In response to the scarcity of applied economic analyses to support a more far-sighted view of the role of protected areas in developing countries, U.S.A.I.D. supported a study carried out by John Dixon and Paul Sherman to address these issues. Although the initial study focused on protected areas in Thailand, this book has expanded the analysis to consider the issues more broadly and has included illustrative material from countries around the world.

This book should help governmental and nongovernmental agencies to consider the benefits and costs associated with maintaining protected areas and to deal with the difficult task of assigning them monetary values. The general approach to estimating costs and benefits, outlined in Chapters 1 to 4, applies to protected areas everywhere. The second half of the book examines how this approach can be applied to protected areas in settings as diverse as Thailand and Indonesia on the one hand and Africa, the Caribbean, and Australia on the other.

As pressures on the world's remaining natural areas will only increase in the future, the development of better economic valuation approaches is both essential and timely. We are pleased that the East-West Center has pursued publication of this book and that U.S.A.I.D.'s initial support has helped make this possible.

MOLLY BOWER KUX
Environmental Coordinator
Bureau for Asia and the Near East
U.S. Agency for International Development

Preface

This book grew out of a desire to apply the techniques of economic analysis to a particularly difficult, yet important, topic— protected areas and their establishment and management. Our goal was twofold: to develop a general economic approach to this subject and to illustrate the application of the approach with actual cases.

The book developed in two stages. The first stage was a research project focusing on Thailand that resulted in a study titled *Economics of Protected Areas in Developing Countries: General Issues and Examples from Thailand*. This report was then revised and expanded to present a broader analysis of the issues and offer illustrations from protected areas around the world; the result is the present volume.

We have benefited from the comments, suggestions, and support of numerous people and organizations. The impetus for the initial study came from Michael Philley of the Asia/Near East Bureau of U.S.A.I.D./Washington. Mr. Philley first proposed the project and then worked closely with us to develop a research plan and secure funding. Thailand was chosen as the site of the initial study for a number of reasons: it has an extensive and mixed protected-area system, it has a rapidly growing economy with increasing tourism and recreational demand for protected area services, and data were available for many of the aspects that interested us. After Mr. Philley's transfer overseas, A.I.D.'s support continued under Harvey van Veldhuizen, Stephen Lintner, and later Molly Kux and Kathryn Saterson. We are grateful for their contributions—both substantive and financial.

In Thailand we received valuable assistance from Nipon Tangtham (Department of Conservation) and Supachat Sukharomana (Department of Economics) at Kasetsart University. Both researchers prepared background papers on different aspects of protected areas in Thailand, assisted with field visits, and reviewed the draft manuscript. Officials of the National Parks Division and the Wildlife Conservation Division, Royal Forest Department, and staff at the U.S.A.I.D./Thailand Mission were consistently helpful during our visits to Thailand. We designed the survey reported in Chapter 6 in conjunction with Robert Dobias and other members of the related Beneficial Use Project, Thorani Tech; the survey was undertaken and tabulated by the latter group.

Earlier drafts of the manuscript were carefully reviewed by a number of people who provided detailed and useful comments. These reviews resulted in a major rewriting and reorganization of the book. Detailed comments were provided by Jeffrey McNeely, IUCN, Gland, Switzerland; Patrick Durst, Forestry Support Program, USDA Forest Service; Edward Barbier, IIED, London; and Robert Dobias, Thorani Tech, Bangkok, Thailand. At U.S.A.I.D., Kathryn Saterson and Molly Kux provided helpful and insightful comments.

In preparing Chapters 8 and 9 we benefited from the comments and materials provided by a number of persons and organizations. Arthur Heyman of the Organization of American States offered numerous references and detailed comments on much of the Caribbean material. Edward Towle of the Island Resources Foundation was similarly helpful, particularly in the case of the Virgin Islands National Park study. Jack Ruitenbeek, a consultant from Ottawa, Canada, allowed us to draw heavily on his study of Korup National Park in Cameroon. We are also indebted to Elizabeth Boo of the World Wildlife Fund, Washington, for the use of material on ecotourism in Latin America and the Caribbean and to Michael Wells, consultant to the World Bank, for the use of material on national parks in Indonesia. All of these people provided materials and reviewed drafts of the appropriate chapters. Although we could not report all the details of the various studies, this assistance was invaluable in allowing us to expand our analysis. We extend our sincere appreciation to all of them.

At the East-West Center, we benefited from comments by James Juvik and Regina Gregory. James Thorsell of IUCN, who spent the latter half of 1989 in residence at the East-West Center, also provided materials and helpful comments. We are also grateful to various East-West Center staff for their contributions: Mary Ruddle, Connie Kawamoto, and Anne Taylor typed the numerous drafts of this book, Laurel

Lynn Indalecio drew the figures, and Helen Takeuchi and Joy Teraoka provided valuable editorial assistance.

Writing and publishing a book is a long, complex process. In this case we were very fortunate to have the excellent support of Island Press. Charles Savitt, president of Island Press, has been a strong supporter of this project. Of special note is the superb editorial help provided by Barbara Dean, executive editor, who guided this book from initial concept through publication. Her attention to detail and her substantive suggestions have benefited us greatly. In this regard note should also be made of the very able assistance provided by Barbara Youngblood and Nancy Seidule of Island Press. Don Yoder, our copy-editor, deserves special thanks for his careful and insightful contributions.

We hope that this book demonstrates what can be accomplished using the tools of economic analysis. More can be done, however, in terms of evaluating the economic dimensions of protected area benefits and costs. Certainly this work is timely given the growing worldwide interest in protected areas and related biodiversity issues. We hope, as well, that the approach outlined here will be applied to protected areas in other countries, and that this book will stimulate others to carry out further work on this important topic.

JOHN A. DIXON
PAUL B. SHERMAN
Honolulu, 1990

Introduction

Natural areas—areas that remain relatively undisturbed by people and close to their natural state—are becoming an increasingly scarce resource in both developed and developing countries. This is particularly true if one excludes those areas that are either so inhospitable to people or so remote that opportunities for substantial human use are severely restricted. Mountains with perpetual snow cover, many desert areas, and the remote parts of a number of countries may all be superb natural areas, but they are not necessarily scarce or at risk. The natural areas of concern here are those that are in danger of conversion, areas that are becoming increasingly scarce.

The division between "remote" and "close" is obviously subjective and influenced by such factors as population density, accessibility, and level of development. The Mount Everest region in Nepal, for example, once very isolated and rarely visited, has become a victim of success. Now there is a major trekking and climbing industry in the area and the Sagarmatha National Park has been established to help manage this fragile environment. Major management problems include garbage and waste disposal and excessive firewood collection. Efforts are under way to work with the local residents to address these problems and maintain environmental quality while allowing a continuing yield of economic benefits from tourism and trekking.

The list of areas at risk is always changing. Technology and wealth can transform an inhospitable or "useless" environment to one that is habitable or useful—witness settlements in Alaska and Siberia or the

1

many arid areas now made habitable through irrigation. While these areas may have been viewed as uninhabitable a century ago, today they are the sites of major settlements. At the same time, these areas contain plant and wildlife resources that are now threatened by the development that has taken place.

Many of the most valuable natural areas remaining are located within the borders of developing countries, especially those in the tropics. These areas often contain a wide variety of genetic resources and support a number of essential ecological functions. This is true in all climatic zones, but genetic diversity often reaches a maximum in tropical settings (Myers 1983). Governments in these countries face the difficult decision of how best to use their natural areas. Should they be preserved intact? Should they be exploited for short-term profits? Should they be converted to another use such as agriculture? How should decisions be made?

One option is to keep natural areas relatively intact, thus preserving the flora and fauna they contain, providing opportunities for recreation, and maintaining the other benefits such areas provide. Establishing natural areas as parks or other types of protected areas is one means of preserving their benefits. Establishing protected areas is not without cost, however. If the areas are not in government hands, they must first be purchased or acquired. Once acquired, they must be managed and protected—often a difficult and expensive task. Moreover, groups that have traditionally used the resources in the now protected areas will suffer a loss. Finally, there is a cost in terms of alternative uses of the area that are no longer possible because of its protected status. The sum of all of these costs may be considerable.

Alternative uses of natural areas often appear extremely attractive. Many tropical forests, for example, contain vast amounts of valuable timber. Other areas can be converted to such uses as agriculture, grazing, or tree crops. In most cases, a traditional economic analysis would show that some alternative uses would provide greater financial returns than the modest direct returns from maintaining an area in its natural state. As a result, there is often substantial pressure to convert and exploit natural areas.

Apart from pressure on natural areas from formal development projects, in many countries an even greater threat is the slow encroachment by nearby residents and their extraction of resources. Whether done in an unsustainable manner (such as clearing for annual crop production on steep slopes) or in a sustainable fashion (such as collection of various minor forest products in wooded areas), these patterns of resource use are not easily stopped by mere creation of a protected area. The economic forces that motivated these patterns of resource use must be taken into account to provide effective protection. These questions too have a major economic dimension.

A financial analysis of the various alternative uses of an undeveloped natural area is often misleading. Since the financial analysis is designed only to examine costs and benefits as measured by market prices, it leaves out key factors that are not bought or sold. Many of the benefits of conserving natural areas are difficult to measure and are not exchanged in markets—consequently, the value of conserving, rather than developing, an area is often underestimated. This leads to a bias toward development and exploitive use of an area; the end result is that fewer natural areas are protected than would be the case if all the benefits of conservation were included in the economic analysis of alternative uses.

The bias toward exploitive use of natural areas is a classic example of what economists call market failure—as a result of incorrect signals from the market, an incorrect decision is made. The benefits of development are seen as large, the benefits from protection small. Since the benefits of protection are underestimated, the *costs* of protection in terms of development opportunities that must be given up (as well as government expenses to acquire and manage a protected area) appear considerable. As a result, a smaller amount of natural area is protected than would be the case if there were a full accounting of all the benefits and costs associated with each alternative land use.

A second major problem is the management of protected areas. Even where adequate amounts of land are given protected status, these areas often receive only limited funds for management—essentially because many of their benefits go unnoticed or are quite dispersed over time and space. Furthermore, since the government receives no compensation for many of these benefits, there may be little motivation to allocate the funds needed to ensure proper management and continued provision of these benefits.

Today, however, citizens and governments in both developed and developing countries are beginning to recognize the need to designate certain natural areas as parks or other types of protected areas such as wildlife sanctuaries or scenic reserves. In developed countries the need for protected areas is widely accepted, and many governments have taken appropriate measures not only to designate protected areas but also to provide funds for their management. In the United States, for example, the National Park Service manages more than 330 national parks, seashores, and other areas covering 32 million hectares. A record 290 million visitors used these facilities in 1987, and the annual operating budget for the service was about $740 million in 1988. In developing countries, however, even if the need for protected areas is recognized, budgetary constraints, poverty, and pressing social and economic needs all work against effective protection. The need for protected areas is especially important in the tropics, where the remaining forests are believed to hold up to half of the world's species of plants and animals (Myers 1983). In addition to protecting biological resources, maintaining sites as protected areas also provides benefits to nearby or downstream areas—improving watershed protection, for example, and maintaining ecological processes.

This book explains how economics can be used to help make decisions involving natural areas. Although we pay special attention to the situation in developing countries, the questions raised are important in all countries—rich and poor. The difference is a matter of degree of urgency and available resources. A number of issues are considered here: the justifications for designating protected areas, how to measure the benefits and costs of establishing and managing protected areas, and how governments can increase the benefits provided by protected areas, both to nearby residents and to the country as a whole.

Our main objective is to demonstrate how economics can be used to improve the decision-making process. The approach outlined here is aimed primarily at resource managers, planners, and analysts in national governments and aid agencies who must make hard decisions on land use and the allocation of funds for protected areas. By illustrating how economics can be incorporated into the decision-making process, better decisions can be made—decisions that take into account all the benefits and costs of the alternatives being considered, thus improving the effectiveness of a protected area system.

The book is divided into two parts. Part I takes a broad look at the economic issues associated with establishing and managing protected areas, especially in developing countries. Chapter 1 begins with a brief look at the history of protected areas and the types of protected areas found today. We then discuss the overall benefits and costs associated with protected areas. Chapter 2 addresses the issue of how to value the benefits of protected areas. After explaining why many of the benefits provided by protected areas are hard to value in monetary terms using market prices, we describe methods that can be used to overcome these difficulties and estimate both the market-based, financial value and the social-economic value of various benefits. In Chapter 3 we turn to policymaking and examine how economics can be used to improve the decision-making process for establishing protected areas. Chapter 4 deals with a number of protected-area management issues.

Part II examines the application of this approach in various locations around the world. Because of its national commitment to protected areas and the availability of data on these areas, Thailand is considered in some detail in Chapters 5, 6, and 7. Chapter 5 looks at the history and development of Thailand's protected area system. In Chapters 6 and 7 the focus turns to individual protected areas in Thailand to demonstrate the valuation methods presented earlier and show how economics can be used to promote more effective protection of these areas. Chapters 8 and 9 consider examples of economic analysis of protected areas in a number of other countries. In Chapter 10 we summarize the lessons learned and the policy implications of the economic issues discussed in this volume.

PART I

GENERAL ISSUES

The first half of this book considers the general economic issues associated with the establishment and management of protected areas. Although largely illustrated with examples from developing countries, these issues are universal. Certainly questions of valuing nonmarketed benefits of protected areas arise in both developed and developing countries. Developed countries, by definition, are richer and therefore less constrained financially in providing funds for effective management. Richer societies, moreover, are usually more willing to make public investments to ensure continuation of intangible or poorly defined benefits and promote actions that are seen as a social responsibility, either on behalf of the country or the world. Developing countries, on the other hand, are usually faced with more pressing economic needs and have fewer resources for investment in what may be considered secondary concerns, such as protected areas. At one level, this ordering of priorities is entirely understandable given the funds available, the level of external debt, and the political and social pressures within a country. As illustrated here, however, there may be sizable—and measurable—economic benefits to be gained from protected areas.

1

Overview of
Protected Areas

The practice of maintaining natural areas for the common good and restricting development to protect the resources they contain was uncommon until this century. When such areas were established, it was generally at the request of—and for the exclusive use of—royalty. Reserves for hunting and riding were set aside for Assyrian noblemen as far back as 700 B.C., and open spaces were reserved for the use of the ruling class in ancient Rome and Medieval Europe (Runte 1979). Overall, however, undeveloped regions were simply considered to be areas that had not yet been tamed and had no particular value in the absence of development and use.

Apart from serving the recreational needs of the ruling class, small areas of land occasionally were designated to protect certain species valuable for hunting or other purposes. In Lithuania, a reserve for the European bison was established in 1541; in Switzerland, a reserve to protect the chamois was set up in 1569 (Boardman 1981). The harvesting of oak forests for shipbuilding in England during the sixteenth and seventeenth centuries prompted calls for controls and protection of forests (Hoskins 1970).

The practice of protecting outstanding natural areas for their scenic beauty and for recreation and enjoyment by the general public is scarcely more than a century old. The first "national park," Yellowstone, was proclaimed in the United States in 1872. The growth of the national park movement continued slowly until World War II. After the end of the war, however, the number of parks around the world began

9

to increase sharply. Figure 1 shows the dramatic growth in the number of national parks since 1900.

Whereas most early parks were established to protect scenic and recreational resources or for viewing wildlife, the idea of protecting entire ecosystems to preserve biological diversity only developed later. Natural areas were thought to be vast and not in any danger; forests and prairies and coastal resources were there to be used as needed. This perception began to change, however, as the availability of undeveloped natural areas declined and the realization grew that untapped biological resources could yield substantial benefits.

Most of these early parks were established in countries that today are considered developed. The establishment of parks in devel-

Figure 1.
Growth in Number and Area of Protected Areas Worldwide: 1870–1985

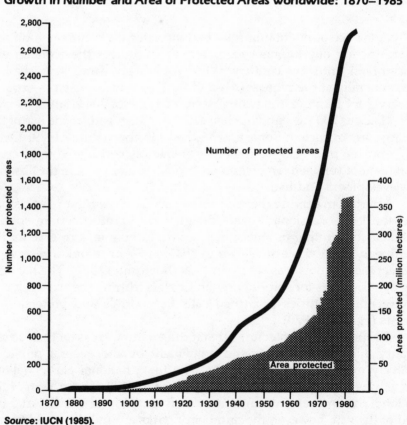

Source: IUCN (1985).

oping countries did not occur until much later. The first national park in Asia, for example, was Corbett National Park, established in India in 1935.

In 1982, fewer than half of the nations classified as developing countries had established any national parks (Blower 1984). This situation is rapidly changing. Since the mid-1970s, most of the new national parks have been located in developing countries (Malik 1984). In 1985 the International Union for the Conservation of Nature and Natural Resources (IUCN) updated its list of protected areas (nature reserves, national parks, natural monuments, wildlife sanctuaries, and protected landscapes or seascapes). This list contains more than 3,500 sites in 136 countries and territories (IUCN 1985b). A total worldwide area of more than 423 million hectares is designated as protected in this sense— equivalent to the combined land area of India, Pakistan, and Bangladesh. Over half of these protected lands are in national parks, and most of the rest are in wildlife sanctuaries.

If we consider only the developing countries (about 100 countries), the total protected area decreases by more than half to about 186 million hectares, of which almost 90 percent is in national parks or wildlife sanctuaries. There is tremendous variation in the absolute area protected by country and the percentage of each country's land area that is protected. India is 70 percent larger than Indonesia, for example, but each country has protected areas of similar magnitude (11 to 14 million hectares)—equivalent to the protected area in Brazil, Botswana, or Tanzania. Other countries have very small areas (a few thousand hectares) or no designated protected areas.

Still, many developing countries are far from possessing protected area systems that are truly protected. Though much progress has been made, many countries are still reluctant to allocate the funds necessary to manage protected areas properly once they are established. This situation can be changed, however, if decision makers can be made to understand the value of protected areas, ecological as well as economic. Moreover, ways must be found to increase the direct economic returns from certain categories of protected areas.

TYPES OF PROTECTED AREAS

Though the national park is probably the most widely known form of protected area, it is only one of many possible categories. Protected areas can play a variety of roles in a nation's economy and provide a range of benefits. They can be managed to meet different objectives ranging from strict preservation of natural ecological processes to provision of sustainable levels of timber, wildlife, water, or recreational use.

The IUCN has been championing the idea of protected areas since 1959, when it was given the task of maintaining a list of the world's national parks and equivalent reserves. Through its Commission on National Parks and Protected Areas (CNPPA), it has defined ten categories of conservation areas representing different levels of protection (from strict nature reserves to multiple-use areas) and varying degrees of local, regional, and global importance. Each category is designed to meet different objectives. The IUCN notes that countries may not need to develop all the categories listed, but through a mix of several different categories a country can design a system that reflects its own objectives and constraints (IUCN 1984).

The IUCN classification comprises eight protected-area categories and two international designations: biosphere reserves and world heritage sites. *Biosphere reserves* are sites of exceptional richness with respect to the diversity and integrity of biotic communities of plants and animals within natural ecosystems—for example, the Sinharaja Forest Reserve of Sri Lanka, Mount Kulai in Kenya, and the Rio Platano Reserve in Honduras. The primary use of biosphere reserves is for research, education, and training. *World heritage sites* are unique natural and cultural sites considered to be of outstanding universal significance. Among the areas designated as such sites are Serengeti National Park in Tanzania, Sagarmatha National Park in Nepal, Galápagos Islands National Park in Ecuador, and Everglades National Park in the United States.

We turn now to the principal management objectives and examples of the eight protected-area categories recognized by IUCN (IUCN 1984; MacKinnon and others 1986). While all protected areas control human occupancy or use of resources to some extent, considerable latitude is available. The following categories are arranged in ascending order of degree of human use permitted in the area:

- *Scientific reserve/strict nature reserve*. Objectives: To protect nature and maintain natural processes in an undisturbed state in order to have ecologically representative examples of the natural environment available for scientific study, environmental monitoring, and education and for the maintenance of genetic resources in a dynamic and evolutionary state. Examples: Yala Strict Nature Reserve in Sri Lanka; the island of Barro Colorado in Panama; Gombe Stream National Park in Tanzania.

- *National park.* Objectives: To protect large natural and scenic areas of national or international significance for scientific, educational, and recreational use under management by the highest competent authority of a nation. Examples: Royal Chitwan National Park in Nepal; Etosha National Park in Namibia; Iguazu National Parks in Argentina and Brazil; Volcan Poas National Park in Costa Rica.
- *Natural monument/natural landmark.* Objectives: To protect and preserve nationally significant natural features because of their special interest or unique characteristics. Examples: Angkor Wat National Park in Kampuchea; Petrified Forests Nature Monument in Argentina; Gedi National Monument in Kenya.
- *Managed nature reserve/wildlife sanctuary.* Objectives: To ensure the natural conditions necessary to protect nationally significant species, groups of species, biotic communities, or physical features of the environment requiring human intervention for their perpetuation. Examples: Manas Wildlife Sanctuary in India; most of the national reserves in Kenya; the biotope reserves in Guatemala.
- *Protected landscape.* Objectives: To maintain nationally significant natural landscapes characteristic of the harmonious interaction of people and land while providing opportunities for public enjoyment through recreation and tourism within the normal life-style and economic activity of these areas. Examples: Pululahua Geobotanical Reserve in Ecuador; Machu Picchu Historic Sanctuary in Peru; the national parks of England.
- *Resource reserve.* Objectives: To protect the natural resources of the area for future use and curb development that could affect the resource pending the establishment of objectives. Examples: Few countries have yet applied this category, but several resource reserves exist in Kenya including Kora and South Turkana National Reserves; other examples include Brazil's Forest Reserves and Tahuamanu Protected Forest in Bolivia.
- *Natural biotic area/anthropological reserve.* Objectives: To allow societies living in harmony with the environment to continue their way of life undisturbed by modern technology. Examples: Gunung Lorentz Nature Reserve in Indonesia; Xingu Indigenous Park in Brazil; Central Kalahari Game Reserve in Botswana; many protected areas in the South Pacific islands.

- *Multiple-use management area/managed resource area.* Objectives: To provide for the sustained production of water, timber, wildlife, pasture, and outdoor recreation; the conservation of nature is primarily oriented to the support of economic activities (although specific zones can also be designed within these areas to achieve specific conservation objectives). Examples: Ngorongoro Conservation Area in Tanzania; Kutai National Park in Indonesia; Jamari and Tapajos National Forests in Brazil; Von Humboldt National Forest in Peru.

Although this listing is being revised, it gives a clear indication of the latitude available for potential use of protected areas. There is a continuum ranging from strict preservation to intensive resource development. The exact mix of resource protection and resource development at any point on this continuum will depend on the situation in each area.

Once the overall objectives have been established for an area, they provide a basis for management and for determining which uses are consistent with these objectives. In most cases, management practices can be designed to allow for a compatible set of benefits—either by focusing on one objective and allowing other uses that do not conflict with the primary objective or by focusing on a set of consistent benefits with no single objective dominating. Different objectives can be met within a protected area. National parks, for example, can satisfy a wide variety of conservation objectives simultaneously. Other categories, such as strict nature reserves, focus on maintaining natural conditions while protected landscapes and multiple-use areas fulfill both production and conservation objectives.

Even when different activities are generally compatible, there may be conflicts between certain uses in specific areas or during certain times of the year. Critical habitats for certain species or important nesting sites during the breeding season, for example, may need extra protection. In such cases, management can address the conflicts by zoning restrictions or by curbing certain activities during specific periods. Obviously some uses will be totally inconsistent with the management objectives—for example, timber harvesting and preservation of ecological processes cannot both be pursued at a single site. By establishing a number of different *types* of protected areas with different objectives, however, a well-designed system can provide a variety of benefits based on the resources and needs of each country.

BENEFITS

Diverse benefits are associated with each type of protected area. These benefits flow from various conservation objectives:

- Maintenance and conservation of environmental resources, services, and ecological processes
- Production of natural resources such as timber and wildlife
- Production of recreation and tourism services
- Protection of cultural and historical sites and objects
- Provision of educational and research opportunities

Some of these benefits are the result of direct resource use and can be valued according to market prices (for instance, logging and fishing). Other benefits, such as recreational uses, depend on direct human use of the protected areas, as well, and these too can be valued in various ways. Most of the benefits from protected areas, however, are hard to measure in monetary terms. These broad benefits to individuals or society at large are frequently referred to as social benefits and are a primary justification for protected areas. This topic is discussed at length later in the chapter.

There is another possible grouping of benefits that is especially useful for discussing various ways of valuing benefits:

1. Recreation/tourism

2. Watershed protection
   - Erosion control
   - Local flood reduction
   - Regulation of streamflows

3. Ecological processes
   - Fixing and cycling of nutrients
   - Soil formation
   - Circulation and cleansing of air and water
   - Global life support

4. Biodiversity
   - Gene resources
   - Species protection
   - Ecosystem diversity
   - Evolutionary processes

5. Education and research

6. Consumptive benefits

7. Nonconsumptive benefits
   - Aesthetic
   - Spiritual
   - Cultural/historical
   - Existence value

8. Future values
   - Option value
   - Quasi-option value

See McNeely (1988) for yet another grouping of benefits; Ledec and Goodland (1988) provide detailed lists of economic benefits of wildland management.

RECREATION/TOURISM. Recreation and tourism are normally the primary objectives in national parks and are key objectives in many other types of protected areas. Unless the primary objective is strict protection of natural conditions or research, some tourism and recreational use are normally allowed. These services not only yield direct financial benefits from protected areas but stimulate employment and rural development in surrounding areas, as well.

WATERSHED PROTECTION. Maintaining the natural vegetative cover helps control erosion, reduces sedimentation and flooding downstream, and regulates streamflows. The extent of the benefit depends on the type of soils, topography, and natural cover in the protected area, the alternative uses available, and the types of investment and land use downstream.

ECOLOGICAL PROCESSES. In their natural state, protected areas provide a number of environmental services in addition to watershed protection. These services often benefit people downslope and downstream by maintaining the productive capacity of nearby areas. Vegetative cover acts as a natural filter to reduce air and water pollution and promotes nutrient cycling. Clearly forests and wetlands are essential to the overall global life support of the planet. Many aquatic species depend on the existence of wetland areas during some portion of their life cycle. Mangroves and their associated fish and shrimp populations constitute just one example.

BIODIVERSITY. The maintenance of biodiversity—short for biological diversity, which includes all species, genetic variation within species, and all varieties of habitats and ecosystems—is currently considered to be one of the most important benefits of protecting natural areas. Biological resources form the basis of numerous industries and are major sources of food, medicines, chemicals, and other products used in both traditional and industrialized societies. By protecting habitats, one protects the variety of species they contain. For detailed discussions of the value of biodiversity, see McNeely (1988) and Wilson (1988).

EDUCATION AND RESEARCH. Research in protected areas may focus on a wide variety of topics from animal behavior to measurement of environmental status and trends. By examining ecological processes in their natural conditions, one can better understand the workings of the environment and thereby improve management and restoration of both undeveloped areas and areas converted to other land uses. Research may involve changing the underlying conditions of the study area in some manner, or it may simply monitor natural conditions with as little interference as possible. Research is often integrated with education, as well, and protected areas provide fertile ground for field study by students at all levels. Moreover, protected areas instill people with an understanding and appreciation of the environment—making them more aware of the harmful consequences of certain types of behavior.

CONSUMPTIVE BENEFITS. Protected areas can yield a number of products including timber, forage, food, wildlife, fish, herbs, and medicines. If an area is to be protected, of course, such products will be harvested only on a sustainable basis. Depending on the objectives of the protected area, consumptive use of the resources may be totally forbidden (as in strict nature reserves and many national parks) or it may be a primary function (as in multiple-use areas).

NONCONSUMPTIVE BENEFITS. These benefits include the values people derive from protected areas that are not related to direct use. Aesthetic benefits may accrue when one passes near the area, views it from a distance, or sees it in films or on television. The cultural value of a mountain or lake may be important in some societies, while urban societies may derive spiritual value from having a nearby asylum from modern life. Certain protected areas may also be key historic sites. Some people, moreover, may derive a benefit simply from knowing that a certain unspoiled area or a certain species exists, even though they themselves will never see or use it. This "existence value" is independent of any direct present or future use.

FUTURE VALUES. Apart from the values people derive from both consumptive and nonconsumptive use, the protection of certain areas ensures a variety of benefits from their potential use in the future—either for visiting or from products that may be developed from the area's genetic or other resources. The question of future value is discussed in the next chapter.

COSTS

Three main types of costs are associated with establishing and maintaining protected areas: direct costs, indirect costs, and opportunity costs. *Direct costs* are costs directly related to establishment and management of protected areas. *Indirect costs* refer to adverse impacts caused by establishing protected areas; these include damage to property or injury to people by wildlife. *Opportunity costs* represent the loss of potential benefits associated with protecting an area rather than harvesting its resources.

Direct Costs

Direct costs represent direct budget outlays, usually paid for by local or national governments. The first category of direct costs are those associated with establishing an area as protected. If the land is not already owned by the government, there may be costs to acquire title to it. If people are already living in the area, they may require relocation depending on the management objectives. There may also be costs associated with developing roads and facilities and preparing a management plan for the area.

Apart from the costs of establishing a protected area, there are a number of ongoing costs of maintaining and managing it. Administrative and staff costs must be considered, as well as maintenance costs for roads and facilities. Protected areas should also have a monitoring and research program to keep track of changes in status and trends. If tourists will be using the area, an educational program is usually required. There is also a critical need, especially in developing countries, for adequate enforcement to protect the area. Poaching of wildlife and timber and clearing of protected areas for agriculture are often acute problems. Thus an effective protection program—including enforcement of regulations combined with other strategies such as education, incentive systems, and a rural development program for nearby residents—must be developed and maintained. The expenses of this protection program are part of the direct costs.

Indirect Costs

Another cost involves damages indirectly caused by the existence of the protected area. For example, wildlife in the protected area may cause damage outside the area itself—crops trampled or eaten by wildlife, for instance, as well as harm to people, livestock, or materials. These are all indirect costs. In Indonesia, elephants living in protected areas frequently wander outside the boundaries and damage nearby plantations or field crops. Though governments are not compelled to compensate for such damages, community attitudes toward protected areas and the wildlife they contain will be much more positive if residents are reimbursed for any damages they suffer.

Opportunity Costs

The opportunity costs of a protected area are the benefits that society or individuals lose when an area is protected. These costs include forgone outputs from the protected area (animals, spices, timber)—not only the resources currently on the site but also those that could have been developed through more intensive exploitation. Opportunity costs also include the benefits that might have been gained from conversion to an alternative use. (These opportunity costs may have already been accounted for in the costs of establishment. If the area was purchased on the open market, the purchase price will reflect the value of alternative commercial possibilities.)

In many developing countries, there may be significant opportunity costs from the need to restrict use by nearby residents. If the local community has to forgo outputs they are accustomed to receiving, compensation or development of alternative sources of these products will be called for. Otherwise the local community will suffer a loss and may be very reluctant to give up its traditional patterns of use.

These three types of costs have important bearing on the pressures for and against protection. Direct costs appear as government budgetary outlays and, when resources are scarce, are always under pressure. Indirect costs may be sizable but are usually dispersed over many individuals who may find it difficult to organize or make known their collective concerns. Opportunity costs, whether large or small, may play an important role in the political decision-making process.

If one person or one industry stands to gain from conversion of a natural area to another use, considerable pressure may be placed on the government to stop creation of a protected area. Frequently private entities have been able to develop potential protected areas for their own personal benefit at society's expense. It is important, therefore, to account for the full range of benefits and costs, both financial and social, when analyzing the creation of a protected area.

COMPARING BENEFITS AND COSTS

There are several ways of weighing benefits and costs when evaluating alternatives. If estimates of both benefits and their associated costs are known, some form of a *benefit/cost analysis* can be carried out. The technique involves the evaluation of a stream of benefits and costs over some chosen period of time. The benefit/cost analysis can result in the calculation of a *net present value* (NPV) figure, a *benefit/cost ratio* (B/C ratio), or an *internal rate of return* (IRR) for the proposed protected area. (For details on the mechanics involved in benefit/cost analysis, especially for environmental decisions, see Hufschmidt and others 1983, Dixon and Hufschmidt 1986, and Dixon and others 1988.) In most cases involving protected areas, the quantifiable benefits (those that can be measured in monetary terms) are less than the total benefits. When the directly quantifiable benefits alone are greater than the costs of protection, the decision to provide protection is easy.

The ultimate decision whether or not to designate an area as protected will depend on a variety of factors—the quantified and nonquantified benefits expected from protection, the costs of providing protection (constructing and maintaining facilities, for example), the potential net benefits from alternative uses of the site, and so on. Even if the expected monetary benefits of protection exceed the direct costs of protection, the potential benefits from alternative uses may be considerable. Usually the decision maker has some notion of the net benefits expected from the development alternative for a site—from timber extraction, agricultural development, housing, or industrial development, for instance. This information, in turn, must be compared to the expected net monetary benefits (if any) of the protected area *plus* the other important (but unquantified) benefits provided by a protected area. (In Chapter 3 we discuss the selection of protected areas.)

There are no firm rules for selecting and designating protected areas. Given the uncertainty of the true magnitude of future value to be gained from such benefits as genetic resources, species protection, option value, and existence value, caution is called for. If the area is not established as a protected area, some of these benefits will be lost forever. Another issue to be considered is that protected areas often increase in value relative to other uses of these areas since they are a finite resource that will become increasingly scarce as time passes.

One approach to these decisions is known as the *safe minimum standard* (SMS) approach originally developed by Ciriacy-Wantrup (1952) and also advocated by Bishop (1978). In essence, the SMS approach uses a modified version of the "minimax" criterion—choosing the alternative that minimizes the maximum possible loss that could result from making the wrong decision. In the modified approach, this alternative is chosen unless the costs of doing so are "unacceptably large" (Bishop 1978). How large is unacceptably large is left to the decision maker. If the costs of establishing a protected area (such as acquisition, management, and other uses forgone) are greater than the quantifiable benefits, the maximum loss associated with establishment will be some amount less than the difference between the quantified costs and benefits (because of unquantified benefits from protection). The cost of not establishing the protected area, however, is unknown but potentially very large—if, for example, some species are lost because the area is not protected, the potential uses for these species will never be known. This means there is a certain unknown probability of a serious social or economic loss in the future. Following the SMS approach calls for avoiding this potential loss unless it would involve an unacceptably large known cost. Essentially the decision becomes a question of accepting some known cost today to prevent a potentially larger cost in the future. This is a political decision.

Another approach to these decisions is to use *cost-effectiveness analysis* instead of benefit/cost analysis. This approach does not attempt to value benefits; rather, it focuses on finding the least-cost method of reaching a desired goal (say, protection of a certain number of hectares of a specific habitat). Cost-effectiveness analysis is described in more detail in Chapter 2.

The opportunity-cost approach can be used when the other techniques do not appear helpful. In this case the analyst compares the net economic benefits from a proposed development of a natural area to the qualitative benefits of protection. Although this is an "apples and oranges" comparison, if the net economic benefits of the alternative use are negative or positive but *small*, it may be easy to justify protection. The economic costs are not large and the benefits of protection, although unquantified, may be substantial. When the economic costs are large, the decision is more difficult.

The opportunity-cost approach can also be used to evaluate different sites for a proposed development project. Presumably an alternative site would not be as advantageous for the project as the natural area (or it would have been considered as a primary choice), but the reduction in project benefits associated with the alternative site may be more than outweighed by the benefits of protecting the original site. In this case, the opportunity-cost approach evaluates the difference in project benefits associated with the two sites and compares it to the benefits of protecting the original site. See Chapter 2 for a detailed description of this approach.

When all of the benefits and costs associated with protection or development of a natural area are considered, the economic analysis yields results that allow any protected area to be placed in one of three categories: privately beneficial, socially beneficial, or undetermined benefits. In *privately beneficial* areas, the economic benefits are directly obtainable by individuals, groups, or firms and are larger than the associated costs or the benefits of alternative uses. In these cases, the individual will provide the "service" (protection of a natural area) without government intervention. Such cases are not uncommon, but the areas tend to be small and the service provided rather specific. Privately run recreational areas such as campgrounds, ski resorts, and game reserves may result in limited portions of an area being kept in its natural state. Outstanding areas such as the Galápagos Islands or Parc National des Volcans in Rwanda, though currently administered by national governments, are also examples of potentially privately beneficial areas. In most such cases, tourism is a primary use of the area.

Some natural areas unprotected by government may be considered so important that individuals or groups feel strongly enough to purchase them from their current owners. Private conservation groups, such as The Nature Conservancy in the United States, have begun acquiring critical natural areas threatened by development. These groups pool donations from their members to acquire development rights or to buy areas that might not otherwise be protected. Supporters of such private conservation efforts must, therefore, perceive benefits in excess of the costs of these actions.

More common is the case where establishment of a protected area is *socially beneficial* (the net benefits to society at large are positive), though an individual could not easily capture all the benefits and therefore would not be willing to provide protection or preservation on a commercial basis. Protection of upper watershed areas, for example, may be justified by preserving the water supply and water quality for a downstream area. National parks are often socially beneficial. Government support of wildlife parks in East Africa, for example, is usually profitable in terms of attracting tourists who spend money both inside and outside the protected areas.

The third category is *undetermined benefits*. In many cases, it may be difficult to determine whether the net benefits of protecting a natural area are positive or negative. The costs of protection may be known, but the benefits may be diffuse or hard to measure. Wilderness areas or remote locations are examples of such sites. Governments may well decide to protect some of these areas, but at what cost and to what extent? These issues must be addressed. The following chapter deals with the problem of assessing the economic value of protected areas— particularly areas that are socially beneficial or have undetermined benefits.

2
Valuing the Benefits

Few people dispute the desirability of protecting selected natural areas. In developing countries, however, the costs associated with establishing and managing protected areas often appear formidable. Faced with acute shortages of funds, governments are reluctant to make the investments needed to provide effective protection.

Many developing countries rely directly on their natural resource base for a substantial portion of domestic employment and national income. The need to exploit resources such as timber and minerals often makes it difficult for governments to forgo using these resources in order to establish a protected area. Growing populations and the need for more agricultural and urban land further increase the pressure to convert undeveloped natural areas to agricultural or urban uses. Such pressures notwithstanding, many developing countries have managed to establish significant amounts of land as protected areas. As noted in the Introduction, more than 100 developing countries have designated more than 185 million hectares as one category or another of protected area. Yet even in these countries, many areas remain threatened due to inadequate funding for management and protection.

The expected benefits from the conversion and development of natural areas can usually be expressed in monetary terms. These benefits include the returns from agricultural, urban, or industrial developments as well as the value of timber, minerals, and other natural resources that can be extracted from protected areas. Many of the benefits that result from establishing and maintaining protected areas

24

are not so easily valued in financial terms, however. As a result, these benefits are often overlooked when decisions are made on budget allocations and how best to use a nation's natural resources. The following section explains why the value of certain benefits derived from protected areas cannot be easily quantified.

OBSTACLES TO VALUING BENEFITS

For most goods and services, prices are established in the marketplace through the process of buying and selling. The price of a kilogram of rice or a piece of lumber is easy to determine. It is not so easy, however, to value other goods and services due to various factors that prevent normal market operations. These factors are referred to as *market failures* (or "market imperfections"). If they are not adjusted for, they result in distorted market prices that do not reflect the true value of the good in question. Many of the benefits of protected areas, such as their ecological, biological, or aesthetic value, are subject to these market imperfections.

Some of these benefits are quite abstract—biological diversity, for example, is recognized as important but exceptionally difficult to value in monetary terms. Other benefits are much more concrete but, owing to their location or other factors, do not have easily determined monetary values—forest products that are collected and used by local inhabitants but not sold commercially, for example, or the downstream impact on water regulation and water quality created by maintaining forest cover in a watershed.

Why are certain goods and services subject to market failures? To answer this question, economists have linked a number of characteristics with these goods and services. Table 1 lists the major benefits of protected areas along with their characteristics: whether or not use of the benefit is rival or excludable, the location and ease of valuation of benefits, and whether change or loss of the benefit will be irreversible. Benefits vary in their extent of "competitiveness" in use, and economists discuss this concept in terms of rivalness and excludability. A competitive benefit is one where different users compete to receive or enjoy it. In the following sections we consider these characteristics in greater detail.

Nonrivalry

In most cases, each person's consumption of a good reduces the amount available for everyone else by the amount consumed. When

Table 1.

Characteristics of Benefits from Protecting Natural Areas

Benefit	Nonrival	Non-excludable	Off-Site Effects	Prevention of Irreversible Loss	Estimation of Value
Recreation/tourism	XC	P		P	S
Watershed values					
Erosion control	X	X	X		S
Local flood reduction	X	X	X		E
Regulation of streamflows	X	X	X		E
Ecological processes					
Fixing and cycling nutrients		X	X		S
Soil formation					S
Cleansing air and water	X	X	X		S
Biodiversity					
Gene resources	X	P	X	P	E
Species protection	X	X	X	P	E
Evolutionary processes	X	X	X	X	E
Education	X	P	X	X	E
Research	X	P	X	X	E
Aesthetic	X	X	X	P	S
Spiritual	X	X	X	X	E
Cultural/historical	X	X	X	X	E
Option value	X	X	X	X	E
Quasi-option value	X	X	X	X	E
Existence value	X	X	X	X	E
Global life support	X	X	X	P	E

C = congestible
P = possibly
S = somewhat difficult
E = extremely difficult
X = attribute is present

someone consumes an apple or purchases a house, for example, the amount of apples or houses available to everyone else is reduced by that amount. These goods are strictly competitive. For nonrival goods, however, one person's consumption does not affect the amount available to anyone else. The total amount of the good available can be enjoyed by anyone without diminishing the supply. A beautiful view or clean mountain air are examples of nonrival goods, as are radio and television signals. These goods are often called "public goods," but increasingly economists are coming to prefer the term *nonrival* (Randall and Peterson 1984; Randall 1983). This property is also known as "joint supply."

Some goods are nonrival up to a certain point; beyond that point, there is indeed rivalry. Recreation is an example of such a good—a protected area can be enjoyed by a number of people without one person's enjoyment being diminished by the actions of another. A stretch of open beach or a mountain trail are examples. Beyond a certain point, however, congestion sets in and each person's enjoyment is reduced as more people use the area. These goods are known as *congestible*.

The problem with nonrival goods is that the market cannot set an efficient price for them. Most nonrival goods have large start-up or establishment costs and then very low or, at the extreme, zero costs of use. Since one person's consumption does not affect the enjoyment of others, the economically efficient price is zero because there is no need to allocate the resource among competing users by means of a price. Air is free, as are scenic views, but if no price is charged then no information on the true value of the good is generated. As Table 1 indicates, almost all the benefits of protected areas are nonrival. When an area is designated as protected, many of the benefits provided are then available to all, and one person's use does not detract from anyone else's (with the exception of overcrowding and congestion). For benefits that accrue only locally, the total amount of social benefits remains within national borders in most cases. When benefits are nonrival and accrue globally, however, the country protecting the area is freely providing these benefits to the world at large.

Nonexcludability

Sometimes it is not feasible to exclude anyone from consuming the good because the cost of excluding them would be greater than the benefit received. Consider again the case of clean air or a view of a distant mountain—to exclude people would be impossible or very expensive at the least. National defense is another example of a nonrival, nonexcludable good: once it is provided, everyone receives the same level of benefits. Nonexcludable goods can also be rival: some fish and animal populations are examples of rival, nonexcludable goods. In many countries near-shore or pelagic fish are definitely rival goods in consumption but nonexcludable in practice. This situation commonly results in overfishing. When goods are nonexcludable, there is no requirement for people to reveal their preferences, and it is difficult to estimate true demand curves. Goods that are both nonrival in consumption and nonexcludable are often called "pure public goods."

Nonexcludable goods often involve what economists refer to as *external effects* or *externalities* (Samuelson 1954, 1955)—that is, the production or consumption of a good or service by one person affects another person involuntarily without benefit of compensation. In the absence of a set of regulations or property rights, the person producing the externality will not take into account its effect on others. If this external effect is negative, too much of the good will be produced (or consumed) since the producer does not consider these external costs in his or her decision-making process. If the external effect is positive, too little of the good will be produced. Consider the case of biological diversity—a country is asked to preserve natural areas in order to maintain genetic stocks for future use. Given incomplete knowledge and weak patent regulations, it may be very difficult for the country to reap the benefits (by *excluding* others) from the development of a new medicine or plant cultivar derived from this protected area. Consequently, the incentives to preserve natural areas are reduced because of nonexcludable and external effects.

Other examples of benefits from protecting natural areas that are, in effect, nonexcludable include the impact of natural forest cover on carbon dioxide levels, the enjoyment people receive by reading about the flora and fauna of natural areas, and the various off-site effects on water and air quality. Though many people may benefit from the establishment of a protected area, they often cannot be forced to pay for such benefits. Table 1 shows that almost all benefits associated with protected areas are nonexcludable to some degree. The one exception is the benefits that require on-site use of the protected area—for example, tourism, recreation, and research. If the number of access points is limited, entrance fees can be charged and some degree of excludability is possible. Hence our characterization of these benefits as "possibly nonexcludable."

Users who benefit from the existence of a good such as a protected area but do not pay for it are known as *free riders*. Since they cannot be excluded from enjoying these benefits (at least not without cost), there is no incentive for these users to reveal how much these benefits are worth to them. As a result, countries establishing protected areas cannot easily estimate and charge for all the benefits these areas provide. (The establishment and management costs, however, are largely paid directly by the national treasury.) In these cases, a protected area may be "socially beneficial" even though no individuals would be willing to provide the required protection by themselves (the "privately beneficial" category described in Chapter 1). Normal market mechanisms, therefore, will not supply the desired amount of protected areas even if they promise net social benefits. Nonexcludability, like nonrivalry, can occur on a local or global scale. To the extent that the benefits of a protected area accrue beyond national borders, the country protecting the area is freely providing benefits to other countries.

Off-Site Effects

Although many important benefits remain within the protected area itself, other benefits extend beyond its boundaries. There may be benefits to nearby farmers, for example, from protecting important watershed land and regulating water supply. Other benefits may even be global in scope (such as maintenance of genetic stocks). These off-site benefits are examples of positive externalities.

Although many off-site benefits are also nonexcludable, not all nonexcludable benefits occur off-site. These two properties often overlap, but they are separate issues. Nevertheless, the same valuation problem arises with both—since individuals do not request these services and do not control their provision, they are not required to pay for them. This does not make these benefits any less real. If the social benefits of protected areas are to be accurately valued, all benefits should be included whether someone pays for them or not. If they are not included, less than the optimum amount of protected areas will be established.

Not all off-site effects are benefits, of course. If wildlife wanders beyond the boundary of a protected area and damages crops or injures people, these effects too must be considered. In this case, the off-site effect is a cost or negative externality. Soil erosion is another example. Suppose a farmer has several cultivation techniques that can be used to grow a crop within a multiple-use protected area; some techniques produce more soil erosion than others but may be less expensive to use. If the main effect of soil erosion is a reduction in crop yields, the farmer will consider the benefits and costs associated with changes in yield and cultivation practice. If, however, the main impact of soil erosion occurs downstream (sedimentation of a reservoir, for instance) the farmer will usually not consider these sedimentation costs and will choose the cheapest, but more erosive, cultivation technique. A negative externality occurs and too much soil erosion is produced.

Uncertainty

As a result of incomplete or inadequate information, it is often difficult to place values on many of the benefits of protected areas and the future demand for these benefits. In most cases there is incomplete knowledge of what resources the area contains, let alone what they may be worth. Bishop (1978) defines two main types of uncertainty: "natural uncertainty" about the potential uses for various known or unknown species and "social uncertainty" about the nature of future human demands. Uncertainty thus exists on both the supply and demand side with respect to biological and genetic resources (Jakobsson and Dragun 1989). The market failures mentioned previously add to the information problem—their presence makes it hard to assign accurate values to many of the benefits of protected areas. Predicting the *future* value of these benefits simply adds to the uncertainty problem.

Irreversibility

Natural areas are complex systems whose resources have adapted to their individual environment and the overall system over long periods of time. If the area is disrupted by harvesting some of these resources or is converted to another use, it may take centuries, if ever, to return to its former state. This may be true in many tropical forests where clearing may so interrupt hydrological and nutrient cycling processes that the original forest cover can never be reestablished (Wilson 1988). As a result of the uncertain consequences of development and the possible losses it may entail, a more cautious approach should be taken when the results of a decision may be irreversible (Krutilla and Fisher 1985).

In a sense, any decision, once implemented, is irreversible. In the context of protected areas, however, the effects are often permanent and potentially substantial. While less important decisions may also be irreversible, mistaken decisions can often be adjusted with only short-term and insignificant effects. In protected areas, however, it may not be possible to make such adjustments, thereby leading to losses that continue in perpetuity. Another factor that affects the degree of irreversibility is replicability. To the extent that the regenerated state does not duplicate the original state, the action can be said to have had irreversible effects. While some economists argue that reversibility is usually possible given sufficient application of technology and money (Cummings and Norton 1974), others maintain that it is impossible to faithfully recreate natural environments in a manner that would be acceptable to many users (Fisher, Krutilla, and Cicchetti 1974).

Biological changes resulting from many uses may also be irreversible. Though some tropical forests may eventually return to a forested state, for example, the changes are likely to be substantial. The regenerated forest may superficially resemble the original forest, but the changes in species composition and other factors may be so great that the replacement forest cannot be considered to be the same as the original forest (Jordan 1986). Destruction of the habitat may also have resulted in local or even global extinction of animal species. In the former case, restocking from other areas may be possible, but if global extinction has occurred the change is truly irreversible.

Development may also cause an effect that has been labeled an "uncertain irreversibility" (Smith and Krutilla 1979). This, perhaps, is best illustrated by the issue of species extinction. If, for example, a proposed development would destroy a significant portion of the remaining habitat of a certain species, it is possible, though not certain, that there may be an irreversible effect: species extinction. In this case, the costs associated with a greater likelihood of extinction caused by development must also be considered.

Pearce (1983) introduces the concept of "shifted irreversibilities." While he assumes that a political representative system would take into account risks to the current generation, he argues that since future generations have no political representation, potentially irreversible damages done to future generations would not be included in decision making. The cost of these irreversibilities are "shifted" to future generations without consideration by current decision makers.

When an irreversible development is undertaken (such as converting a natural area to field crop production), future alternatives become limited. For every species, for example, there is a certain probability that a new use will be discovered that can yield benefits (Randall 1986). If the species is made extinct by the proposed conversion, this opportunity is lost forever. The value that arises from delaying such an irreversible decision has been termed *quasi-option value* (Arrow and Fisher 1974) and can be characterized as the expected value of information that might be gained by delaying an irreversible decision (Conrad 1980). (Note, however, that development may also generate quasi-option value if it leads to better information for future decisions; see Freeman 1984 and Miller and Lad 1984.)

Irreversible changes may also result in a loss of existence value and option value. Many people derive a sense of well-being simply from knowing that these areas exist (so-called existence value). Others hope that they may someday have the opportunity to visit a certain area or observe a certain species in the wild (option value). If these opportunities are no longer available due to development and the consequent irreversible loss of the resource, there will be a loss in terms of social welfare. Such losses, though difficult to quantify, may be significant.

Toward More Informed Decisions

As a result of all these problems, the benefits of protected areas are often simply considered intangible. As such they are frequently ignored or undervalued during the decision-making process, and potential protected areas are lumped into the "undetermined benefits" category discussed in Chapter 1. This policy creates a major problem. Since most protected areas are social or public investments made by governments on behalf of society, undervaluing or failing to estimate monetary benefits results in insufficient government funds being provided for management. Rather than regarding protected areas as valuable resources with measurable economic and ecological benefits, they are commonly considered "welfare cases" and a drain on the public treasury. Yet monetary estimates of many of these benefits can be made in order to indicate their true value to society. By accurately estimating benefits, decision makers can make better and more informed decisions on the key questions they face:

- What are the benefits to society from protected areas?
- How significant are these benefits?
- Which areas should be protected?
- How large a budget allocation for protected areas can be justified?
- What are the best decisions when faced with difficult trade-offs between exploitation and protection?

The next section discusses the methods that can be used to quantify some of the monetary benefits of protected areas. For more background on these methods, see Hufschmidt and others (1983), Dixon and Hufschmidt (1986), and Dixon and others (1988).

WAYS OF VALUING BENEFITS

Valuation, the process of placing monetary value on goods and services, is an essential part of any political decision or economic analysis of a proposed project. When faced with deciding on a project (a factory, a port, a national park), both the economist and the decision maker need answers to similar questions. The decision maker asks: "What will it cost and what are the returns?" The economist inquires: "What are the levels of expected benefits and costs over the appropriate time horizon?" Though the language may differ, the concerns are similar.

For many activities, valuation is not a problem—the market yields useful information on prices for inputs and outputs. Distortions created by government intervention can be handled by means of shadow prices. In the case of protected areas, however, the situation is different. Although the costs of protection are clear and usually easy to quantify, the benefits frequently appear indistinct. Valuation, therefore, plays a major role in providing monetary estimates of the various benefits (and occasionally costs) associated with protected areas. Without estimates of the monetary value of the benefits of protection, it is much harder to justify the budget outlays needed for establishment and maintenance of these areas.

Considerable progress has been made in the past few decades on developing techniques for placing monetary values on many of these benefits. Though not exhaustive, this section presents a number of the main approaches that have proved useful in this work. Many of these techniques rely on market prices of related goods and services, both to value benefits and to estimate costs. Others rely on survey-based approaches to infer values. Most of these approaches have been formulated in the United States or in other developed market economies. Their application too has largely been in developed countries, although increasing work is being done in developing countries. Here we give the entire range of techniques but stress the approaches that are most likely to be useful in developing countries.

Techniques Based on Market Prices

Valuation techniques in this category can be used to value effects that change the quality or quantity of outputs that are eventually exchanged on the market. Deforestation, for example, may result in increased erosion that deposits sediment on farmland downstream. If this reduces crop production, the income of farmers falls. Alternatively, the sediment may enter a reservoir downstream and reduce its storage capacity. Reduced hydropower or irrigation water production may result. Such effects can be valued by estimating the change in value of production of the good or service that occurs as a result of the change in land use—in this case crop yields, hydropower, or the forgone benefits due to reduced irrigation water. This specific technique is known as the *change-in-productivity approach.*

It is essential to evaluate the effects in a *with-and-without* context. (That is, effects should be compared to some preexisting baseline situation.) In valuing the off-site productivity effects of a protected area compared to converting the land to agriculture, for instance, only the additional external effects resulting from the conversion should be included, not the total effect. An example might be downstream damage from sediment originating in a protected area. Even with complete protection, there will normally be some naturally occurring background level of soil erosion and sedimentation. If downstream sedimentation damages are worth $X when the upstream area is protected and damages would increase to $Y if the upstream area were converted to agriculture, only the additional damage (equal to Y minus X) would be attributable to the conversion of the protected area.

The change-in-productivity approach can also be used to value on-site resources, those located within the protected area. A recent study (Peters, Gentry, and Mendelsohn 1989) estimated the market value of nonwood or "minor" forest products found in a tropical forest. These benefits are usually ignored in the decision-making process about preserving or converting a tropical forest. But this analysis, reported in more detail in Chapter 9, found that the value of minor forest products in the Peruvian Amazon was surprisingly large. In fact, total net revenues generated by sustainable exploitation of "minor" forest products are two to three times higher than those resulting from logging and forest conversion. Since conversion would destroy the forest ecosystem, protected status with continued sustainable harvest of minor forest products has some win/win aspects: generation of income and maintenance of this rich ecosystem.

Another technique that relies on market prices is the *loss-of-earnings approach.* Rather than evaluating a change in output of some *product*, in this case the change in productivity of human beings is used to measure the effect of a change in environmental conditions. Another possibility is to measure the medical costs associated with some increased (or decreased) level of environmental damage. In many cases, lost productivity and medical costs will have to be evaluated. This technique is most appropriate when applied to minor illnesses caused by changes in environmental quality; when more acute illnesses or deaths are involved, there are strong objections to the use of this technique.

Although the loss-of-earnings approach may initially appear to have limited usefulness for assessing the benefits of protected areas, this technique can be used when a protected area produces air or water quality benefits. The maintenance of natural areas as "green lungs" has long been accepted as part of urban planning. Similarly, some wetland and coastal ecosystems have major water purification benefits. If these air and water quality effects reduce the incidence of disease associated with poor air or water quality, the loss-of-earnings approach can be used to estimate these health benefits. The data problems may be significant, however, especially in most developing countries.

Techniques Based on Surrogate Market Prices

Because of the market shortcomings described earlier in this chapter, many environmental effects have no established market price. In some cases, however, it may be possible to estimate the value of an environmental good or service by examining the price paid for a closely associated good that is traded in the market. These goods are referred to as *surrogate market goods*. In essence, this approach uses observable market prices for one good to estimate the value of an environmental good that does not have its own price.

When the surrogate good is a perfect substitute for the environmental good, this technique should provide very accurate information. To the extent that the goods are not perfect substitutes, adjustments must be made. The issue of market clearance must also be considered. That is, one cannot assume that the full quantity of the service or amenity would be demanded if it were priced the same as an expensive substitute (Randall and Peterson 1984).

The most widely used technique in this category is the *property-value approach*. Property values (that is, prices for housing or other real estate) are affected by a number of variables including size, construction materials, and location, as well as environmental quality attributes. A study using this approach gathers data on the price and characteristics of a number of houses. After controlling for all other variables except environmental quality, the residual price difference can then be ascribed, at least theoretically, to differences in environmental quality.

The increased value of property located next to natural areas or with scenic views is one example of this effect. A related technique, the *land-value approach*, is based on the same principles. (These techniques are discussed in detail in Hufschmidt and others 1983, but because of their limited applicability in developing countries, they will not be discussed further here.)

Another technique in this category is the *wage-differential approach*. The difference in wage levels for similar jobs in different areas is ascribed to differences in working and living conditions after other variables are controlled for. Environmental variables—the level of air pollution, for example, or risks to life and health from working conditions—can then be valued by looking at differences in wages. For this technique to provide accurate information, many assumptions pertaining to labor market competitiveness, mobility, and information are necessary. These conditions are more likely to be met in developed countries. The diffuse nature of many protected-area benefits means that the wage-differential approach is hard to use. One can observe the result, however, in many resort areas. Wages are frequently low since workers are willing to accept lower wages for a higher level of environmental quality or natural resource availability (the "sunshine tax"). If these environmental benefits are provided by a protected area (a Yellowstone or Yosemite National Park, for instance, or a marine or coastal park in the Florida Keys), measurements based on the wage-differential approach capture the value of certain benefits of protection.

A final technique in this category is the *travel-cost approach*, which has been widely used to value recreation benefits from protected areas. The fees for park use are often much lower than an individual would actually be willing to pay. The difference between what a person actually pays and the maximum amount he or she would be willing to pay is known as *consumer's surplus*. The travel-cost approach looks at the pattern of recreational use of a park and uses this information to derive a demand curve to estimate the total amount of consumer's surplus. To do this, visitors are divided into a number of origin zones of increasing distance from the park. Then a survey is used to determine the time and monetary cost involved in getting to the park. (Normally, per capita use of the park will decrease as distance to the park increases.) The technique assumes that people react to increased travel costs as they would to increased admission fees at a park. At some level of cost, therefore, demand for park use is reduced to zero. The technique then traces out a demand curve based on all this information. Note that the value of the park is *not* equal to the amount of travel costs; this information is simply used to derive the demand curve.

In essence, then, increasing travel costs are used as a surrogate for increasing admission fees to determine consumer's surplus. This technique is an excellent way to estimate the recreational value of an area such as a national park. It has been used extensively in developed countries and increasingly in developing countries. (Interested readers should consult the references given earlier for more details.)

Even when a complete travel-cost study cannot be carried out, information on tourist expenditures can yield valuable information. In the analysis of the Thai protected areas reported in Chapters 6 and 7, it was found that the tourism-related expenditures generated by these areas were from 20 to 100 times greater than their annual operating budgets. In studies of safari tourism to East African wildlife parks, sizable values have been attributed to lions, elephants, and other "major" animals. In one analysis for Amboseli National Park in Kenya, for example, the value of a lion (as a visitor draw) was estimated at $27,000 per year; an elephant herd was worth $610,000 per year (Western and Henry 1979). Another observer noted that, by way of comparison, a lion's "value" as a hunting or sport resource was about $8,500 (the cost of a 21-day lion hunt) or $960 to $1,325 as a skin (Thresher 1981). Although these numbers are "back of the envelope" economics that mix together a number of issues, they do indicate the sizable values of large animals as tourist attractions. These issues are explored in greater detail in Chapter 9.

Survey-Based Approaches

Lack of market prices or incomplete information may make it impossible to use the market and surrogate market techniques described in the previous section. This is often the case where markets are not well developed or one is dealing with goods that are traded (rather than bought or sold) or goods that never enter the market (minor forest products, for example, or subsistence economy products). If market prices or surrogate market prices cannot be obtained, it may be possible to question people directly about how they would react to a given situation. Based on their answers, the value of a good or service to each person can be determined and then extrapolated to determine the aggregate effect on everyone affected.

These survey-based approaches have been largely developed in industrialized countries and are the subject of considerable academic debate. Although their usefulness in developing countries, especially in rural areas, is limited, carefully done they can yield useful information in some situations. In fact, these methods are one of the few ways to place monetary estimates on certain intangible effects. For these reasons, the main approaches are outlined here.

As noted earlier, one is interested in the total value of an effect, not just the observed price. This total value includes the price paid plus any consumer's surplus that may accrue to the individual. *Contingent valuation methods* (CVM) use two measures of consumer's surplus. The first is *compensating variation* (CV), which estimates how much payment would be required to keep an individual at a certain initial level of satisfaction if he or she were forced to face new circumstances that were not as favorable. That is, there will be a certain payment which, combined with a new situation, would leave the individual equally well off as he or she was in the initial situation; this payment would be the compensating variation. The second measure is *equivalent variation* (EV). This measure looks at the satisfaction level of the individual after a change is made (rather than before as CV does). It measures how much he or she would be willing to pay to avoid returning to the initial situation (assuming the new situation is preferable) or how much he or she would have to receive in compensation to forgo returning to the initial situation (assuming the initial situation is preferable). (These consumer's surplus measures are explained in detail in most microeconomics textbooks.)

Depending on which measure of consumer's surplus is used (CV or EV), very different answers may result. Though the differences should be small theoretically (differing only by the income effect of whether payment is made or received and by the fact that willingness to pay is constrained by income), empirical research indicates they are often quite large. The "correct" measure depends on the distribution of property rights—that is, who is given the initial rights to use the resource? This determines whether the appropriate question refers to compensation (for giving up the right) or willingness to pay (to get the right). Not surprisingly, compensation demanded is consistently higher than willingness to pay—often several times larger (Knetsch and Sinden 1987).

One common type of contingent valuation method is the *bidding game*. Here a hypothetical situation is described to a person who is then asked the maximum amount he or she would pay for the item in question. For example, urban residents might be asked how much they would pay to have a certain area protected as a national park. Alternatively, people could be asked about the minimum amount they would accept to avoid a hypothetical situation. For example, villagers might be asked how much they would have to be paid to give up the right of using a protected area to collect plants, hunt animals, or gather fire-wood. Or one could ask park users how much they would have to be paid to give up the opportunity of using a park for recreation.

There are two major types of bidding games: single-bid games and iterative-bid games. In the first type, the survey describes a situation and asks the person for a single bid that would make him indifferent between having the good described at that bid price or not having the good (assuming the good is something he would want). In an iterative-bid game, rather than asking for an open-ended bid, the survey asks the person if he would pay $X for the situation or good described. The amount is then varied iteratively until the maximum willingness to pay (or minimum willingness to accept compensation) is reached.

A variation of the bidding game is the *take-it-or-leave-it experiment*. In this variation, rather than being asked for a bid, the respondent is given a situation and offered a certain amount to accept this situation that he can accept or reject (take it or leave it). Different respondents are given different dollar amounts and the final result is a series of subsam-ples, each of whom has been given a different amount yielding some percentage of people who have accepted the offer and another percent-age who have rejected it. These answers can then be analyzed using a logit model to yield an average willingness to pay.

Yet another variation is the *trade-off game* in which people are asked to choose between two different bundles of goods. One could, for example, ask respondents to choose between (1) a certain sum of money plus a certain level of an environmental good and (2) a different sum of money plus a different level of the environmental good. The answer can then be interpreted as the marginal willingness to pay for the additional level of the environmental good. This technique could be used to find out people's valuations for different-size protected areas, different total amounts of protected areas, or even different types of protected areas.

One problem with these CVM approaches is that they all involve money. In remote villages or areas with migrating tribes, many things may be exchanged rather than bought and sold. One way to overcome this dependence on a monetary alternative is the *costless-choice method*. Here people can be given the choice of a certain environmental good and several alternative goods. Villagers might be asked, for example, what they would be willing to accept in exchange for not hunting in a wildlife sanctuary. The choice could be given in terms of cattle, rice, firewood, or even land. This method could be very valuable in deter-mining the value of different uses of protected areas to villagers.

One last survey approach that is potentially valuable is the *Delphi technique*. Here "experts" rather than consumers are interviewed and attempt to place a value on a certain good through an iterative process. First they are independently asked to place a value on a good and then these values are discussed as a group. After considering all the opinions, each expert reevaluates his or her decision and makes a new estimate. Ideally the values will become less divergent in each round, eventually clustering around a mean value. Care must be taken to avoid confrontations and not to allow a single member of the group to dominate.

Since surveys rely on hypothetical situations rather than the observed behavior common to market-based approaches, the situations must be described clearly and completely. There can also be "information bias" if surveys are not undertaken in an unbiased manner. Another problem is that people may give answers to influence the results in a manner favorable to them—this is known as "strategic bias." If people think they may actually be charged for the good in question, they may give an answer that is less than the amount they would truly be willing to pay. Alternatively, they may exaggerate their answer if they believe they will not have to pay the amount but are nevertheless in favor of the proposal under consideration.

Although one may be justifiably skeptical about the use of such approaches in poor countries or with people who are suspicious of outside interviewers, there are many situations where these techniques can be used. The use of trading games, visual cues, and examples appropriate for different communities may yield surprisingly robust results. One should remember that contingent valuation methods are usually used only when other direct market or surrogate market approaches cannot be used.

Various aspects of using surveys and CVM approaches are discussed in Hufschmidt and others (1983) and Freeman (1979). Cummings, Brookshire, and Schulze (1986) and Mitchell and Carson (1989) discuss the uses of CVM and its applications in considerable detail. The extensive use of survey-based approaches in the United States to value wildlife and other environmental values is outlined in these references as well as in survey articles such as Kellert (1984) and Loomis and Walsh (1986). Despite their potential shortcomings, properly conducted surveys can often provide estimates of value that cannot be obtained by other means.

Cost-Based Approaches

Rather than attempting to measure benefits directly, another approach focuses on the costs that would be imposed if areas were converted from their natural state to an alternative use. By establishing or maintaining a protected area, these costs can be avoided and can thus be viewed as benefits. There is no difference between a cost avoided and a benefit received except the perspective from which the impact is viewed. Cost-based approaches, therefore, rely on information on actual or potential costs that are determined using market prices. These techniques are very useful since, as previously indicated, the benefits gained from protection may be quite diffuse or hard to measure. The costs associated with forgoing development, however, or redesigning development projects, may be much easier to translate into monetary terms.

The first approach described here, the opportunity-cost approach, measures what would have to be given up to ensure continued protection and receive some (presumably unquantifiable) level of benefits from the protected area. The second technique, the cost-effectiveness approach, attempts to find the least-cost means of achieving some predetermined level of benefits. The final two approaches measure the value of certain adverse environmental impacts that would occur if a protected area were converted to some other use.

OPPORTUNITY-COST APPROACH. In this approach, rather than trying to measure the benefits of some action (such as the establishment of a protected area), the forgone income from an alternative use is measured instead. One might attempt, for example, to value the benefits of the best alternative use of the land rather than the benefits of the protected area. If this forgone value is low, it may be wise to protect the area since the benefits of protection are more difficult to quantify.

A corollary of this approach could be used to look at the benefits of a proposed development project in a valuable natural area. In this case, one would examine other alternatives to the project or perhaps other sites where the project could be located and evaluate the difference in benefits of the alternatives. For example, one might examine the net benefits of building a coal-fired electrical plant on degraded or abandoned land rather than building a dam and hydroelectric plant in a potential protected area. The difference in net benefits between the two alternatives would then indicate the opportunity cost of protecting the natural area. If this cost is low, it may be prudent to develop the alternative project.

A slightly different use of this approach can be found in the classic Hells Canyon analysis carried out in 1969 and reported in Krutilla and Fisher (1985). The project in question, construction of hydroelectric power developments in the Hells Canyon reach of the Snake River along the Idaho–Oregon border, would have irreversibly altered one of America's last great wild rivers. Several different dams were proposed, and the analysis showed that all but one of the alternatives were unprofitable based on traditional benefit/cost criteria even before environmental considerations were included. One alternative, however, the High Mountain Sheep project, was justifiable on strictly economic grounds and, therefore, an analysis comparing the net benefits of this project to the net benefits of preserving Hells Canyon intact was performed.

Construction of the dam would have greatly altered the environment of the area. To account for this effect, the analysts estimated benefits from recreational use of the canyon in its current state and compared these benefits to the net benefits anticipated from the proposed dam. After taking into account the asymmetric effects of technological progress—that is, preservation benefits would be expected to grow more rapidly than benefits from the dam—the analysts found that the value of preservation benefits was substantially greater than the level needed to establish a case, on economic grounds, for preserving Hells Canyon. In this case the environmental opportunity cost of development was sufficiently large to ensure protection. Krutilla and Fisher concluded that although they counted only part of the environmental benefits of preservation, "the estimates of the benefits of preservation that we were able to measure turned out to be sufficient to answer the question in the High Mountain Sheep case" (1985:142).

A recent analysis in Thailand of the proposed Nam Choan Dam used a more traditional opportunity-cost approach. In this case the analysts examined the expected increase in net power generation costs if the dam were not built as planned in a wildlife sanctuary. The additional costs associated with alternative thermal generation were substantial but thought to be justifiable to protect the wildlife sanctuary. Construction of the dam was indefinitely postponed. (This project is discussed in Dixon, Talbot, and Le Moigne 1989.)

As shown by these examples, the opportunity-cost approach is especially useful for areas with unique resources that might be irrevocably lost if the area were not protected. This measure indicates what will have to be given up to protect a unique resource. The final decision is political: the decision maker has to weigh the benefits that would be received in the short run against the losses to future generations who might have wished to preserve this resource.

COST-EFFECTIVENESS ANALYSIS. When the benefit of reaching a certain policy objective cannot be valued but the objective is believed to be important, attention can be focused not on estimating benefits but on how to achieve the objective in the most cost-efficient manner. *Cost-effectiveness analysis* (CEA) involves setting a goal and then analyzing different means of achieving it. It can also be used to analyze how to allocate the funds available so they are used most effectively. A variant of this technique, incremental cost-effectiveness analysis, examines how much additional money would be needed to reach a more stringent goal of environmental or resource protection. For example, CEA could be used to determine how to protect a certain species or habitat type in a least-cost manner. The cost of establishing, managing, and protecting the resource in a number of different areas could be compared and the least-cost alternative would then be chosen.

The first step of a CEA is to decide on a target—for example, maximum acceptable levels of soil erosion, a certain level of water quality, a minimum population of a certain species, or a desired output of timber. The target must be set at an appropriate level. Even though benefits cannot be valued precisely (which is why this technique is used), trade-offs among different targets and the costs involved in achieving them must be considered. Once the target is established, the CEA examines various ways of reaching it. The costs of these alternatives are then evaluated and the least-cost alternative is chosen. As we will see, cost-effectiveness analysis can also be used in guiding national policies and decisions.

EXPENDITURE-BASED APPROACHES. Sometimes the establishment of a protected area will provide benefits, such as improved air or water quality, that are hard to measure using traditional approaches based on market price. These benefits can be produced both within the protected area (on-site) or outside its boundaries (off-site). Although hard data on the value of benefits may be difficult to obtain, one can use information on expenditures, both actual and potential, to define the issues. For example, if the establishment and maintenance of a protected area will either improve or maintain the water quality in an area, one can obtain information on expenditures for water quality improvement that are thus avoided. This information, although based on costs avoided, gives some indication of the minimum magnitude of benefits produced by avoiding the adverse environmental impact. Similarly, information on potential expenditures can also be useful. These two approaches are explained in the following paragraphs.

One method of analyzing the value of adverse environmental impacts on those affected is to examine responses to these impacts. If costs are voluntarily incurred to alleviate damage, these costs indicate the victim's minimum valuation of mitigating the damage. The amount is only a minimum for two reasons: the response may be constrained by the ability to pay for the defensive measures, and the benefits of the measures taken may be far greater than the costs involved. The approach that examines these reactions is known as the *preventive expenditures* method. This procedure examines actual expenditures made to alleviate an environmental problem. It is based on the idea that a person would incur these costs only if he felt that the reduction in damage was at least equal to the amount spent. Moreover, the person would continue to incur more costs up to the point where the additional expenditure is just equal to the value of the additional reduction in damages or until income constraints become binding. (In economic terms, additional costs would be incurred until the marginal benefits of the reduction in damages were equal to the marginal costs of further reduction.)

The second category of expenditure-based approaches involves potential expenditures. These techniques examine the investments that would be needed to offset or mitigate environmental damage. In some cases, these techniques can reveal whether it is more efficient to prevent damage from occurring or whether the damage can be repaired at reasonable cost. Unlike the techniques based on actual preventive expenditures, these techniques are based on potential (but as yet unmade) expenditures.

The first technique in this category is the *mitigation-cost approach*. This technique examines how much it would cost to mitigate or reverse the damage caused by a change in land use or a development project. This involves estimating the cost of labor and materials needed to counter the effects of the change. If a change in land use or implementation of a project would result in increased erosion, for example, one effect may be increased sedimentation in irrigation channels downstream. The additional cost of clearing the increased sediment should also be considered a cost of the project. As with the other techniques, only the additional costs attributable to the change, not the total cost, should be included.

Another technique in this category, the *replacement-cost approach*, looks at how much it would cost to replace productive assets that are damaged by a project or development. These costs must then be compared with the cost of preventing the damage from occurring. If the replacement costs are greater than the cost of prevention, then the damage should be avoided—assuming, of course, that the benefits of repairing the damage are greater than the costs. For example, deforestation may result in increased peak streamflows during the rainy season. If these increased flows would result in damage downstream, such as washing out roads or bridges, the costs of replacing these structures should be compared with the costs of preventing the damage from occurring. A less obvious application of the technique might be the cost of physically replacing soil and nutrients that would be lost if land-use practices that increased erosion levels were allowed. Kim and Dixon (1986) examined such a case.

A variation of this approach is the *shadow project*. If a development or change in policy would cause the loss of some environmental good or service, the cost could be approximated by examining the cost of a supplementary project that would provide a substitute for the good or service. If villagers depend on a nearby forest for fuelwood, for example, and consideration is being given to restricting this use, the cost of providing the fuelwood by developing a nearby woodlot could be examined. Another example might be to analyze the cost of providing alternative wildlife habitat if development of a wildlife-rich area is proposed.

The shadow project approach was used in analyzing the options for protecting or replacing a natural estuary in the Netherlands. Although not a protected area per se, the Oosterschelde region is a low-lying coastal area that has important wetlands and estuaries. Flooding and consequent loss of life and property were the immediate problems. The initial solution proposed a major dike to hold back the sea, but the dike would have closed off the estuary and many biological and recreational resources would have been lost. In the analysis of various options, one shadow project was considered: an artificial estuary in another location to replace the lost environmental benefits. An economic analysis of the various alternatives is reported in Hufschmidt and others (1983); the final decision was to build a special dam with large gates that would only be closed when flooding threatened. The shadow project analysis was a key component in the argument for the benefits of preserving the natural ecosystem and thereby avoiding the costs associated with the shadow project. In assessing the benefits to be gained from protection, the shadow project approach can indicate the costs that would be incurred if the natural system's benefits were to be replaced in another location.

Yet another variation of this technique is the *relocation-cost approach*. Here the costs of relocating a physical facility that would be damaged by a change in environmental quality are used to estimate the value of the damage. For example, if a development project would affect water quality to such an extent that people would no longer be able to use this water, the cost of relocating the intake upstream of the project would also be a project cost. Some of the examples given previously could also be evaluated by this technique if they could be relocated rather than replaced.

All of these cost-based approaches can be valuable in many situations, especially when benefits are difficult to estimate. Moreover, they provide a means of evaluating the benefits and costs of preventing or mitigating harm *before* the damage is done.

APPLYING VALUATION TECHNIQUES

The variety of benefits outlined in Table 1 range from directly usable benefits centered on production of goods and services to such intangibles as global life support and evolutionary processes. Table 2 indicates how some of the valuation techniques just described could be used for valuing certain categories of benefits. This listing is not exhaustive—it merely suggests where one can begin to determine values.

The best valuation technique to use in each case will depend on the circumstances. The value of a protected area for preserving certain ecological processes, for example, can be estimated by various means: a CVM approach estimates willingness to pay to retain this function; an opportunity-cost approach examines what net benefits must be given up to protect an area; a loss-of-earnings approach may be useful if the ecological process has clearly defined health benefits. In general, approaches that rely on data regarding the production of goods and services, changes in resource productivity, or cost-based information are directly applicable. Survey-based approaches present substantial conceptual and operational difficulties but can be very useful in certain situations. As a result of increasing work on these issues, the ability of the economics discipline to recognize and quantify the benefits of protected areas is growing.

An alternative way of considering valuation of protected areas is to follow the flowchart in Figure 2. Originally developed to handle any environmental effect (Dixon and Bojö 1988), the flowchart can also be used for protected areas and the anticipated effects of protecting or losing a natural area. The chart divides impacts into two broad categories: those that result in a measurable change in production of some

Table 2.
Ways of Valuing Various Benefits

Valuation Technique	Benefits
Change in productivity	watershed values ecological processes
Loss of earnings	ecological processes (health impacts)
Opportunity cost	ecological processes maintenance of biodiversity global life support
Property value	aesthetic
Wage differential	aesthetic
Travel cost	recreation/tourism cultural/historical
Bidding games	aesthetic spiritual
Take-it-or-leave-it experiments	cultural/historical recreation/tourism
Trade-off games	ecological processes option value
Costless choice	existence value global life support
Preventive expenditures	watershed values
Cost-effectiveness analysis	maintenance of biodiversity watershed value ecological processes

Replacement cost/
  shadow project/
  relocation cost
	watershed values
	recreation/tourism
	maintenance of biodiversity
	ecological processes

good or service and those that result in a change in environmental quality. The former impacts are quite straightforward and can be handled using market prices or appropriately adjusted shadow prices. The latter effects, changes in environmental quality, include a number of the more subtle valuation topics such as change in habitat, health effects, and air and water quality.

As shown in Figure 2, a number of valuation techniques can be applied to any impact. The ultimate decision on which approach to use depends on the exact conditions in each case. In the case of habitat change (or loss), for example, the analyst may use the opportunity-cost approach, replacement-cost approach, land-value approach, or contingent valuation method. Similarly, air and water quality changes can be addressed by several cost-based approaches. Figure 2 merely suggests where one can begin. Note also that certain potential benefits and costs mentioned earlier (biodiversity, cultural values) do not appear here. Estimation of benefits is still an evolving discipline and is as much an art as it is a hard science.

**Figure 2.
A Simple Valuation Flowchart**

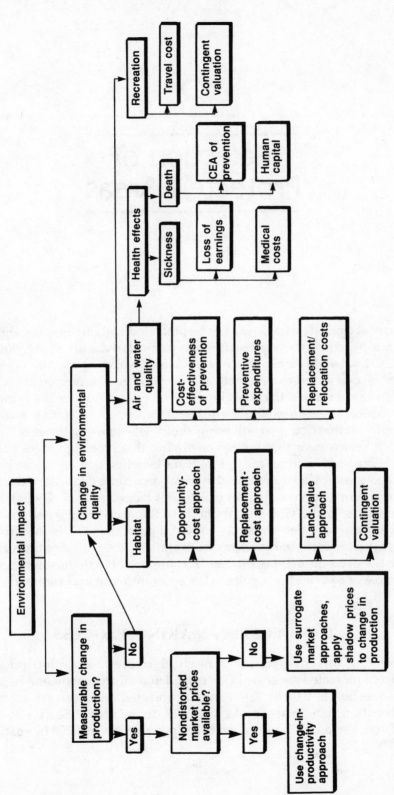

Source: Dixon and Bojö (1988).

3

Selection of
Protected Areas

In most countries, few areas can be protected without forgoing significant benefits. These pressures are particularly acute in developing
countries. Land is often scarce, and many developing countries believe
they cannot afford to designate a large number of protected areas and
forgo the revenues that development of these areas might bring. If
governments are to establish additional protected areas, they must be
convinced that doing so will bring about net economic benefits.

It seems clear that by demonstrating that protected areas have a
wide range of economically significant benefits, one can more easily
promote the case of enhanced natural area protection. But such an
"accounting" approach neglects a crucial factor: politics. Though economics can make vital contributions to the decision-making process,
few government decisions rely solely on economics. There are fundamental differences in how economics and political considerations enter
into the decision-making process. It is important to understand clearly
the role of each and recognize what economics can and cannot do.

THE DECISION-MAKING PROCESS

Protecting the environment is rarely the government's top priority.
Indeed, protected areas are often considered an environmental issue—
the question is usually "how many protected areas can we afford?"
rather than "how many protected areas do we need?" Since very few
protected areas fall in our category of "privately beneficial," it is usually

up to the government to establish them. In many cases, establishment of protected areas can be justified as "socially beneficial." When information is lacking or valuation is difficult, areas fall into the third category as having "undetermined benefits." Whatever the category, most government decisions to support protected areas are *social decisions* whereby some magnitude of social benefit (frequently undefined) is used to justify a clearly defined cost (both budget outlays and development benefits forgone).

Social benefits are frequently important in deciding the allocation of government resources—witness allocations for education, health, and the arts, among others. The political case for protected areas, however, is harder to justify: not only are the benefits more difficult to value and more diffuse in nature, but the forgone costs are easier to see. As a result, establishment of protected areas may well rank below most other environmental issues, such as control of air or water pollution. In considering the process whereby governments and countries decide on the allocation of resources for protected areas, it is therefore important to understand which decisions are essentially "political" and which ones are "economic." (One should never underestimate, however, the potential contribution of economic arguments to the making of political decisions.)

The Political Dimension

Politics often enters the decision process right from the start by affecting which areas are given consideration as potential protected areas (see Figure 3). Political pressure from domestic citizens, from interna-

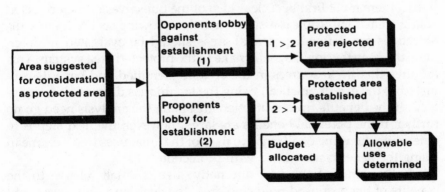

Figure 3.
The Political Decision-Making Process

tional organizations, or from government agencies often plays a significant role here. Pressure from within the country may come from university researchers, local government, students, or private environmental groups. Outside pressure may be from foreign governments or
international conservation groups.

Once an area is proposed, its opponents organize quickly. Forest
industries, mining industries, ranching and agricultural interests, or
any other group that sees potential uses in the area often object
strongly. Depending on their political power and the strength of their
arguments, the proposed area may be withdrawn from consideration.
In developing countries, such interests frequently have close ties with
government officials and can block the establishment of a protected
area. Less influential groups such as local villagers (who often have the
most to lose) rarely receive much attention; as a consequence, these
groups are often overlooked. If no opponents voice strong protest or if
the protected area's supporters are well organized and have a high
profile, the proposed area may continue through the administrative
process and become established as a protected area. Further decisions
are then made on budget allocations and which uses will be allowed in
the area. In some cases, compromises are made allowing certain commercial uses.

Note that economics has not played a central role in this scenario. It
has entered only as a motivating factor for opponents of the protected
area. The proponents rarely bring economics into the picture; their
arguments are usually based on biological or ethical considerations.

The Economic Dimension

Figure 4 shows a different decision-making structure incorporating
greater use of economics. Before areas are considered for protected
status, there must first be a clear idea of the objectives of the protected
area system. (This topic is discussed in the following section.) Once the
objectives are defined, potential areas should be evaluated to determine the contribution they will make to the protected area system. This
requires that the resources in the area be identified and benefits estimated to the extent practical, using the techniques discussed in Chapter 2. If the benefits from protection are small, the analysis need go no
further. If the potential benefits are large, however, the next step is to
determine the value of alternative uses of the area, uses that may mean
losing the benefits associated with protection.

If the value of the best alternative use is small relative to the
benefits of the proposed protected area, the decision is fairly easy and

Figure 4.
The Economic Decision-Making Process

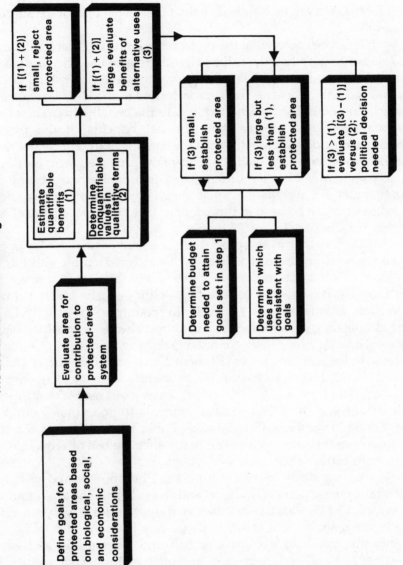

the area should be established as a protected area. When the value of
the alternative use is large, however, the decision becomes more difficult. Unlike the earlier process where such cases usually resulted in the
rejection of an area as a protected area, now the net benefits of the
protected area can be weighed against the net benefits of the alternative
uses.

If it can be shown that the protected area's quantifiable net benefits
alone are greater than the value of the alternative use, then the area falls
into the "socially beneficial" category and should be established as a
protected area. This was the approach used in the Hells Canyon example discussed in the last chapter, where the benefits from direct recreational use were greater than the net benefits of the proposed
hydroelectric development. When the benefits of the alternative use are
greater than the quantifiable benefits of the protected area, the decision
becomes harder. Here the difference in quantifiable benefits of the two
uses must be weighed against qualitative considerations. Several
frameworks can be used in this process. (See "Comparing Benefits and
Costs" in Chapter 1.)

It is clear that in the proposed economic framework for decision
making, political input has been reduced considerably and has been
replaced with a goal-oriented, economically influenced framework. It
is utopian, however, to believe that politics can be taken out of the
decision-making process. In developing countries, the benefits forgone
by establishing protected areas will almost always be considerable, and
strong interest groups will continue to fight against restrictions to their
access to valuable resources. Economic analysis of the direct and indirect benefits of protected areas is a powerful tool to wield against these
groups. The proponents of protected areas must realize that they have
to sell the economic and social arguments to policymakers, much as
was done in the Hells Canyon case. Public interest groups can play a
vital role in this process and can make effective use of economic argu-
.ments to further their cause.

A recent study carried out on the Philippine island of Palawan
illustrates these points (Hodgson and Dixon 1988). The area around the
town of El Nido and Bacuit Bay is the locale for a very interesting
resource management conflict. Bacuit Bay is famous for its beautiful
water and coral reefs, abundant fish and marine life, and isolated
setting. Fishing, both near-shore and offshore for pelagic species, is an
established industry. A resort-based scuba diving industry has also
developed, dependent on clear waters and the fish and coral of the bay.
The bay is not a protected area, but both fishermen and resort operators
have a vested interest in maintaining the natural ecosystem processes

for their economic gain and have in fact cooperated in managing and preserving the marine resource.

The system has recently been disturbed, however, by the operations of a large commercial logger. Although the bay's watershed forms only one small part of the company's logging concession area (Figure 5), logging creates considerable soil erosion and sediment deposition in the bay's water, thereby causing coral death and declining fish populations—a classic example of an economic externality. Hodgson and Dixon examined the gross benefits generated for the three industries under two scenarios. Scenario 1, a logging ban, allowed continued and growing fishery and tourism benefits but at the cost of forgone logging income. Scenario 2, continued legal logging within the watershed, produced short-term logging benefits but major costs in terms of reduced fishery and tourism revenues.

The results of this simple ecological/economic analysis have been used as a persuasive argument in policy discussions in Manila. Since all three resource-using groups have legal rights to operate, any change in use rights will have property rights implications. It now appears that as a result of the attention focused on the El Nido case, the bay may be made a marine park and some restrictions will be placed on further logging in the watershed. Conflicts over the use of resources are never easily resolved but, as this case illustrates, fairly simple analytic techniques can be used to prepare a case for resource protection.

In the decision-making processes described thus far, little emphasis has been given to the overall goals of a protected area *system*. In most cases individual areas are evaluated according to the opportunity costs associated with establishing them. Little thought is given to how each area contributes to a national system of protected areas. In the next section we examine the essential steps in creating such a system.

DEVELOPING A NATIONAL SYSTEM

A national system of protected areas can be developed in two ways. One alternative is to establish the system area by area in a process of individual decisions. This is a commonly used but ad hoc approach. The other alternative is to establish goals for a national system and then determine which areas can best contribute to the system. Here we focus on the latter method. In countries where the former ad hoc process has already been initiated, it is still possible to convert to the latter system by making some changes in regulations to fit the new goals of the national system. Regardless of the process, enabling legislation at the national level is necessary before the system can be established. (See Lausche 1980 for a discussion of protected area legislation.)

The process of classification was covered in Chapter 1. Regardless of what classifications a country ultimately decides on, the next step in creating an integrated protected-area system is to assign potential sites

Figure 5.
Bacuit Bay, Palawan, Philippines

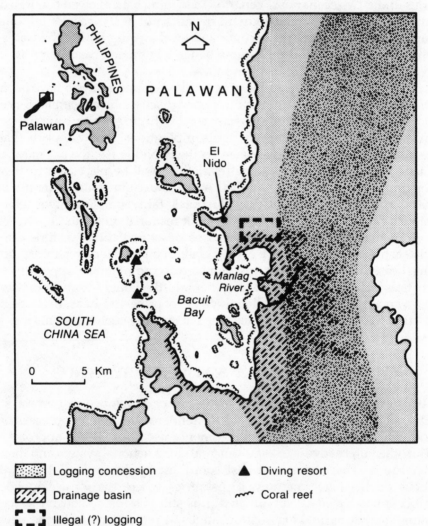

	Logging concession	▲	Diving resort
	Drainage basin	∿	Coral reef
	Illegal (?) logging		

Source: **Hodgson and Dixon (1988).**

to a number of these categories, depending on the area's specific attributes, the objectives for the area, and the forgone opportunities implied by the uses that would be prohibited in the area.

Another consideration is the availability of alternative areas that could provide similar benefits. If two sites would be equally valuable habitat for a rare species but one would involve much greater forgone benefits if designated as a wildlife sanctuary, it would be more efficient to establish the wildlife sanctuary in the area involving fewer forgone benefits. (This is an example of the cost-effectiveness approach discussed in Chapter 2.) The other area could then be established as, for example, a managed resource area where the species would still be protected, though at a lower level, and the forgone benefits would be much less.

For various aspects of establishing a protected area system see Thorsell (1985) and McNeely and Miller (1984). MacKinnon and colleagues (1986) provide a particularly thorough review of managing protected areas in the tropics. The following sections focus on the basic steps involved in establishing a protected area system and the key issues that need to be considered at each step.

STEP 1: CLARIFY THE OBJECTIVES OF THE SYSTEM. Why is the system being established at all? Presumably the reason for establishing a national protected-area system is to fulfill certain objectives that will benefit the country as a whole; in some cases it may also be expected to provide benefits to the world at large. These objectives must be carefully considered since they will guide all future decisions on protected areas, including which types of protected areas will be established. Each country will need to decide for itself which objectives it wants to meet and which objectives will be given priority. For example:

- Protection of watershed areas important to other areas and users downstream
- Protection of rare ecosystems
- Protection of areas with concentrations of economically important or potentially important species and varieties
- Protection of areas with concentrations of threatened species
- Protection of ecosystems with exceptional diversity
- Protection of fragile areas that may be easily degraded
- Protection of important aesthetic, cultural, historical, or recreational areas
- Providing enough open space in densely populated areas
- Providing enough areas to meet anticipated demands for recreation

- Protecting areas that will attract foreign tourists
- Protecting areas important for research and education
- Protecting areas important to local residents
- Protecting areas whose best use has not yet been determined

STEP 2: LIST THE POTENTIAL PROTECTED AREAS. The next step of the process is to identify all areas that might play a role in the protected area system. To do this, a broad inventory of the nation's land and its current patterns of use is necessary. Depending on the resources available for this task, current information may have to suffice; if more resources are available, selected areas may be investigated to see what resources the lands contain and what constraints might preclude certain uses. Areas currently uninhabited or with few settlements may be appropriate for a number of different protected-area designations, while other areas may have current uses or known alternative uses that limit the economic or political feasibility of their establishment as a protected area.

In countries with a high population density, very little land may be left for protected areas. In this case the country may wish to move quickly to protect, at least temporarily, all such areas before they disappear. In countries with vast natural areas remaining, there may be a variety of areas from which to choose.

It is essential that public opinion be solicited during this process. Information should be gathered from as many sources as possible—especially from those who will be most affected by the decisions to be made. Many areas will have people who depend on them for food, firewood, and other forest products; their needs will have to be reconciled with the needs of the protected area system. Failure to foresee potential conflicts will mean problems in protecting these areas once they are established. This land identification survey should result in a listing of all the potential protected areas and the categories appropriate for each.

STEP 3: ASSESS THE RESOURCES AND CONSTRAINTS. Once all the potential protected areas are identified, the next step is to determine the key functions and assets of each area. Some sites might provide outstanding recreational opportunities, for example, while others are important watershed areas or habitat for rare species. Certain areas may have more than one key function—for instance, they may provide watershed protection, scenic beauty, and wildlife habitat.

Along with the area's natural functions, its human uses must also be identified. The number of settlements, the existence of private property or leased concessions, the number of people who depend on the area—all must be given consideration. Some of these constraints may not be insurmountable: settlements can be relocated, concessions can be withdrawn, and alternative employment opportunities can be created. Eventually, however, the costs of these changes will have to be included.

STEP 4: DETERMINE THE PRELIMINARY CATEGORIES. Once resources and constraints are assessed, all the potential protected areas can be categorized. This is only a preliminary list, however, for some areas may eventually be put into other categories. Trade-offs may be necessary to ensure that all the system's objectives are met. Areas can be assigned a primary designation based on their anticipated most valuable use but should also be given secondary designations for other categories for which they could also be considered. Constraints and potential problems identified in Step 3 must also be considered.

STEP 5: DETERMINE NEEDS. If the protected area system is to bring about the intended benefits, certain requirements must be met. One primary consideration is the need to include as many different types of ecosystems as possible in order to maximize the number of species in the system. Since species distribution can vary widely even within an ecotype, further consideration must be given to ensure that species with limited spatial distributions are also included.

Adequate land to provide recreational opportunities for both national residents and foreign tourists (if desired) is another consideration. This includes areas for different types of recreation involving both dispersed and high-density uses. Projections need to be made based on expected population growth, participation rates, and potential for tourism. Important cultural, historical, and archaeological sites must also be noted. In general, then, all the objectives listed in Step 1 should be considered. This initial examination of the number of areas that fit into various categories will indicate the relative difficulty of meeting different objectives.

STEP 6: RECONCILE NEEDS AND COSTS. This step in the process is by far the most crucial. Since the system must be designed to meet a number of objectives simultaneously, an iterative process will be necessary to make trade-offs among different objectives and address shortcomings in certain areas. Thus far no detailed economic analysis of the benefits and costs of placing different areas in different categories has been carried out. Though detailed economic analysis will be necessary in some cases, it need not be performed until difficult decisions are made. Some decisions will be relatively easy given the obvious attributes of certain areas relative to the cost of protecting them.

To begin the process of assigning categories, a few simple guidelines can be followed:

Start with the easiest decisions first. Certain areas will have obvious assets and few constraints on their prospective status. Remote, inaccessible areas with a large number of species or rare species found at few sites are obvious candidates for protection as wildlife sanctuaries or strict nature reserves. Large, undisturbed scenic areas near major population centers are ideal candidates for national parks.

Identify areas with critical environmental roles. These areas may include forested upland watersheds with large capital projects downstream (such as dams or urban areas) or areas that protect water supplies for settlements or agricultural areas. Other areas in this category might include critical habitat for rare or economically important species, valuable areas for scientific research, or important open space.

Identify unique areas with few substitutes. Once the needs to meet the objectives of the protected area system are determined, the different habitats or sites where rare species are found should be identified. Rare habitats and species should be given early consideration since they will have few substitutes and thus are especially valuable due to their scarcity. Scarcity can come about for two reasons: some areas may be naturally scarce such as montane areas, wetlands, or coastal zones, while other areas may have formerly been abundant but are now scarce due to another, high-valued use. This second category of scarce areas, as well as certain areas in the first category, such as lowland forests and mangrove areas, are likely to entail significant forgone benefits if they are established as protected areas. Here it is likely that economic analysis of various uses will be necessary.

Identify important recreational areas. Some recreational areas may already have been identified by this point. Additional areas should now be identified based on the prior assessment of needs. Considerations should include establishing areas within reasonable distance from all population centers and tourist destinations.

STEP 7: DETERMINE FINAL CATEGORIES. The areas initially chosen are those that have large benefits for one reason or another. Where the costs of protecting these areas are relatively low, decisions are relatively easy. If there are significant alternative uses, the choices will be harder. The economic techniques discussed in the previous chapter, combined with the process portrayed in Figure 4, should help guide these decisions.

Determining the best status for the remaining areas is often difficult. Gaps in the system (both physical type and habitat type) should be addressed first. Areas with low opportunity costs that can fill these gaps should be assigned to the appropriate protection categories. If alternative areas are available that will fit the needs as well, those with the lowest opportunity cost should be chosen.

Areas that appear to be valuable to the system but would involve high costs should now be given consideration. In areas containing mining or timber concessions, the value of the resources that would be lost must be weighed against the benefits the area would provide if protected. If the benefits of protection are high, it may be possible to give the concessionaire another area and take away the concession in this valuable area. This is being done in the El Nido example cited earlier in this chapter. If the benefits are very high but no alternative areas are available, it may be worthwhile to buy back the concession if this can be done at a cost less than the value of the net benefits of the area as a protected area. Another possibility is to regulate the use of the concession to minimize the harm done to the area. If none of these alternatives is feasible, a less restrictive category such as a multiple-use managed area could be considered or boundaries could be redrawn to omit the concession area.

The final areas on the list of potential protected areas will be the most difficult to deal with. These are likely to be areas with few quantifiable benefits or areas with high-valued alternative uses. An economic evaluation would look at the additional benefits these areas would provide versus the costs associated with them. Exact valuation, however, may not be possible. One possibility is to designate some of these areas as resource reserves—a category designed to protect them temporarily until decisions can be made as to their best uses. Areas that have high-valued alternative uses and are not essential to the system should be dropped from consideration.

Though the overall process outlined here may seem straightforward, this is rarely the case. Filling all the gaps in the system while attempting to meet all the objectives is seldom a painless procedure. Carefully done, however, the process can yield a system that will provide a variety of benefits, both domestic and international, for many generations. Establishing a protected area system is only the first phase, however. The next chapter considers the key management issues vital for effective protection.

4

Management of Protected Areas

Identification of priorities, selection of sites, and formal designation as protected areas are all essential components of the process of protecting natural areas. Without these steps, only "privately beneficial" areas will be protected. Formal designation of an area as protected, however, is often one of the easier steps. *Effective* protection requires management; management, in turn, requires money; and this, ultimately, is often the most serious constraint on protection. Here we emphasize how economics can be used to guide management—in designing incentive systems, accommodating nearby residents, generating revenues, finding outside sources of funding, and allocating funds. (For the general aspects of protected area management see MacKinnon and others 1986; McNeely and others 1987; Moore 1984; and McNeely and Miller 1984.)

PROTECTING ENDANGERED RESOURCES

The fact that protection is required means there is some threat to the natural area. Threats may come from big developers, from individual resource users, or from nature itself. While threats from nature (such as fires or insect outbreaks) may be important, here we concentrate on threats from humans since economics is better equipped to deal with these issues.

A crucial issue in management is designing policies that benefit both the protected area and nearby communities. In many settings, effective protection will require changing current patterns of behavior to limit or prevent uses that endanger the resources of the protected area. Finding ways of accomplishing this without imposing a burden on these residents is the focus of our discussion.

Threats to Protected Areas

While preparing the list of the world's most threatened protected areas, the Commission on National Parks and Protected Areas of the IUCN (CNPPA 1984) found that the most commonly reported threats were inadequate management of resources and human encroachment. Though many developing countries have impressive protected-area systems on paper, the situation in the field is often very different. There is virtually no government presence in many reserves, and many areas are already degraded. Even where workers are present, they often have neither the numbers nor the equipment to protect their area. Human encroachment includes both permanent activities, such as shifting or permanent agriculture, as well as transient use. Poaching is a major example of sporadic human encroachment and ranges from timber poaching in some of Thailand's protected areas to the well-publicized poaching of elephants, rhinos, and other animals in many East African national parks.

The problem of human encroachment is consistent with the three basic issues that underlie many problems in developing countries, including threats to protected areas (Malik 1984): poverty, ever-increasing need for land, and development processes. All three of these issues are interrelated and are compounded by another problem facing most developing countries: rapid population growth.

Threats to protected areas can be of human or natural origin. Sometimes the source is a combination of the two: fire can have either human or natural causes and can be affected by both natural and human-induced conditions; floods can be exacerbated by human activities both inside and outside the protected area's boundaries; overgrazing by wildlife can sometimes be traced back to human activities (such as removal of predators).

Some occurrences may be considered threats in one type of protected area, yet not in another. For example, natural occurrences such as droughts, floods, fires, and insect outbreaks may be tolerated in strict nature reserves but not in national parks. The decision on when to intervene is not always clear-cut—witness the controversy over the recent fires in Yellowstone National Park. Controversy may also arise about intervention on behalf of a particular species. When natural conditions threaten a species considered important by humans, the threat may be mitigated through human intervention while another species may not be given similar assistance.

Human-induced threats to protected areas are numerous and widespread. Moreover, these threats often change as the development process proceeds—protected areas in developing countries face different threats than those in the developed world. According to Machlis and Tichnell (1987), the threats most often cited in developing countries include unlawful entry, fire, harassment of animals, illegal removal of animal life and vegetation, and conflicting demands. The threats reported most often by developed countries were invasion by exotic plants, chemical pollution, legal removal of animals, noise pollution, and mining. Fast-growing tourism industries have also created problems, both in developing and in developed countries. (See McNeely, Miller, and Thorsell 1987 for a discussion of appropriate tourism development.)

Work forces in protected areas are often paid extremely low wages, especially in developing countries. This lack of adequate financial compensation makes it difficult to attract and retain well-trained staff to protected areas, leads to morale problems, and can end in corruption. To supplement their income, workers may violate restrictions themselves or accept payments to allow others to violate the restrictions.

Encroachment and overuse of protected area resources by nearby residents are common and understandable phenomena. When a natural area is protected, the people who have traditionally used its resources are usually denied access and receive no compensation. They pay a sizable private cost to help the country obtain social benefits. As a result, many people continue to extract resources and pose a critical threat to the area. The following sections deal with the issue of balancing protection and use of protected areas.

Determining Allowable Uses

What constitutes a threat? Activities can be divided into four categories: (1) uses consistent with the objectives of the protected area that do not require restriction within the foreseeable future; (2) uses that do not currently require restriction but may become threats in the future; (3) uses that could be allowed in restricted amounts but whose current level is damaging some resource; and (4) uses inconsistent with the objectives of the protected area. Both category 1 and category 4 are relatively easy to manage—the former can be allowed without restriction and the latter must be totally banned. Categories 2 and 3, however, involve more difficult choices.

Many uses are no problem at low levels but will constitute a threat if the use increases beyond a certain point. Collecting certain plants, gathering firewood, and hunting wildlife may all be tolerable at low levels in certain areas but will endanger the long-term viability of the resource if allowed to expand beyond the capacity of the resource to replenish itself. Here one must decide whether to allow the use at all or restrict the use to some acceptable level. Although management and enforcement are usually easier if the use is totally banned, this may not be the optimal policy. If a certain level of use would not damage the resource, banning the use altogether will result in forgoing the benefits gained from limited use. Such benefits are often extremely important to local residents. These forgone benefits (which can also be viewed as a cost) must be weighed against the damage that might occur if the restrictions are not effective (causing the resource to become damaged) plus the cost of enforcing the regulations.

Direct harvesting from protected areas has worked well in a number of situations. MacKinnon and colleagues (1986) cite the systems in use in Chitwan National Park in Nepal and Matobo National Park in Zimbabwe, both of which permit grass harvesting for thatching purposes. In both cases, controlled harvesting is allowed to provide some compensation to local people for their loss of the park's natural resources. The Matobo National Park scheme was developed in 1962 to permit strictly controlled harvesting of thatching grass within the park in exchange for a promise that those benefiting from the program would not poach, trespass with cattle, or set fires within the park. As reported by Child (1984), the annual harvest quota of 40,000 to 115,000 bundles, worth at least 50 cents each, represents an income of $200 to $600 for each villager involved for six to eight weeks of work per year. The park receives payment of one in every ten bundles cut and uses its share to maintain park facilities. This program has resulted in increased income to the local population, sustainable use of the park's grass resources, and fewer management problems from human encroachment.

Reducing Demands on Resources

Most of the threats arising from uses that may require limitations are threats to individual species—overhunting of a wildlife species, for example, or overcollection of a plant species. For uses such as gathering fuelwood, more than one species may be threatened. In addition to direct regulation of the use, two other responses can be taken. First, actions can be taken to increase the supply of the resource. Alternatively, steps can be taken to reduce the demand for the resource.

Increasing the supply normally involves development of an alternative supply, usually outside the protected area's boundaries or in a buffer zone. Woodlots for fuelwood, captive breeding for wildlife, farms or plantations for plant species—all are examples of alternative supply sources. A number of sources can be tapped to develop these supplemental supplies including aid agencies, governments, universities, nonprofit organizations, and national research organizations. If alternative sources of supply are made available, there is less need to poach these resources inside the protected area.

There are a number of alternatives for reducing demand for a resource. When the motivation behind a use is to supplement income, any alternative that increases income will reduce the demand for the resource in question. Rural development schemes that raise income, whether or not they involve the protected area, will reduce the need of nearby residents to encroach on a protected area. Another means of reducing demand is to develop supplies of another resource as a substitute. If the resource is used for food, developing alternative crops that can be grown intensively in buffer zones or outside the park will reduce demand. Again, many organizations can help with this task. The Matobo National Park example illustrates the development of sustainable harvests within the protected area.

If the endangered resource is poached for commercial use, actions can be directed to regulate sale of the product in the marketplace. If the penalties or level of enforcement are increased, both poachers and dealers will be less apt to participate in the sale of the resource. This will reduce the demand for the resource, thus limiting poaching. Stronger enforcement of existing laws and eliminating loopholes will be necessary for this option to succeed.

The recent worldwide campaign to reduce the international ivory trade and associated killing of African elephants is a case in point. The African elephant population is now estimated at only about 700,000—less than half the number that existed only ten years ago. Efforts to reduce poaching, however, have produced some undesirable side effects. Greater use of police power to reduce poaching has led to escalating levels of violence and increased use of weapons—not only against elephants but also against police or even tourists who are in the wrong place at the wrong time. At the same time, the shrinking supply of ivory brings higher market prices and, in turn, greater incentives for illegal ivory harvesting. Even though the weight of an average tusk has declined steadily due to poaching of younger animals (tusks now average 7 pounds versus 15 to 20 pounds previously), one poached animal can yield a return to the poacher that is equal to the annual per capita income in many African countries (WWF 1989a). The economic incentives are certainly a major factor in the continued slaughter of elephants.

There is no easy solution. Gradually reducing the international trade in elephant ivory will help, but it will take some time to be reflected in lower ivory prices. Legal ivory supplies, from existing stocks or as a product of sustainable management of elephant herds in some countries, may gradually increase and will help to keep ivory prices down, thus discouraging poaching. Unlike the demand for whale products such as oil and meat, for which there are many acceptable substitutes, the demand for elephant ivory is less likely to disappear completely. Unless properly regulated, the demand will continue to put growing pressures on elephant herds in game parks as well as protected and unprotected areas in Africa.

Another option for reducing demand is to relocate people who are using the resource. Forced relocation should only be used as a last resort; providing incentives that get people to relocate voluntarily is far preferable. Incentives such as guaranteeing employment or providing allotments of land may benefit both the protected area and the people being relocated—especially where populations cannot be sustained in their current location. In some cases, education can be used to reduce demand. If local residents are made aware of the damage being done, they may be persuaded to reduce or stop their use of the resource. If residents consider the use to be vital to their survival, however, no amount of education will be effective.

Direct Regulation and Restricted Community Use

In addition to these supply and demand options, direct regulation of the use of resources may be necessary. Perhaps the best form of regulation is to provide guidance and allow a community to regulate use of the resource on its own. This option is best suited to situations where a single, cohesive community can be given sole access to the resource, even within a protected area. If community members are all willing to act in the best interests of the community, they can be given control of the resource subject to outside monitoring to ensure that its use stays at an acceptable level. One advantage of this option is that the need for enforcement is greatly reduced; the community can police itself and simultaneously prevent outsiders from using the resource. Khao Yai National Park in Thailand has benefited from an innovative program set up in Ban Sap Tai, a neighboring village. This program promotes nature tourism and uses villagers as guides and hosts; there are also village development activities designed to increase village income (Dobias 1988).

A number of other examples where such a policy has succeeded are described in McNeely (1988). The case of traditional Masai herders and Kenya's Amboseli National Park is one example. Both the Masai cattle and the area's wildlife depend on water and pasture lands located inside and outside the park; the needs and range of both cattle and wildlife change during the year according to the amount of rainfall and pasture availability. Restricting wildlife to the park's boundaries and excluding all cattle would result in a lower population of both. A compromise between the local Masai and the park authorities resulted in substantial economic gains to both parties. The solution included payment of a grazing compensation to the Masai to cover their livestock losses to wildlife migrants. According to Western (1984), the net monetary gain of the park per year from use of Masai lands would be about $500,000 and the benefits from the park to the Masai would result in an income 85 percent greater than from cattle herding alone.

In a different type of setting—Sagarmatha (Mount Everest) National Park in Nepal—Sherpa (1988) describes how the local population, largely Sherpas, continue to live within the park boundaries. The government of Nepal seeks to integrate conservation objectives into the country's social and economic structures. By allowing continued use of park resources, but with certain restrictions, the management goal is to promote resource conservation as well as economic improvements for the local population.

When community-based management is not possible, other regulatory schemes will be needed. If a limited amount of use is not detrimental to the protected resource, a permit system can be established to regulate the number of users. Thus the collection of herbs and spices is permitted in Thai national parks, grass for thatch and construction in several Asian countries, and firewood in many European protected forests. Implementing such a system is often problematic, however. Decisions need to be made on who gets permits, and penalties must be established for users who do not hold permits. The cost of enforcing the permit system may be considerable.

Another alternative is to allow everyone to use the resource but restrict the amount that can be harvested. The state of Florida, for example, has a two-day "sport fisherman lobster season" before the opening of the commercial lobster season. Harvesting is allowed in state park waters (as well as outside) but is limited to six lobsters per person. Spot checks and heavy fines help ensure compliance. These schemes have their drawbacks, however, since enforcing the quotas may be difficult and expensive.

As in the case of lobsters in Florida, certain uses can be restricted to particular areas or certain times of the year. This approach involves determining where or when such uses will not be detrimental. Buffer zones can be established, for example, where certain uses are allowed. To implement this type of policy effectively, penalties must be imposed on those who disregard the regulations.

In general, penalties and monitoring will always be needed to enforce regulations (unless resources are regulated by the community). The degree to which regulations will be effective depends on three factors: the benefits to be gained by disregarding the regulation, the probability of being caught, and the penalty for being caught. All of these factors can be affected by management policies. The first factor, the benefits to be gained from illegal harvesting, can be handled through the supply and demand options discussed in the previous section. The probability of being caught will depend on the effectiveness of enforcement measures—which in turn depends on the enforcement budget and the dedication of the guard force. Penalties should reflect the damage caused by the action in question. For actions that require regulations, all three factors must be considered when regulatory policies are being designed.

Though penalties and enforcement are necessary tools, they are the least desirable way of regulating activities. They create hostility between local residents and guards that can lead to violent confrontations, as with elephant poachers in Africa. Eliminating the need for villagers to poach protected areas in order to survive is far more desirable.

Protected Areas and Alternative Development

Most of the regulations just described rely on a system of penalties and enforcement or integration of local communities into the management of the protected area. These can be looked at as ways of reducing actions that adversely affect protected areas. Another approach is to create incentives for communities to change from harmful patterns of resource use to other income-generating activities that are less damaging to protected areas. (Community-based regulation can also be looked at as a positive incentive since it gives the community a reason to protect the resource.)

Protected areas can be managed to provide a number of incentives for the community. When management plans are being designed, it is important to consider how to maximize the direct economic benefits of the protected area to the community. One method of benefiting the community is to provide as many employment opportunities as possible for local residents. Residents can work as guards, help in construction activities, build trails, and take care of daily maintenance. Someone employed by the protected area has much more incentive to protect it and ensure its continued existence. Another source of employment is through the promotion of nature-based tourism. Tourism provides jobs in restaurants and accommodation facilities and as guides. It also provides a market where local artisans and craftsmen can sell their handiwork. Durst (1988) and Whelan (1990) discuss a number of ways in which nature tourism can benefit local communities. A useful bibliography on nature tourism has been prepared by Ingram and Durst (1987).

Local residents should be allowed to profit from the protected area by giving them the right to continue harvesting resources if such uses are sustainable and not detrimental to the objectives of the area. The examples from Nepal and Kenya illustrate this approach. Constant monitoring is needed to ensure that the protected area is not being damaged by such uses. In many cases, however, establishment of a protected area will mean that some uses must be restricted or prohibited altogether. For local residents who are forced to give up such practices, there will be a loss of income that is bound to create hostility. Those who suffer direct losses from the establishment of a protected area must be compensated in some manner, either directly or via alternative income-generating opportunities.

Community development activities including schools, sanitation facilities, electricity, water systems, and health clinics are also potential forms of compensation. But residents should be made aware that these facilities are, at least in part, compensation for previous activities that are no longer allowed. Provision of such facilities does not make up for a loss in income, however. If damaging activities are to be reduced, they must be replaced with other forms of income-generating activities. For example, agricultural inputs can be provided free or at subsidized cost. Inputs that improve crop yields will increase incomes and reduce the need to engage in activities detrimental to the protected area.

Many of the programs mentioned in the section on supply and demand options are also forms of community development. Development of alternative sources of supply to replace prohibited activities can often reduce reliance on protected areas. Village woodlots and captive wildlife-breeding programs are two good examples since timber and wildlife poaching are often serious problems.

Revolving loan funds are another means of helping local residents improve their quality of life. This approach involves establishing an initial capital fund that is loaned to villagers to invest in agricultural inputs, machinery, or other income-producing activities that are currently restricted due to a lack of available funds. The loans are made at low rates of interest and are repaid into the loan fund. This type of activity has been initiated at Ban Sap Tai, a village outside of Khao Yai National Park in Thailand, with a great deal of success (Dobias and Khontong 1986).

One common feature of all these programs is that they reduce the need for local residents to degrade the protected area by providing alternative opportunities. In essence, they attempt to guide behavior into less damaging patterns by creating incentives. Similarly, eliminating policies that encourage damaging activities will help to reduce the pressures on protected areas. McNeely (1988) details a number of ways in which incentives and disincentives can be used to encourage the conservation of biological resources.

All of these programs involve costs. In addition to funding from the national government, two other sources of funds are available. First, international organizations may be interested in such projects since they will benefit both local residents and protected areas. Nongovernmental organizations (NGOs), national governments, or universities can help design projects, apply for funds, and assist with implementation. Another potential source of funds is to allocate a percentage of revenues generated by the protected area to development projects. Since it is local residents who often end up losing the most when protected areas are established, returning some of the fees collected is both equitable and a means of getting local residents to take an active interest in the area. If protected areas and local communities are to coexist and flourish, nearby residents must not be forced to pay major costs associated with establishment.

Few protected areas generate sufficient revenues to support substantial management activities and community development. In many cases, however, there is at least some potential for increasing the revenues generated.

INCREASING THE FINANCIAL RETURNS

Although protected areas can be shown to yield many benefits, these benefits are not always easily captured by governments. Even if governments are convinced of their importance, budget problems will continue to limit the establishment and management of protected areas. If, however, these areas are able to provide greater returns to the government to offset their costs, the chances for larger budget allocations and increased political support are enhanced.

Difficulties in Capturing Benefits

Many of the economic factors that make it difficult to estimate the benefits from protected areas are also responsible for the difficulties governments have in capturing such benefits. Perhaps the key factor is nonexcludability. Once a protected area is established, many of the benefits are enjoyed by everyone—not only visitors to the protected area. Nearby residents are all able to enjoy scenic views of the area. Local farmers and villagers benefit from animals that breed in the park but wander beyond the boundaries to areas where they can be legally killed. Regulation of streamflow provides hydrologic benefits to downstream areas.

All these effects are social benefits. The problem for governments, however, is that they are forced to bear the cost of providing them (such as the cost of establishing and managing a protected area) without receiving direct monetary returns from them. The benefits described here mostly remain within national borders, which at least means that the country's social welfare is improved, even if at government expense. These benefits justify the use of general tax revenues to support protected areas. Many of the most significant benefits, however, are not confined within national borders—if a species is protected through the creation of a protected area, all mankind benefits. If a tropical forest is protected, this adds to the entire global life-support system. In these cases, developing countries are providing benefits to everyone, including residents of countries far richer than their own, without compensation.

The central problem with nonexcludable benefits is that people have no incentive to pay for them. Since they cannot be excluded from enjoying the benefits, they are in essence free riders. The only means of encouraging people to pay for the benefits they receive is to make them aware that without outside help, some of these benefits may no longer be provided.

Table 1 characterizes some of the benefit categories (recreation, genetic resources, education, research) as "possibly nonexcludable." Often fees are not charged for these benefits because of existing laws such as patent rights or because of the difficulty in obtaining payment. In some cases, however, governments can change their practices and require payment for access to these resources. Charges for off-site benefits are also difficult to collect since people have no choice in the decisions that result in such benefits. The governing authority, however, may be able to require at least partial payment for these benefits as long as the area where the benefits accrue is in the same jurisdiction as where the benefits originate. For example, a regional irrigation authority could charge beneficiaries who live downstream from a protected area for the benefits they receive provided that these people reside in an area subject to the irrigation authority's jurisdiction. Even though people may not have any alternative but to receive these benefits, charging them a portion of the value would still leave them better off than if the area were no longer protected and the benefits lost.

Generating Revenues

Though it may not be possible to capture all the benefits that protected areas provide, it is certainly possible to increase the returns. Some of the methods described here can be implemented by the country where the protected area is located; others involve international cooperation.

USER FEES. The easiest method of generating revenue is to charge on-site users a fee based on the benefits they receive from using the area. Many countries already charge entry fees for recreation, but often the charges are minimal. Developing countries should institute a two-tier fee system with a lower charge for visits by domestic residents and a higher charge for international visitors. China, for example, uses a two-tier fee system for most cultural and historical sites. Given the high cost of international travel, the additional cost of an entrance fee to a major protected area, even a relatively high fee of US$10 or more, will have only a negligible effect on the total number of foreign visitors to a site. Fees for accommodations within protected areas should be comparable to those charged for privately run accommodations. Camping fees too could be set on a two-tier system.

A less common type of user fee is one charged to researchers who wish to enter protected areas. Though some fields of research will benefit the host country, many other research topics yield benefits that accrue outside the country. An additional fee charged for research would be insignificant compared with the cost of international travel and thus would probably not affect the demand for research in protected areas.

A more controversial type of user fee charges people to collect firewood or other forest products where such uses are compatible with the objectives of the protected area. Caution is required for this type of policy, however. In many protected areas, poaching and encroachment represent the single greatest threat. If the overall aim is to reduce poaching, allowing villagers to make limited use of the area without charge may be more beneficial than imposing a user fee. In such cases, local villagers should be allowed to use the area at no cost but permits should be required for people living outside a given radius of the park or for certain uses that need to be regulated.

CONCESSION FEES. In addition to charging fees to people who directly use protected areas, fees can also be charged to those who provide services to park users—by licensing concessions for food, lodging, transportation, and retail stores, for example. By auctioning or leasing the rights to operate such concessions, governments can control development in and around protected areas and simultaneously raise revenues to help maintain the area. Moreover, governments can impose conditions on concession leases to address other objectives such as hiring local employees or selling locally produced goods.

Charges can also be levied on off-site facilities. In prewar Cambodia, for example, the famous complex of ruins associated with Angkor Wat was maintained by the government but was completely open to visitors without any formal payment. This policy enhanced the visitor's enjoyment of the site and allowed casual exploration. The government, however, collected a special tax on all hotel rooms in the nearby town of Siemreap to support its conservation and preservation efforts. Since virtually all visitors to Angkor stayed in these hotels (and the ruins were the main reason for people coming to the town), this was an unobtrusive means of revenue collection. In fact, since the charge was built into the room rates, the visitors did not even realize how the system worked.

PATENTS AND ROYALTIES. Maintenance of biodiversity is one of the principal benefits of preserving protected areas. Improvements in plant and animal food sources through biotechnology and development of many drugs and other products can often be traced back to new species or new varieties found in a developing country. The direct benefits to the country itself, however, are no greater than for any other country. (They must purchase the improved seed or new product, for example, on the open market just like everyone else.) Naturally occurring plant germ plasm has always been a public good exchanged freely between countries. Naturally occurring species and varieties are considered the common heritage of mankind. Given the current costs of protecting as yet undiscovered species, however, this policy denies countries the opportunity to benefit from their sacrifice. Some countries have already restricted the availability of germ plasm for economically important species. Ethiopia, for example, has completely restricted exports of plant germ plasm (Myers 1981).

Clearly, changes are needed. One change that would create a strong incentive to protect species-rich areas would be to extend patent rights to newly discovered species or varieties. The benefits from any plant or animal that is found to have commercial applications should be split between the country of origin and the individual or organization who discovers the new application. Such a policy would not only encourage developing countries to maintain biodiversity but would also promote expenditures to discover new species. It would also be consistent with the United Nations' recognition of the right to national sovereignty over natural resources (United Nations 1974).

Patent law distinguishes between "invention" and "discovery." Discovery of something that exists naturally is not given any exclusive rights; invention, however, which is the development of some new creation, is given exclusive rights. (See Sedjo 1988 for a discussion of this topic.) Such a distinction does not recognize that discovery may not be possible if no incentives are created to protect the resource. Overhauling the international code of law is not something that can be done by one country. It may be possible, however, to restrict entry to protected areas by scientists unless written agreement is given in advance that rights to any inventions based on materials found in the area will be shared between the host country and the researchers. Many scientists may initially refuse to participate in such a system, but if it is adopted by a number of countries, they may eventually accept it.

This policy is not without cost. Initially it may inhibit research in countries adopting such a policy and thereby delay important discoveries. Moreover, scientists in the developed countries are sure to complain bitterly; this has already occurred where this idea has been advanced (see Wilkes 1987). Given the potential value of unknown genetic resources, however, incentives for protection are urgently needed. In addition to royalties on research products, royalty systems could also be established for other activities undertaken in protected areas. For example, permission for books, photos, or films made in protected areas could be exchanged for a certain percentage of the revenues made on these items.

PLANT BREEDING AND IMPROVEMENT PROGRAMS. If current international laws cannot be restructured, developing countries themselves, or with the help of developed countries, can establish their own research institutions to develop new products from naturally occurring species. Some countries have already begun such programs—for example, the Pharmaceuticals and Natural Products Department of the Thailand Institute of Scientific and Technological Research. Such programs, however, are often subject to severe budget limitations. If developing countries can learn to develop new products on their own, they will be able to increase the benefits they receive from protecting their genetic endowment.

INTERNATIONAL COMPENSATION SCHEMES. There are a variety of ways in which developed countries or NGOs can promote improved protection of protected areas and the genetic resources they contain. International schemes are necessary in this case, since many of the benefits are not confined within the country though the government bears all the costs. Sedjo (1988) discusses the possibility of designating genetically rich areas as global assets. Countries would retain sovereignty over their land but would be paid "interest" based on its asset value. Payments would also reflect how well the area is maintained and thus would create a financial incentive for proper management. Potential problems with the system, however, include decisions on who should pay what share and how an area's asset value would be determined. A less complicated arrangement would be to have developed countries or NGOs make individual arrangements on particular areas or with specific countries. This approach would reduce the problems and simplify the transaction. An initial payment would be made to help establish the area, and annual payments would depend on its effective management.

A variation on this idea is the "debt-for-nature swap," which has already been used to protect valuable areas in Latin America, Asia, and Africa. Basically an environmental group such as Conservation International or the World Wildlife Fund buys debt at a discounted rate on the open market and then exchanges it for a newly created obligation by the developing country to fund a conservation program with local currency. In Bolivia, for example, the government granted legal protection to the Beni Biosphere Reserve and established a fund in local currency to manage the area (Palca 1987). The swaps implemented to date have reduced external debt of the participating countries by almost US$100 million (World Resources Institute 1989). Given the total debt burden of the developing world, such programs may not be effective in eliminating the debt problems but could help in protecting individual areas. In 1989, for example, the Worldwide Fund for Nature signed a US$3 million debt-for-nature agreement to support conservation of Madagascar's unusual and varied wildlife. The money will go for protection and management of high-priority protected areas (WWF 1989b). For a recent review of the issues involved in debt-for-nature swaps, see Hansen (1988).

Another possibility is the formation of a new multilateral lending agency that would concentrate on funding conservation projects. A recent project commissioned by the United Nations Development Program has recommended the formation of an "International Environmental Facility" (IEF). Rather than a new venture, they see the IEF as a jointly financed, interagency facility of the Organization for Economic Cooperation and Development's bilateral development agencies and the multilateral development banks that would collaborate with relevant UN agencies, developing countries, and NGOs (World Resources Institute 1989). As envisioned, the IEF would identify, design, and fund conservation projects that might not be attractive to private lenders because of their long gestation times and payback periods. In general, the IEF would serve as an intermediary between developing countries, bilateral and multilateral aid agencies, and NGOs. Its financial role would be to assemble cofinancing packages combining standard development financing with special funding for components of a project with long-term, noncapturable paybacks.

The potential scope for arrangements like these is impressive. In addition to the government-led schemes discussed here, NGOs also have the potential to provide significant aid. Environmental awareness in the developed countries concerning the problems of deforestation and species loss is growing rapidly. More and more people are recognizing that developing countries will not be able to establish and maintain protected areas without outside help. All of these measures can help developing countries to increase the financial returns from protected areas. The more benefits these countries can derive from protected areas, the more incentive there is to establish and maintain them.

FUNDING AND MANAGEMENT

The most common constraint on effective protection and management is lack of funds. Funds are needed for a wide variety of activities—from boundary marking and infrastructure development to staff training and interpretive/educational programs. Establishing a protected area without allocating funds for management is simply a token gesture.

Once a protected area is established, a management plan should be prepared and implemented. (For guidelines on preparing management plans, see Miller 1978 and MacKinnon and others 1986.) Among other details, the plan should indicate the costs of different suggested activities along with a priority ranking. Most countries simply do not have the funds to fully implement management plans for all their protected areas. Indeed, it may be difficult even to obtain the funds to prepare a management plan. Once governments understand the true benefits generated by protected areas, however, they may be more willing to allocate the funds needed.

Sources of Funding

Few protected-area systems generate enough revenues to pay the cost of maintenance, let alone the opportunity costs of establishment. This does not mean that protected areas do not pay for themselves, however; when all the direct and indirect benefits of protected areas are calculated, the total will be much higher than the financial receipts they generate and, indeed, may be higher than the total costs.

In the previous section we examined a number of methods for increasing the funds generated by protected areas. Some of these were based on direct funding for establishment and management from outside sources; others involved using the resources of protected areas to generate funds, although there is no guarantee that these funds will remain within the protected area itself or even within the protected-area system. Overall, there are four major sources of funds for protected areas: national budgets, revenues from activities in protected areas, private-sector funding, and international assistance.

NATIONAL BUDGETS. Since protected areas provide a number of benefits to nearby residents and to the nation as a whole, it is only reasonable to expect national governments to contribute to the protected-area system. Budget constraints make it unlikely that the system will receive enough funding from the central government to effectively manage all protected areas. At a minimum, however, national funding should be large enough to develop a central planning and administrative agency of sufficient size to oversee the protected-area system along with enough funds to provide at least a nominal presence at each protected area. This will provide a primary funding base for the system, which can then be supplemented by several sources. National-level funding can come from general tax revenues or from earmarked taxes from specific sectors. For example, a portion of taxes from natural-resource-based industries, such as forestry or mining, can be directly allocated to protected areas.

REVENUES FROM ACTIVITIES IN PROTECTED AREAS. User fees and concession charges can be applied to a number of activities in protected areas. Entry fees, accommodation charges, tour guide services, stores, restaurants—all are potential sources of revenue. Other sources might include charges on research, royalties from books, photographs, and films, as well as a percentage of revenues from products developed from biological resources originating within the protected area. Fees for permits to hunt, fish, or collect materials from the area are another possibility. Fines from those caught violating regulations are yet another source of funds.

In some cases it may be possible to assess fees on people outside the protected area who benefit from its existence, as in the case of Angkor Wat in Cambodia. This idea might also extend to charges for water where water supplies are dependent on a protected area (McNeely 1988). Another possibility is a fee for permits to harvest wildlife that wanders outside of park boundaries. Some protected areas may be able to support commercial harvests of certain wildlife or plant species. If these products are traded internationally, taxes on their export may be a source of income.

Fees generated from protected areas should ideally remain within the system itself. At least a portion of the fees should remain within the area to provide an incentive for collecting them. These fees can then be used in a variety of activities aimed at increasing the effectiveness of protection or improving management. Consideration should also be given to applying some of these fees to community development programs to offset any losses incurred by local residents from the establishment of the protected area.

McNeely (1988) discusses a number of ways to promote conservation of biological resources at the community level. These include direct incentives in cash (rewards, fees, compensation for losses, grants, loans) as well as direct incentives in kind (food, livestock, access to resources where sustainable harvesting is practiced). As McNeely notes, direct incentives in kind normally work best in less developed areas, conditions commonly found in the villages close to national parks in developing countries. Cash incentives may be more difficult to administer and monitor.

PRIVATE-SECTOR FUNDING. Funding can be solicited from a variety of sources in the private sector including individuals, corporations, and nonprofit organizations. Such funds may be given directly to a protected area, to a national agency, or to an intermediary established to collect and distribute funds. As awareness of the importance of protected areas grows, so will private-sector funding.

INTERNATIONAL ASSISTANCE. A variety of mechanisms for international assistance have been noted here. These mechanisms are becoming increasingly popular as developed countries begin to recognize that they too have a responsibility to protect these globally important resources. Debt-for-nature swaps are one example of these mechanisms. But international assistance is not limited to money. Important contributions can be made through assistance in education and training, establishing information and monitoring systems, or providing equipment. Though these actions do not increase the amount of funding available, they are valuable in improving the effectiveness of protection efforts. Press and television coverage of the plight of the African elephant has been an important factor in the recent bans or restrictions on ivory trade announced by a number of countries.

Allocation of Funds

Where funds are scarce and many areas are under immediate threat, it may be necessary to undertake a policy analogous to the medical concept of triage. Used in emergencies, triage is a method of allocating resources according to a system of priorities designed to maximize the number of survivors. First priority is given to those who, though injured, can be expected to survive if given adequate attention. Those who are in reasonably stable condition are left until resources are available. The most seriously injured cases, those with little chance of survival even with intense treatment, are simply made comfortable without expending scarce resources that are likely to be ineffective anyway. In the protected area context, scarce resources must be allocated in a similar manner. Areas that are still relatively intact with little pressure on them may need little or no immediate attention. The bulk of the resources should be applied to areas that stand a significant chance of benefiting. Areas seriously degraded and facing severe pressures may not warrant significant resources even if that will mean further degradation.

The analogy between medical triage and allocating funds among protected areas cannot be taken too far, however. Unlike the medical case where every patient's life is considered to be of equal value, protected areas differ in their importance. Therefore, along with the assessment of how effective resources will be, consideration must be given to the importance of protecting a particular area. Balancing the importance of an area with an assessment of the probable effect of investments on protection is not an exact science. An area's importance depends on each country's objectives and how crucial the area is in both a regional and a national context. The effectiveness of investments in protection and management is difficult to foresee and depends on a variety of factors. Clearly there are no easy answers.

To make matters even more difficult, there is yet another factor to consider: Are resources better spent responding to existing threats or preventing future threats? In many cases, prevention is much cheaper than treatment. Though triage may be necessary in extreme situations, proper emphasis on prevention may avert such emergencies from ever arising. Thus consideration must be given to potential threats as well as current ones. Attention should also be given to those areas that have the potential to provide large returns from recreation and tourism. Developing facilities in these areas can provide a source of revenue that can then be used to protect other areas. Management plans will be necessary to ensure that development does not threaten the areas to be protected.

The issue of allocating funds, then, is important and complex. Various economic frameworks such as those discussed in Chapter 1 offer some guidelines. Cost-effectiveness analysis can be used in situations where targets have been established, though quantification of benefits is difficult. Safe minimum standards to protect important species or habitats can be developed and implemented. Alternatively, benefit/cost ratios can be used to decide which expenditures will bring about the greatest returns per dollar spent. Whichever method is chosen, decisions should be based on agreed-upon criteria. Allocations should also be made in the context of the entire national protected-area system rather than in a series of ad hoc decisions.

INSTITUTIONAL ISSUES

Effective protection requires a clear commitment at the highest levels of government. This commitment must be backed up with adequate budgets and enough political power for the administrative agency in charge of protected areas to carry out its duties. Ideally the government agency in charge of management should be an independent agency or department whose sole function is to establish and manage protected areas. Too often these areas are managed by a division (or divisions) within a department with other competing goals. In many cases the division has little power within its own department, let alone at higher levels of government.

The agency in charge should establish links with other government departments whose actions will affect protected areas. Cooperation with other agencies over land-use decisions is essential if protected areas are to remain intact. Coordination with interested nongovernment parties such as conservation groups and tourism agencies also will be valuable.

Many protected area systems suffer from a top-heavy administrative structure. Too often the central offices of the agency in charge are well staffed while the protected areas themselves have few or no workers. Without an on-the-ground presence, management of these areas is almost always inadequate. Of course there must be a central administrative agency to set policy and keep track of national issues. Often a set of regional offices is needed also to oversee protected areas within a region and provide guidance when needed. But the most important level of administration is at the site itself.

To be effective, area superintendents should be required to attend a training course to help them understand the issues and problems they will face. They should also be required to spend a certain portion of their time on-site. Too often managers are located far from the areas they serve and have little knowledge of the true situation in the field.

Field-workers and guards form the backbone of the protected area staff, but frequently these workers are poorly motivated and have little or no training. Salaries are low, field conditions difficult, and essential equipment in short supply. In some protected areas, guards are not only ineffective but contribute to the problem themselves by poaching or allowing others to poach. If field-workers are to control poaching and encroachment, adequate supervision and training are needed. Improvement of living conditions and salaries may also be necessary. In many countries, insufficient field staff and inadequate resources are the weakest aspects of protected area management.

PART II

APPLICATIONS

The second half of this book considers applications of the approach in a number of countries around the world. Chapters 5, 6, and 7 focus on Thailand, a country that has made a major commitment to protected areas. Thailand is still grappling with the questions of how much and which areas to protect and how large a budget to allocate to protection and management. As is true elsewhere, the government's resources are limited, many programs compete for scarce funds, and data and staffing limitations restrict the ability to carry out in-depth analysis.

This examination of the situation in Thailand points out what can be done within the constraints faced by the Thai government. Chapter 5 outlines the history and present situation of protected areas in Thailand. As is true in many countries, early conservation efforts focused on protecting economic resources, especially forested areas. The development of a formal protected area system came later. Chapters 6 and 7 examine examples of three different types of protected areas: a national park, a nonhunting area, and a wildlife sanctuary. Although the areas we have chosen may be better than average examples of each category, they do illustrate the diversity of protected areas and the main benefits and costs associated with each type. The relative richness of Thai data also makes it possible to illustrate the application of a number of valuation techniques. In some cases, data constraints prevent a complete economic analysis but in these cases we outline the approach and report general findings.

Chapters 8 and 9 present examples from a number of other countries in Asia, Latin America, the Caribbean, and Africa. Although our coverage is brief, these examples illustrate the growing interest in economic analysis of protected areas. Chapter 8 presents analyses of complete protected areas whereas Chapter 9 analyzes selected components of protected areas.

In Chapter 10 we present our main conclusions and outline the policy implications suggested by the various case examples. We highlight not only the potential contributions but also the limitations of an economic approach to protected area establishment and management.

5
Protected Areas In Thailand

In recent years Thailand has implemented an ambitious program to establish and maintain a variety of protected areas. This campaign offers a useful context for examining the issues and approaches discussed in earlier chapters. Thailand has a land area of 514,000 square kilometers and in 1988 had a population of more than 54 million people. Bordered by Laos, Kampuchea, Malaysia, and Burma (now known officially as Myanmar), Thailand is one of the emerging ASEAN economic success stories—indeed, it has graduated to the World Bank's list of middle-income economies with a 1987 GNP of $850 per capita. During the 1965–1987 period, per capita GNP grew at a very respectable rate of 3.9 percent per year. Thailand represents one of a growing number of countries that are achieving considerable success in their economic objectives and, at the same time, trying to protect their dwindling natural resource base.

In one way, economic growth is a two-edged sword. Economic development means greater pressure on natural resources not only from direct exploitation but also from environmental degradation and pollution; yet economic development also provides the financial means to protect and manage areas once they have been selected. This tension is both a challenge and an opportunity for those concerned with the protection of natural areas.

HISTORICAL DEVELOPMENT

As in many other parts of the world, in Thailand the first protected area was established to provide a recreation site for the country's rulers. Dong Tan Park was established in the thirteenth century by King Ram Khamhaeng the Great. Thailand's Buddhist culture was another factor in promoting the conservation of its natural resources. Many Buddhist temples were surrounded by forests that helped to create a peaceful sanctuary in the temple precincts. Since Buddhist strictures forbid the taking of life, these areas also served as de facto wildlife sanctuaries. Such oases still exist and grazing animals, monkeys, and other forms of wildlife often wander freely within the outer temple walls though they no longer survive in nearby areas.

Elephants have held an important place in Thai culture for centuries and, at different periods in Thai history, have had considerable economic, military, and cultural value. Capture of wild elephants was initially regulated during the Sukhothai period (thirteenth century), and various restrictions on the capture and use of elephants have evolved over the years. Another important natural resource, teak, also became an object of concern, and its depletion was a major spur to the establishment of the Royal Thai Forest Department in 1896 (Kasetsart University 1987).

Other than these few economically important plant and animal species, little need was seen to take special action to protect wildlife and natural areas before World War II. Until then, forests covered more than 60 percent of Thailand, and herds of large animals were common, as were large flocks of birds in the plains. Following the war, however, a number of factors including increased population, increased availability of firearms, and increased export of timber combined to initiate a steady depletion of wildlife and wildlife habitat throughout Thailand (TDRI 1987).

In 1961, surveys showed that Thailand had 27.4 million hectares (274,000 square kilometers) of forest. By 1973, forest area had been reduced by almost 19 percent; by 1985, another 26.5 percent of the original forest had been destroyed (see Figure 6). Official figures for 1985 indicate that 14.9 million hectares of forest remain, which represents approximately 29 percent of the country's land area. Conversations with Thai officials indicate that many believe that the true figure is closer to 25 percent and that some of this is degraded forest. In response to the rapid loss of forest cover, the new Thai government of Prime Minister Chatichai banned all logging in Thailand's forests in

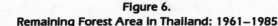

Figure 6.
Remaining Forest Area in Thailand: 1961–1985

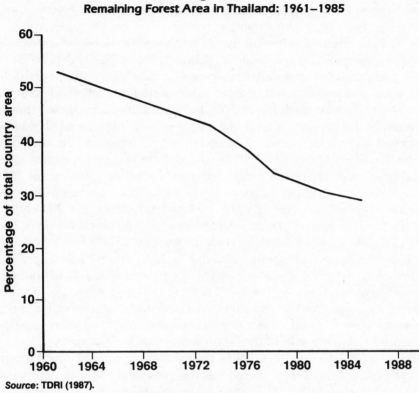

Source: TDRI (1987).

early 1989. How effective this bold and almost unprecedented step will be remains to be seen.

Along with this decrease of forest cover has been a concurrent reduction in wildlife populations. Other than in a few remote regions, there are few surviving herds of large animals outside the protected areas. Moreover, of the 578 known resident forest bird species, 15 percent are thought to be endangered, threatened, vulnerable, or indeterminate in status (Round 1985). Other vertebrate species thought to be in danger of extinction (or already extinct) include five species of fish, seven species of reptiles, and eight species of mammals. The status of many other species is still unknown (TDRI 1987).

Though the Royal Thai Government enacted the Wild Animals Reservation and Protection Act (WARPA) in 1960 to regulate the hunting, capture, and trade of wildlife, many species are still under considerable pressure. Subsistence hunting and trapping are common in rural areas, and there is extensive trade in many wildlife species. The Royal Forest Department lists 228 types of vertebrates on reserved and protected lists, but enforcement of the laws has not been effective.

Conservationist interests initially focused on forested areas and their management and protection. Although not primarily designed as a park and protected area measure, these efforts helped reduce encroachment into and loss of forested areas. Thailand's first National Economic and Social Development Plan (1960–1964) contained a provision that 50 percent of the country, a total of 256,000 square kilometers, should be reserved as national forest. The second plan, however, allowed for a reduction of forest area to 200,000 square kilometers, or 40 percent of the total land area. This latter target remains unchanged. Under the 1964 Forest Reserve Act, permanent forests were to be gazetted by royal decree as forest reserves. By the end of 1985, some 218,000 square kilometers had been declared forest reserves. Of this area, however, less than 150,000 square kilometers remains forested (TDRI 1987).

Land administration in Thailand is highly complex. There are twenty-four agencies in six ministries along with several land committees involved in this task. In 1979, the cabinet approved a program to allow illegal squatters to continue to cultivate forest areas that had been previously encroached. Other encroached forest reserve areas were reclassified following a land use and ownership policy approved by the cabinet in 1982. In December 1985, the cabinet approved a new national forest policy. This policy maintains the previous goal of keeping 40 percent of Thailand's total land area under forest cover. Of this about two-thirds, or 25 percent, is to be economic or productive forest including forest reserves, plantation areas, community forests, private tree farms, and timber concession areas. The other 15 percent is to be conservation or protection forest including headwater source areas (first-class watersheds), national parks, wildlife sanctuaries, nonhunting areas, reserved parks, arboretums, botanical gardens, and reserved areas for specific studies. Table 3 shows the current area in each category.

TYPES OF PROTECTED AREAS

A separate set of rules and regulations covers protected areas. Although largely found in forest areas, protected areas also include a number of coastal and marine sites. In fact, a recent focus in Thailand is development of tourism in coastal areas and offshore islands.

Protected areas in Thailand stem from two major pieces of legislation: the Wild Animals Reservation and Protection Act (WARPA) of

Table 3.

Forest Areas by Function in Thailand: 1985

Function	Number	Area (rai)
Logging	621	122,479,056[a]
National forest reserve	1,158	136,347,175
Prereserved forest	84	15,506,075
National park	52	16,724,600
Forest park	57	938,200
Wildlife conservation area	28	12,909,050
Nonhunting area	38	1,871,250
Wildlife park	2	15,344
Botanical garden	5	6,250
Arboretum	42	19,544

Note: 1 hectare equals 6.25 rai.
[a] Only about 15 million rai are actually open for logging.
Sources: RFD (various years); TDRI (1987).

1960 and the National Parks Act of 1961. The major classes of protected area in Thailand are national parks, wildlife sanctuaries, and nonhunting areas. These three classes include about 10 percent of Thailand's total land area, or more than 51,000 square kilometers. National parks account for 52 percent of protected areas, wildlife sanctuaries about 42 percent, and nonhunting areas the remaining 6 percent. Currently the Thai government is sponsoring a detailed survey of upper watersheds. Areas deemed fragile and critical for protection of downstream areas will also be strictly protected.

Thai protected areas span the categories outlined in Chapter 1. Wildlife sanctuaries are fairly strict preserves, national parks have a major recreational use component, and nonhunting areas combine commercial use with species-specific protection. The locations of these protected areas are shown in Figure 7. They are administered by two separate divisions of the Royal Forest Department.

National Parks

The first national park in Thailand, Khao Yai, was established in 1962. Currently, there are fifty-two national parks (including fourteen marine

Figure 7.
Location of National Parks, Wildlife Sanctuaries, and Nonhunting Areas in Thailand

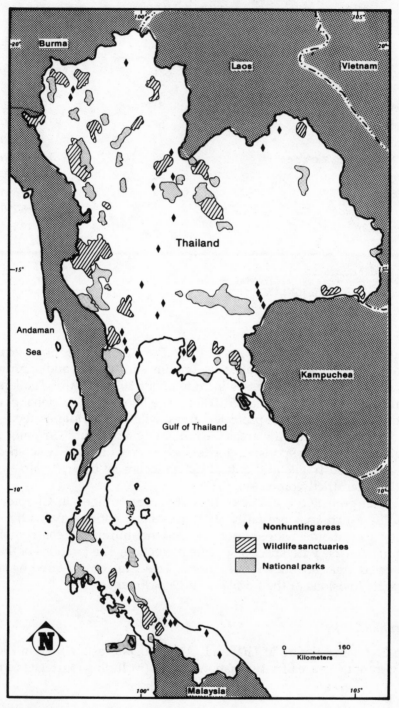

parks) covering 5.2 percent of the land area of Thailand. Of this total, thirty-six parks have been established since 1980.

The National Parks Act states that a national park is "land . . . preserved in its natural state for the benefit of public education and enjoyment." These areas are administered by the National Parks Division (NPD) of the Royal Forest Department (RFD), which has established the following guideline for the use of national parks: "National parks are lands preserved for protection of the environment, especially forests, wildlife, and unique scenery, which impresses the viewer as worthy of preservation in its natural state. National parks shall be protected from destruction, alternative uses, and incompatible activities so that future generations may enjoy and study these natural treasures in perpetuity."

Visitation at national parks has increased dramatically in the last decade. In 1976, park statistics reported approximately 1 million visitors to national parks whereas 1985 figures report more than 4 million visitors. Actual visitation rates are believed to be higher due to incomplete compilation at certain parks (Kasetsart University 1987). Increasing numbers of foreign tourists are also discovering Thailand's national parks; though specific numbers are unavailable, it is believed that foreign tourists comprise nearly 10 percent of visitors (TDRI 1987). The rate of increase of park visitors between 1976 and 1985 was about 15 percent per year. Although it is unlikely that future growth in visitor numbers will be so rapid, even with a 10 percent annual increase park visitors will total more than 10 million by 1995. Rising incomes in Thailand and increased numbers of foreign tourists both contribute to this rapid growth in demand for park use.

The NPD budget has also increased steadily in recent years, though budget constraints still hamper many activities. Its 1986 budget was 125 million baht (or about $4.8 million at an exchange rate of approximately 26 baht = $1.00); this is 80 percent higher than the 1982 budget. In the same period, budget allocations to the individual parks increased from 30.5 to 57.6 million baht. Income derived from entrance fees, lodging fees, and fines was 15.9 million baht in 1985, or less than 15 percent of the amount budgeted to operate the NPD.

Each national park has a permanent headquarters. Most have living quarters for resident officials, workers, and guards, but these are of varying quality and often inadequate in number. There are visitor centers in eighteen parks, but few of these provide many services to visitors. Most parks also have outposts for guards to help with enforcement of park regulations (to control poaching of animals or timber, for example), but the number of outposts is only one-quarter the number thought to be needed by the NPD for effective protection (Kasetsart University 1987).

Wildlife Sanctuaries

Thailand's first wildlife sanctuary, Salak Phra, was established in 1965. There are now twenty-eight wildlife sanctuaries covering an area of 21,638 square kilometers, equal to 4.2 percent of Thailand's land area. As defined in the WARPA, a wildlife sanctuary is "land declared for the conservation of wildlife habitat so that wildlife can freely breed and increase their populations in the natural environment." Wildlife sanctuaries are managed by the Wildlife Conservation Division (WCD) of the RFD to "conserve the habitat of various wildlife species, including conservation of essential requirements such as water, food, protective habitat, nesting habitat, breeding habitat, and rearing habitat, as well as salt licks, wallows, dusting areas, and sunning areas so that wildlife may freely exist and propagate."

Recreational tourism is generally discouraged in wildlife sanctuaries. Education and research, however, are considered important activities. Nearly all sanctuaries provide at least basic services to visiting researchers, but the level of research is considered far below its potential (Kasetsart University 1987). There are seven nature education centers located in these sanctuaries. These centers are visited by schoolchildren and local residents.

Since 1980, the WCD budget has grown rapidly. The 1986 budget was 116.2 million baht, of which 37 million baht was allocated directly to wildlife sanctuaries. Another 4.4 million baht went to the seven nature education centers. Despite recent large increases in the WCD budget, most wildlife sanctuaries still cannot afford the equipment or manpower needed for effective protection.

Nonhunting Areas

In addition to wildlife sanctuaries, the WCD is also responsible for administering nonhunting areas (NHAs). Nonhunting areas are "areas which have been designated by the government for protection of certain specified wildlife species. . . . [They] differ from wildlife sanctuaries in that: (i) they generally are of smaller size; (ii) only the specified wildlife species are protected; and (iii) other uses such as fishing, lumbering, recreation, and tourism are permitted." Thus, unlike national parks and wildlife sanctuaries, the government permits commercial activities such as logging and fishing and other consumptive activities such as the collection of plants and herbs in nonhunting areas.

The country's first nonhunting area, Thale Noi, was established in 1975. There are currently forty-one NHAs covering approximately 3,000 square kilometers, or about 0.6 percent of Thailand's total area. Many nonhunting areas are located in wetlands while others protect a variety of small habitats and populations or colonies of particular species. Often they are located near settlements and make important contributions to the daily lives of the residents in the area.

In 1986, the budget allocation for nonhunting areas was 12.9 million baht. On a per hectare basis, this is twice that of national parks and 2.5 times the budget per hectare of wildlife sanctuaries. Like national parks and wildlife sanctuaries, however, the nonhunting areas suffer from inadequate manpower and equipment. Small NHAs do not even have an administrative center but are administered by larger NHAs in the region.

Unlike wildlife sanctuaries, many NHAs do receive significant numbers of tourists. Certain NHAs have fairly developed tourist facilities including lodging and some visitor services. Due to administrative rules, however, NHAs cannot charge fees for their lodging facilities, which denies them an opportunity to gain supplemental funds in this manner. Since many NHAs do not keep a visitor count, total visitation rates are unknown.

Other Protected Areas

Apart from the three main types just described, there are other categories of land that can be considered protected areas:

- *Forest parks.* These are scenic areas too small to be considered national parks but still valuable for recreation. They often include such attractions as waterfalls, caves, or other features of natural interest. The RFD has the authority to designate areas as forest parks without cabinet approval. Thailand has fifty-seven forest parks, twenty-two of which are administered by the RFD with the remainder administered by regional or provincial forest offices. They cover about 1,500 square kilometers.
- *Botanical gardens.* These are "locations established to collect indigenous and exotic plant species that are considered rare or have

economic value as ornamentals and are planted in taxonomic order
for purposes of research and dissemination. These species are
propagated for the benefit of the public and the country"
(Khomkris 1965). Five botanical gardens totaling 10 square kilometers are located in different regions of the country.

- *Arboretums.* These are "smaller than botanical gardens and are
  established to collect various plant species, especially economically
  useful plants and flowering plants, which are indigenous to that
  area. . . . Arboretums contain roads and walkways for tourism,
  recreation, and research" (Khomkris 1965). There are currently
  forty-two arboretums totaling 32 square kilometers throughout
  Thailand.
- *Biosphere reserves.* These belong to a protected area category developed by the Man and the Biosphere International Coordination
  Council. They are designed to combine nature conservation with
  scientific research, education, training, and environmental monitoring. A major goal of biosphere reserves is to promote economic
  activity but at the same time safeguard the environment. Thailand
  currently has three biosphere reserves: the Mae Sa-Kog Ma Reserve, the Sakaerat Environmental Research Station, and the Huay
  Tak Teak Reserve. These reserves are not an integral part of the
  protected area system administered by the NPD and WCD.
- *Protected watersheds.* The Thai government is currently sponsoring
  an inventory of important watershed areas and classifying them
  according to the types of activity that will be allowed. Class I
  watersheds will be considered protected forests, and cutting trees
  in these areas will be prohibited. These are mostly at higher elevations with steep slopes. Since the watershed classification process
  is still under way, it is unknown how much area will eventually be
  included in this category.

Though these other types of protected areas serve many useful
functions, our focus here is confined to national parks, wildlife sanctuaries, and nonhunting areas. These three types of protected areas,
covering about 10 percent of Thailand's total land area, form the core of
the protected area system and are the primary means of protecting
plant and animal species *in situ*. Protected watersheds may become key
parts of the protected area system in the future, but this will depend on
the area eventually included as Class I watersheds, the percentage of
this area that is not already protected, and a determination of how
these areas will be protected from development and encroachment.

THE ESTABLISHMENT PROCESS

The establishment of protected areas in Thailand follows a process similar to the one depicted in Figure 3. For national parks, local government officials usually initiate the process. In most cases, the local official has his representative in parliament write a letter to the RFD proposing an area as a national park. Proposals are then submitted to the National Park Committee, which is chaired by the permanent secretary of the Ministry of Agriculture and Cooperatives and contains representatives from approximately a dozen different government divisions. The committee evaluates the area to see if it passes certain criteria: size greater than 10 square kilometers; scenic beauty; and good recreational opportunities. If there are no constraints such as legal settlements or timber concessions in the area, and the committee determines that the area merits national park status, the committee submits the proposal to the minister of agriculture and cooperatives. If he approves, the minister then takes the proposal to the cabinet where the ultimate decision is made. If no objections have been made to this point, the cabinet normally endorses the proposal.

The role of economics in this process is limited. No concerted effort is made to quantify the benefits of an area as a national park. Instead, it is evaluated in reference to the general criteria previously listed. The primary issue is not benefits but whether or not there is already some constraint such as a timber or mining concession already granted or whether an agency foresees some alternative future use. If any prior use has been established or any department voices strong argument against the proposal, the area is unlikely to gain protected status.

Establishment of wildlife sanctuaries and nonhunting areas follows a similar process. A local official, a provincial forester, or someone else reports to the RFD that they feel an area is suitable for a wildlife sanctuary. The WCD then sends a staff member to evaluate the area to see if it warrants protected status by examining such characteristics as the number of species it contains and whether endangered species are present. If the area appears promising, WCD consults with other divisions to determine if there are any constraints to establishment such as mineral or timber concessions in the area. In most cases, the area is not given further consideration as a wildlife sanctuary if such constraints exist. On rare occasion, the RFD may ask a concessionaire to withdraw from a very valuable area. If this approach does not

succeed but there is strong interest in protecting the area, the boundaries may be redrawn to omit the concession area. Areas that are still
considered viable are then evaluated by the Wildlife Conservation
Committee in a process very similar to that governing national parks. If
the committee approves the proposal, it is sent to the minister of
agriculture and cooperatives. If approved by him, the proposal is then
submitted to the cabinet where the final decision is made.

Even if an area does not make its way successfully through this
process, there is still a chance it will be partially protected. If the area is
too small to be considered a wildlife sanctuary or there is a prior
concession in the area, it can still be designated a nonhunting area
(NHA). This designation will protect any valuable species in the area,
at least from hunting, though all other uses are still allowed. Establishment of a nonhunting area does not require cabinet approval. If the
Wildlife Conservation Committee approves the proposal, a recommen-
dation is sent to the minister of agriculture and cooperatives who has
the power to declare the area an NHA. As in the case of national parks,
economic inputs into the decision are limited. Little or no attempt is
made to quantify benefits. An area largely succeeds or fails based on
the strength of the arguments against it.

THREATS TO PROTECTED AREAS

Many of Thailand's protected areas remain vulnerable to a number of
threats. Though the major types of protected areas (national parks,
wildlife sanctuaries, and nonhunting areas) have resident guards (unlike protected watersheds), the guard force has not been sufficient to
prevent poaching and encroachment. Wholesale clearing of land within
a protected area is not uncommon. The strong demand for agricultural
land, combined with the scarce supply of unoccupied or undeveloped
land, has resulted in growing pressure on protected areas.

Even when the land is not cleared, many areas are subject to heavy
poaching pressures. Illegal commercial logging, collection of firewood,
cutting of poles for building materials—all are common practices in
many protected areas near villages. Poaching of wildlife for food or for
sale to commercial dealers is another serious problem. Collection of
plants for food, medicine, and sale is widespread. In the north and
northwest regions, moreover, hill tribes who engage in shifting agriculture have deforested large areas both inside and outside of protected
areas. At least four national parks and eleven wildlife sanctuaries in

these regions are subject to deforestation by resident hill tribes (TDRI 1987).

Most of the encroachment and poaching are carried out by inhabitants of nearby villages who were traditional users of the resources within the protected area. Although they have no property rights to the now protected areas, the old patterns of resource extraction represent an important source of income. Since these villagers tend to be quite poor, it is understandable that these practices continue even after an area has been given protected status. Providing alternative sources of income to these villagers and incentives for them to respect the protected areas and help in their conservation are major management challenges.

Development goals pursued by the Royal Thai Government also threaten protected areas—especially the development of multipurpose dams and reservoirs. Many of these projects would have adverse effects on protected areas. After years of controversy, the cabinet recently dropped its plans for the Nam Choan Dam, which would have inundated significant wildlife habitat. Other potentially harmful projects include those designed to increase access (such as roads) or development of tourist facilities in inappropriate areas. Moreover, use of protected areas by the military for training and security purposes has had negative impacts. While some of these cases are unavoidable due to national security concerns, other cases appear to be more expedient than necessary. As well, there are reports of illegal logging by the military in some protected areas.

Recently wildlife sanctuaries have been exposed to a new threat. Until early 1988, national parks and wildlife sanctuaries were the only forms of protected area where commercial activities were prohibited. A 1988 court decision, however, has allowed commercial loggers to reopen their former concessions in wildlife sanctuaries. The 1989 ban on all commercial logging in Thailand, however, eliminates this threat at least in the short term.

POLICY ISSUES

Thailand has made a major commitment to the establishment of various types of protected areas. With more than 10 percent of the country's land area currently designated as protected, the government has a stated goal of placing 15 percent of its land area under protected status. The potential benefits of this action are considerable, but so are the costs. Thailand, therefore, is not unlike other countries that have established protected area systems. Among the questions that must be addressed are the following:

- What are the direct economic benefits of protected areas in Thailand? How can they be measured?
- What are the indirect benefits? How can they be measured or evaluated?
- What are the costs of protected areas in direct "out-of-pocket" costs, indirect costs, and forgone opportunities?
- How can Thailand generate revenues from protected areas to offset these costs? What other financing approaches can be used?
- What are the benefits and costs of protected areas for local people? How can the benefits be enhanced and the costs reduced?
- How much area should be designated as protected?

In Thailand most decisions concerning establishment of protected areas have already been made, though questions about certain individual areas remain. As a result, our analysis is mostly an ex post facto examination rather than a study of how large an area to allocate for protection and which areas to select. Nevertheless, the Thai case can be used to examine the benefits and costs associated with protected areas. Management issues, especially the problem of determining the appropriate level of management and then paying for it, remain crucial. In the next two chapters we examine three different types of protected areas—a national park (Khao Yai), a wildlife sanctuary (Khao Soi Dao), and a nonhunting area (Thale Noi)—to explore these issues. Although these areas are better than average in terms of their level of development and management, they still illustrate the broad range of issues associated with protected area management in Thailand.

6

Analyzing a National Park (Khao Yai)

Khao Yai, Thailand's first national park, is located at the southwestern edge of the Khorat Plateau in northeastern Thailand (see Figure 8). Its 2,168 square kilometers extend into four provinces: Prachin Buri, Nakhon Nayok, Sara Buri, and Nakhon Ratchasima. Located about 160 kilometers northeast of Bangkok, Khao Yai has been one of Thailand's most popular parks since its establishment in 1962 and is one of ten ASEAN Heritage Parks and Reserves (NPD 1986).

Khao Yai is situated at the western edge of the Dangrek mountain range, and most of its terrain is mountainous. Limestone peaks dominate its western side while the eastern side is primarily low, undulating hills. Evergreen forests cover most of the park along with smaller areas of deciduous forest and grassland. Average rainfall is more than 2,000 millimeters per year, most of this during the rainy season from July to October.

The northeast region of Thailand has the smallest proportion of forested area of any of the country's regions. Between 1961 and 1985, the region's percentage of forest declined from 42 to 14.4 percent (TDRI 1987). In the vicinity of Khao Yai, almost all forests outside the national park system have been degraded or totally cleared for agriculture and settlements. Deforestation rates of 2 to 10 percent per year in the four neighboring provinces over the 1961 to 1985 period resulted in very little remaining forest land by 1985. Deforestation within Khao Yai itself was made illegal when protected status was given in 1962. Even with its protected status, however, forest cover in Khao Yai declined

Figure 8.
Location of Khao Yai National Park

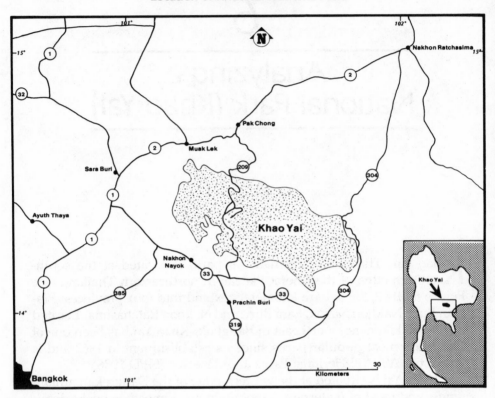

Source: **Santiapillai and others (1987).**

from 94 percent in 1961 to 85 percent of land area in 1985 (RFD various years). Although the annual rate of forest loss in Khao Yai is very low, it is not zero.

Khao Yai provides a number of benefits both to the surrounding region and to the nation. It is a premier tourist destination in the region with between 250,000 and 400,000 visits per year. Since it contains most of the remaining forest in the region, it is of critical importance for wildlife and also profoundly affects the hydrology of the region. Four river basins have their headwaters in Khao Yai, and two major reservoirs are dependent on water from the park.

The main threats to Khao Yai are of human origin. Clearing of forests inside the park's border for agricultural land continues. Poaching of timber, wildlife, and other forest products degrades the park and threatens its resources. At one level, this depredation is under-standable—low-income villagers living on the park's borders end up paying a major cost of protection since they are not allowed to use the park's resources. The direct benefits of protection, however, largely accrue elsewhere.

The following sections discuss the major benefits and costs associated with the protection of Khao Yai. Our analysis benefits from the extensive research done on Khao Yai over the years, including a recently prepared management plan for 1987–1991 (NPD 1986), the on-going Beneficial Use Project (Dobias 1988; Dobias and others 1988), and our own research project on Thai protected areas (Sherman and Dixon 1989).

BENEFITS

In placing monetary values on the benefits derived from protection, one is faced with a wide variety of data reflecting everything from direct personal gain (market values of animals caught or plant products collected) to broad social benefits. Approaches to valuation vary in their sophistication and reliability. Reasonable estimates of consumer's surplus from tourism can be estimated by a carefully done travel-cost survey. Hydrologic benefits can be estimated if data on affected down-stream areas are available. Educational or research values are much harder to determine, although expenditures can be measured.

The following sections examine a number of these benefits in the case of Khao Yai. Although the estimates are based on the specific situation in Khao Yai and the data that are available, our approach can be extended to other parks, both in Thailand and elsewhere. The types of benefits are generic; the monetary estimates are site-specific. Thus our detailed analysis of Khao Yai is designed to show how the approach presented in this book can be applied to the economic aspects of protected areas, including both their benefits and their costs.

Biodiversity and Ecological Processes

Khao Yai contains one of the largest remaining areas of rain forest in mainland Asia (Dobias 1982). More than 60 percent of the park is considered tropical rain forest (NPD 1986), mostly between the 400- and 1,000-meter elevation level. This type of forest is multistoried with many epiphytes. Within this category, different stands contain quite different vegetation communities (Kasetsart University 1982).

Dry evergreen forest is the second most common vegetation type, covering approximately 26 percent of the park. These forests, found mostly between the 100- and 400-meter elevation level, occur in the west, north, and south of the park. Because of their valuable timber species, many have been disturbed by timber poaching (NPD 1986).

Areas above 1,000 meters in elevation are covered with hill ever-green forest. These forests cover only 2.2 percent of Khao Yai's area. The National Parks Division has called for special protection of these areas. There are also small areas of dry, mixed deciduous forest. Due to past disturbances, only isolated patches of this forest type remain.

Khao Yai's size and range of habitats make it a valuable storehouse of plant genetic diversity. MacKinnon and MacKinnon (1986) note that Khao Yai is considered a plant conservation priority site, the only such area in Thailand. Overall Khao Yai is estimated to have more than 2,000 plant species (NPD 1986). Cumberlege and Cumberlege (1964) report finding 121 species of orchids in a series of visits between 1962 and 1963. Eighteen of these species had not been previously reported in Thailand, and three were believed to be new species previously unre-corded anywhere.

The diverse habitats harbor a rich variety of wildlife as well. More than sixty species of mammals live in the park, including larger species such as elephant, tiger, gaur, serow, sambar deer, pileated gibbon, white-handed gibbon, and pig-tailed macaque. The park also contains eighteen species of amphibians and thirty-five species of reptiles (Kasetsart University 1982). For all of these species, the protected areas remain their last refuge in the area. Even within the park, few of the larger species are abundant outside the headquarters area of the park due to widespread poaching (NPD 1986).

Khao Yai is the only known area in the world where the ranges of pileated and white-handed gibbons overlap. This zone of contact is considered an important research area, and the hybrid offspring be-tween the two species are of great interest to scientists (Dobias 1982; Brockelman 1975). Warren Brockelman, a professor at Mahidol Univer-sity, goes so far as to say that Khao Yai could become the most impor-tant gibbon study area in the world.

Khao Yai is also considered a key site for forest bird preservation (Round 1985). More than 295 species of birds have been recorded (NPD 1986). This list includes four species of hornbills—species that require large areas of mature forest for their survival. As one of the largest protected areas in Thailand, Khao Yai offers the best chance for long-term survival of hornbills in the region.

Overall, Khao Yai's rich diversity of plants and animals makes it a major conservation area for maintenance of biological diversity. There are few places in Thailand where such a large area of forest has remained intact. These few remaining reserves are critical to maintaining viable populations of wild species. Khao Yai may harbor as much as 10 percent of Thailand's total population of elephant, gaur, tiger, and pileated gibbon (Kasetsart University 1985).

It is very difficult to attach a monetary value to the benefits of biodiversity in Khao Yai. Indeed, there is no widely accepted methodology for valuing the benefits of biodiversity. One can, however, value some of the goods and services that flow from protecting certain species. For example, one category of values arising from maintaining biodiversity is consumptive value. In this case one measures the value of the sustainable level of use of products directly consumed, sold, or bartered. *Aquilaria crassna*, for example, a plant that grows wild in Khao Yai, is illegally collected by villagers to make incense valued at about $250 per kilogram (ASEAN 1982). Rattans are collected by villagers, as well, as are a number of food and medicinal plants (NPD 1986). The value of collected products cannot be calculated at this time, however, because data are not available. To estimate the value, a survey of nearby villagers would be needed to find out the resources collected, their value, and the time needed to harvest them.

Apart from these resources with known uses, consideration must be given to the possibility of future discoveries of new uses of the plants and animals in Khao Yai. Gaur, for example, a threatened species, may help to improve domestic cattle at some point in the future. A variety of plants in Khao Yai are used for medicinal purposes by local villagers; most of these have not been studied by scientists for medicinal properties. Also potentially valuable is the discovery of plants and animals not yet known to science. Given the uncertainty of the probability, number, and magnitude of these discoveries, future values arising from these resources are difficult to estimate.

Ruitenbeek (1989) attempted to value the genetic resources in a park in Central Africa by estimating the "expected production value." This is equal to the value per research discovery multiplied by the number of research discoveries. For the value per research discovery, he uses a figure of £5,000 from a study of patent values derived from an all-industry mix (Schankerman and Pakes 1986). Ruitenbeek notes, however, that the capturable value may be much lower depending on institutions and patent laws. Applying this methodology to Khao Yai would require estimates of the number of discoveries expected, average value per discovery, and the percentage of value that is capturable.

The option and existence values for maintaining biodiversity may also be substantial. The Beneficial Use Project survey questioned park users on their maximum willingness to pay to ensure the continued existence of elephants in the wild in Thailand. The average maximum willingness to pay indicated was 181 baht (approximately $7.00).

The National Parks Division recorded approximately 4 million visitors to national parks in 1985, 90 percent of whom were Thai. If we assume that the average Thai visitor visits national parks twice a year, this figure implies that 1.8 million Thais (out of a population of approximately 54 million) are park users. Assuming that Khao Yai visitors are representative of park visitors throughout Thailand, this would imply that the option and existence value associated with the continued existence of elephants in the wild in Thailand is 325 million baht (1.8 million × 181 = 325.8 million). Note that this figure includes only park visitors; if we assume that non-park-users have an option and existence value equal to one-tenth that of park users, the additional amount would be approximately 900 million baht (50 million × 18.1 = 905 million).

Now further assume that, in the absence of Khao Yai, the probability of the continued existence of elephants in the wild in Thailand would be reduced by 10 percent. This figure seems reasonable since Khao Yai is one of the few large areas of elephant habitat still relatively intact and, moreover, contains approximately 10 percent of Thailand's wild elephant population. If we assume, therefore, that 10 percent of the option and existence value associated with the continued existence of elephants in the wild in Thailand is attributable to Khao Yai, this gives a combined option and existence value per year for all Thai residents of 122 million baht (0.1 × [325 + 900] = 122.5), which is equal to $4.7 million. Clearly this is a substantial amount. Given that elephants are especially important in Thai history and culture, one would expect elephants to have the highest value of any species. But even if we consider these figures to represent the total value of protecting all the species in Khao Yai, the amount involved is still significant.

Another set of benefits are indirect benefits gained from protecting biological diversity. Tourism, including activities such as wildlife watching and jungle walks, is an important benefit that depends on the maintenance of biological diversity. Similarly, maintenance of the forest ecosystems in Khao Yai yields hydrologic benefits that accrue to downstream areas. Both tourism and hydrologic benefits, as we will see, can be valued.

Tourism

Khao Yai is not only the oldest national park in Thailand, it is also one of the most popular and well-developed parks for recreation. Located approximately three hours away from Bangkok by car, Khao Yai attracts large numbers of both Thais and foreigners. Tourism in Khao Yai has increased dramatically during the last decade (see Table 4). Between 1977 and 1985 (the peak year), the number of visits tripled, reaching more than 460,000 in 1985. The number of visits has dropped in the last two years, but it was still more than 400,000 in 1987.

In a joint effort with members of the World Wide Fund for Nature Beneficial Use Project, we designed a survey undertaken between March and May 1988. (More detailed responses from this survey can be found in Dobias and others 1988.) The survey showed that visitors come to Khao Yai for a number of reasons. For foreigners visiting the park, enjoying the scenery was given as the most important purpose of the trip by the largest percentage of people (25.9), followed by relaxation (22.2), wildlife viewing (20.4), and hiking (7.4). More than 62 percent of the foreign respondents stated that wildlife viewing was one of their three main reasons for coming to Khao Yai. This was followed in turn by scenery (58.1), relaxation (42.8), and hiking (41.4).

Thai nationals answering the survey overwhelmingly said that enjoying the scenery (54.3) was their main reason for coming to Khao Yai. (Note that relaxation was not given as a separate choice in the Thai-language version of the survey, so percentages are not directly compa-

Table 4.

Visitor Statistics for Khao Yai National Park: 1977–1987

Year	Visitors
1977	115,675
1978	118,912
1979	159,627
1980	161,240
1981	169,409
1982	196,730
1983	275,108
1984	258,803
1985	461,794
1986	426,320
1987	401,661

Source: NPD (various years).

rable.) Following scenery, the other most commonly reported reasons for coming were to see the waterfalls in the park (10 percent), overnight camping (8.6), and picnicking (7.4). Adding the percentage of people indicating any specific activity as one of their top three reasons for coming to Khao Yai showed that viewing scenery was still number one (86.4 percent), followed by seeing the waterfalls (58.0), wildlife viewing (35.7), picnicking (28.6), and overnight camping (25.4).

Both the National Parks Division (NPD) and the Tourist Authority of Thailand (TAT) operate lodging facilities in Khao Yai. NPD oversees twenty-two bungalows, two dormitory-type buildings, two open-air sleeping platforms, and six large tents. These facilities can accommodate up to 920 people. TAT operates a motel and bungalows that can accommodate an additional 200 people. Park campgrounds (run by NPD) can hold up to 1,000 people. Revenues from NPD-operated accommodations were almost 1.5 million baht in 1987. Gate fees from admission to the park reached a peak of 2.38 million baht in 1986 before declining to 1.56 million baht in 1987. Adding the gate fees and NPD-operated accommodation charges, we find that tourism directly contributed 3.03 million baht in 1987. NPD also receives 150,000 baht in concession fees from the four restaurants and food stalls within park boundaries.

Dobias and colleagues (1988) report that the TAT income from lodging in 1987 was almost 5 million baht, while TAT-run restaurants received 4.2 million baht in income. TAT also received 400,000 baht from golf course fees, 318,000 baht from their souvenir shop, and 230,000 baht from wildlife lighting activities. Adding these figures, we find that TAT's income was more than 10 million baht in 1987 while its expenditures during that year were approximately 3.3 million baht. Although these figures do not include prior capital expenditures to build the facilities, it is nonetheless clear that TAT's operations are profitable. All profits from TAT's operations go to TAT, however, and not to the NPD and thus do not contribute to the park.

The economic value of tourism can be measured in various ways. At the simplest level, one can examine the expenditures of tourists for transportation, guides, food, accommodations, and souvenirs. Portions of these expenditures are made in the Khao Yai area and generate employment, demand for services, and income. Some expenditures (especially transportation) benefit other regions. The totals involved are substantial. The Beneficial Use Project (Dobias 1988; Dobias and others 1988) has produced some interesting data on both Thai and foreign visitors. In general, foreign visitors spend more per person than do

Thai visitors. Based on data from organized bus tours, average daily per person expenses for foreign visitors range from 500 to 800 baht, of which the formal admission fee is less than 1 percent. Although the distribution of expenditures varies, one tour company reported spending the following percentages in 1988 for small (ten-person) overnight tours: transport, 42 percent; food and drink, 33 percent; accommodation, 19 percent; guide service, 5 percent; park admission, 1 percent. Clearly gate receipts are only a very small fraction of people's willingness to pay to visit Khao Yai.

Bangkok tour companies offered organized one- and two-day trips to Khao Yai aimed largely at Thai visitors. These tours included meals, transport, accommodations, and other costs. The prices ranged from 350 baht for a day trip with two meals up to 1,450 baht for overnight trips with five meals (Dobias 1988). Expenditures by private visitors are not recorded but probably average from 350 to 600 baht per person per day.

With more than 400,000 visitors per year, the total expenditures generated by Khao Yai tourism are considerable—from 40 million to 200 million baht ($1.5 to $7.7 million) if per capita expenditures are 100 to 500 baht. These expenditures, of course, are not an economic measure of the value of the park. To determine the true economic (social welfare) gain from visiting Khao Yai, one would need to measure consumer's surplus. This would require carrying out a travel-cost study carefully controlling for origin, visitor background, and other variables. A travel-cost study is an example of the surrogate market approach described in Chapter 2. Using this approach, the pattern of recreational use of a park provides the data from which one can estimate a demand curve and, in turn, consumer's surplus.

No travel-cost analysis has yet been performed for Khao Yai. In a 1980 travel-cost study of Lumpinee Park in Bangkok, however, the estimated consumer's surplus for the 2 million visits per year was more than 13 million baht (Eutrirak and Grandstaff 1986). Although this value was estimated for short visits to an urban park, the study illustrates the use of this approach in Thailand. The average consumer's surplus from Khao Yai is certainly larger due to the difference in price levels between 1980 and the present and the broader nature of the visitor experience in Khao Yai.

Though Khao Yai is one of the more developed parks for tourism activities, the Beneficial Use Project survey showed that many people would visit Khao Yai more often if improvements were made. Approximately one-half of the foreigners and three-fourths of the Thais interviewed at the park said that improvements would encourage them to come more often. When foreign visitors were asked to list the most important improvement needed, 38.6 percent indicated a need for more English information followed by better hiking and camping opportunities (12.9), more wildlife viewing (11.4), and better transportation facilities (11.4). When asked which activities should be increased, foreign visitors indicated a desire for more wildlife viewing opportunities (24 percent), organized multiple-day hikes with overnight camping (24.0), more scenic viewpoints (19), more day hikes (16.5), and more birdwatching opportunities (15.7). (Note that more than one answer was allowed.) Thai nationals indicated that more scenic viewpoints were the most important thing needed (35.8 percent), followed by more wildlife viewing (18.7), access to more waterfalls (12.0), and more hiking trails (10.4). In addition, 85 percent said they would like to see more areas of the park opened to tourism.

It is obvious from the surveys that although Khao Yai is a popular tourist destination, increasing the activities available would further spur tourism. The Khao Yai Management Plan (NPD 1986) estimates that tourism could grow at a 17 percent annual rate over the next five years if visitor improvements were undertaken.

In sum, tourism is a major and growing use of Khao Yai. Both Thais and foreigners enjoy the facilities and opportunities offered by the park. Although the overwhelming majority of visitors are Thai (more than 95 percent of the total), foreign visitors spend more per day and this could be a growth area given Thailand's international tourism boom. Most visitors stay overnight. In a 1985 survey (NPD 1986), it was estimated that 60 to 70 percent of Thai visitors and 80 percent of foreign visitors stay at least one night. This use pattern creates considerable demand for accommodations and meals—two items that account for 50 percent or more of total expenditures of Khao Yai visitors.

The financial impact of tourism to Khao Yai is impressive: probably somewhere between 100 to 200 million baht per year is spent by visitors for transport, accommodations, food, and other services. The economic benefits in terms of consumer's surplus have not been measured. If, however, we make the conservative assumption that the average consumer's surplus of a Khao Yai visitor is five times that measured for visitors to Lumpinee Park in Bangkok, the total is 13 million baht. If the average consumer's surplus is ten times the amount estimated for Lumpinee Park visitors, the total becomes 26 million baht. Although this is only about $1 million, it is more than ten times the total amount of entrance fees collected.

Tourism value can only grow in the future. Khao Yai lies close to Bangkok and, as incomes rise and fewer alternative open areas remain, it will become increasingly valuable. Foreign tourism could also increase with improved facilities and promotion. Today virtually all Khao Yai tourism activities are restricted to a very small part of the park accessible from the one north–south road; more than 90 percent of the park is completely undeveloped and inaccessible other than on foot. Thus there are prospects for future expansion of facilities.

Watershed/Hydrology

Khao Yai plays an important role in regulating the water resources of the surrounding region. The headwaters of four river basins are located within the park's boundary. Because of its importance in supplying water, the water resources of Khao Yai are relatively well studied. The implications of drastic changes in land use in Khao Yai cannot be forecast with certainty, but it is possible to make some generalizations about expected impacts.

Figure 9 shows the location of the major watersheds in Khao Yai. The two watersheds on the western edge, Muak Lek and Huai Yai, are mostly outside the park's boundaries and are not considered further. The remaining four watersheds—Prachin Buri, Lam Praphloeng, Lam Takhong, and Nakhon Nayok—are all of considerable importance.

Khao Yai's effect on water supply and water quality downstream is a function of climate, topography, geology, and land use. Of these factors, only land use is affected by management policies. The use of forests, the future rate of deforestation, and the subsequent land uses will determine what happens downstream in terms of water quality and quantity. At present the major areas of forest loss are around the perimeter of the park, although deforestation is moving farther inward (NPD 1986). The areas suffering the greatest losses in forest cover are in the northeast (from Pak Thong Chai district west to Pak Chong district), the southeast (Nadi district and Prachantakham district), the northwest (from Pak Chong district to Muak Lek district), and the west (Khaeng Khoi district) (NPD 1986).

Three types of encroachment are most common: illegal logging, cultivation of crops, and collection of minor forest products. Valuable timber species such as *Dalbergia cochinchinensis*, *Hopea odorata*, and *Afzelia xylocarpo* have been heavily logged and are now scarce in the park. Poaching of *Aquilaria crassna* for incense is also substantial. Small trees of many species are also cut by villagers to make construction

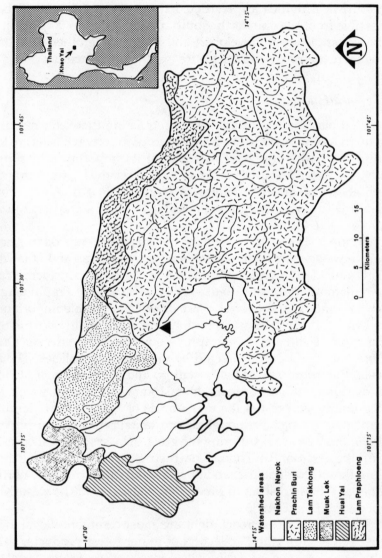

Figure 9.
Watersheds in Khao Yai National Park

Watershed areas

☐ Nakhon Nayok
▨ Prachin Buri
▧ Lam Takhong
▨ Muak Lek
▨ Huai Yai
▨ Lam Praphloeng

Kilometers
0 5 10 15

Source: NPD (1986).

posts, firewood, and tool handles. Moreover, as in many areas of Thailand, Khao Yai's forests are often cut by villagers who then grow crops on the land. Approximately 900 villagers cultivate cash crops such as corn within the park and another 1,670 villagers cultivate rice. Since the fertility of many of these areas is limited, the land is often abandoned after a few years. Many of these areas then revert to *Imperata* grasslands. Collection of minor forest products is another problem. Villagers often supplement their incomes by collecting forest products including mai hom (*Aquilaria crassna*), rattans, orchids, and medicinal plants.

All these activities have different effects on soil and water. Undisturbed closed forest is considered to be the most effective watershed cover. As the degree of disturbance increases, erosion often increases concomitantly. If one looks at a hierarchy of human uses, collection of forest products is a relatively minor disturbance, logging has more severe effects, and shifting cultivation has the most profound effects (Hamilton 1983). If protection or management measures are taken, however, the adverse effects of these practices are less severe.

With its high percentage of forest cover, Khao Yai is currently a source of clean water gradually released throughout the year. With widespread deforestation, one would expect a decrease in water quality. A Kasetsart University study (1982) found that river basins with less than 70 percent forest cover contained streams with higher values of pH, turbidity, electrical conductivity, total dissolved solids, and hardness. Though the water in these basins was of lower quality than more forested basins, it was still acceptable for public water supply. Further deforestation, however, may result in an even greater decline in water quality.

A study of the effect of topography and land use on the water balance in Khao Yai has shown that conversion from forest to agricultural land results in reduced runoff (Kaeochada 1984). While this result runs counter to standard thinking (see Hamilton 1983, for example), this conclusion was also reached in a Kasetsart University study (1982) which estimates that for every 10 percent decrease in forest area of Khao Yai, runoff will decline by about 1.5 centimeters or about 47 million cubic meters (mcm) per year. The change in runoff will, however, depend on the uses to which the land is put. At the time of the study, based on a forest area of about 89 percent and a basin average of 1,600 millimeters rainfall per year, the runoff discharge was estimated at 1,889 mcm a year.

Large-scale deforestation in the higher elevations of Khao Yai could also reduce precipitation in these areas. Results from studies in other areas have shown that removal of high-elevation cloud forests has caused significant declines in annual rainfall after forests have been harvested (Hamilton 1983). Forest cover has also been shown to affect the timing and peaks of streamflow. Tangtham (1988) summarizes these effects based on previous studies and data collected in Khao Yai. Lam Praphloeng, the basin with the least amount of forest cover, was shown to have the shortest half-flow and quarter-flow intervals of all basins. This means that this basin had the most concentrated flows in the shortest periods of time, indicating rapid runoff during high rainfall periods. The bulk of surface streamflow from Khao Yai takes place during the rainy season (May to October) with peak flows from August to October. From 77 to 98 percent of total annual runoff occurs during the wet season (Tangtham 1988). Overall the ratio between wet season flow and dry season flow is 10 to 1 (Kasetsart University 1982).

If the steep slopes in Khao Yai were to be deforested, there is no doubt that significant erosion would occur and sediment levels in streams would increase. The extent of this increase depends on the use of the forest and whether it is subsequently allowed to regenerate or is converted to another use such as agriculture. In northern Thailand, for example, hill evergreen forests converted to growing ornamental flowers and strawberries caused erosion to increase thirty-nine times over the base rate (Chunkao and others 1983). In an extreme case, up to 10 centimeters of surface soil can be lost in one growing season (Messerli 1978). In cases where trees over 10 centimeters in diameter were removed, erosion increased significantly but returned to precutting levels in three to five years (Chunkao and Pricha 1976). On the other hand, if *Imperata* grass colonizes areas burned after harvesting, soil erosion may be even less than when covered by forest, assuming that the grass itself is not burned annually as often occurs (Chunkao and others 1983).

One way to examine the hydrologic benefits of continued protection of Khao Yai is to estimate the costs that would be imposed on downstream areas if deforestation and land-use conversion were to spread. For example, increased erosion and subsequent sedimentation would adversely affect irrigation in areas downstream from Khao Yai. The increased levels of sediment would result in a shallowing and eventual clogging of irrigation channels. This would increase the maintenance costs necessary to clear the channels. The extent of these costs is unknown for Khao Yai but could be estimated by determining how often the channels would need to be cleared, how many kilometers of channels would be affected, and the cost of clearing each kilometer.

This is an example of the mitigation-cost method. These costs could then be compared to current maintenance costs, and the difference would then be the cost of the increased sedimentation due to erosion or the benefits from preventing the erosion.

Another cost of erosion is the increased sedimentation in the dams downstream from Khao Yai. Sediment inputs into the reservoirs reduce the potential water storage volume and thus the benefits of the reservoir. Two main reservoirs are fed by watersheds located, at least partly, within the northern part of Khao Yai. Both the Lam Takhong and the Lam Praphloeng reservoirs are designed to provide irrigation water. The Lam Takhong reservoir stores about 325 mcm of water and irrigates some 238,000 rai (about 38,100 hectares). Sedimentation of the Lam Takhong reservoir has not been a major problem to date. The Lam Praphloeng reservoir initially stored 152 mcm and provided water to 66,800 rai (about 10,700 hectares). In Lam Praphloeng reservoir, however, deforestation upstream has already resulted in a loss of 20 percent of storage capacity in seventeen years (Royal Irrigation Department 1985).

Costs of sedimentation can be estimated by examining the impact of lost storage capacity on irrigated agriculture, power generation, and flood control. In the case of Khao Yai, the primary impact is on irrigated agriculture. In a study of the Nam Pong reservoir in northeastern Thailand, Srivardhana (1986) estimated the costs of sedimentation from reduced hydropower, irrigation, flood control, and fishery benefits. Using data on annual erosion rates in the watershed, channel and bedload erosion, and a sediment delivery ratio, Srivardhana estimated the loss in reservoir benefits associated with increased sedimentation.

Applying this methodology to Khao Yai, the base case would first analyze the effects of existing erosion rates. With increased loss of forest cover, erosion and sedimentation would increase. The costs associated with this increased rate of erosion will reflect the effects on downstream structures and water users affected by increased sedimentation. The additional costs associated with the increased erosion and sedimentation rates would then be a cost of deforestation. Sufficient data are not available at present to estimate these costs. Based on the Srivardhana study and some limited data for Khao Yai, however, the following "synthetic but realistic" estimates can be made.

Present erosion rates in Khao Yai watersheds average about 0.05 millimeter per year, equivalent to about 0.65 ton per hectare per year. This is a very low erosion rate. If deforestation occurred and land use changed, erosion rates could easily increase many fold—for example, erosion rates of 40 tons per hectare for disturbed lands are not uncommon. If loss of protection of the watershed for Lam Takhong reservoir resulted in an increase of erosion rates to half of this level, or 20 tons per hectare, the following calculations could be made:

> Total catchment area: 143,000 hectares
> Erosion rate per hectare: 20 tons
> Channel and bedload erosion factor: 1.56
> Sediment delivery ratio: 0.2

or

> 20 tons/hectare × 143,000 hectares × 1.56 × 0.2 = 892,320 tons

With an average volume of 0.67 cubic meter per ton of sediment, this means that 892,320 tons of sediment delivered to the Lam Takhong reservoir each year would result in a lost storage capacity of about 600,000 cubic meters, or 0.2 percent of the total capacity of 325 mcm. If the erosion rate doubled to 40 tons per hectare and the sediment delivery ratio were 0.4, the yearly loss of reservoir capacity would be 2.4 mcm, or 0.7 percent of total capacity.

There are several ways to translate these hypothetical sedimentation rates into monetary costs. As outlined in Chapter 2, one can use the mitigation-cost approach to calculate the cost of dredging sediment to retain full reservoir capacity. These costs are fairly easy to calculate (and are probably quite high). One could also use the change-in-productivity approach to estimate the loss in agricultural output from reduced water availability. Depending on how much of the sediment goes into live storage, the amount of water available for irrigation would be reduced. This would either result in reduced water being available per hectare or a reduced area being irrigated. In either case, a with-and-without analysis would demonstrate the magnitudes involved.

Given the data from the Khao Yai study, it does not appear that reservoir sedimentation is a major problem for the Lam Takhong reservoir. The Lam Praphloeng reservoir, however, has already been affected by sedimentation; using the approach outlined earlier plus additional data, rough estimates of these costs could be obtained.

Research and Education

Only a few formal statistics describe the extent of Khao Yai's role as a research and education facility. The park's visitor center contains a number of displays on various aspects of the park that provide an introduction to its resources. There is also a meeting hall that holds up to 500 people for lectures and films.

Individuals and groups who go to Khao Yai to learn about nature would be included within the overall visitor statistics, so revenues from these people would be captured in the tourism benefits. An additional (but nonquantifiable) value would be the effect of this education on the future actions of visitors. Certainly environmental sensitivity gained by visiting Khao Yai would tend to promote a greater awareness of the importance of natural resources and encourage conservation. The magnitude of this benefit could be measured by a survey inquiring about the visitors' knowledge and opinions before and after their visit to Khao Yai.

As described earlier in the section on biodiversity, Khao Yai has been a popular site for research, especially on its wildlife. Gibbons, elephants, and hornbills have all been studied extensively in Khao Yai by both Thais and foreigners. Foreigners who come to Khao Yai to do research add to the overall tourism statistics for the country and bring in foreign exchange. Some projects also hire Thais to assist in the study and therefore provide employment and training opportunities.

The reports on the Khao Yai Beneficial Use Project (Dobias 1988; Dobias and others 1988) present some data about scientific expenditures within the park. Although expenditures do not represent economic values per se, they do indicate a minimum willingness to pay to take advantage of the park's resources. The Beneficial Use Project identified some twenty-five research activities (many focused on gibbons, hornbills, and elephants), several broad research and demonstration projects, and some fifteen M.Sc. and Ph.D. theses based on Khao Yai data since 1976. The research activities involved expenditures of more than 3.6 million baht; the research-cum-demonstration projects were considerably larger and totaled more than 7.1 million baht in expenditures (not all in Khao Yai). These expenditures, however, merely reflect the current levels of research and education activities; they do not provide any information on the potential returns to research or the potential value of educational activities.

As mentioned earlier, most of the plants gathered for medicinal purposes have not been scientifically tested for their effectiveness. The Royal Thai Government should encourage such a program, perhaps under the guidance of the Thailand Institute for Scientific and Technological Research. Research on the wildlife in Khao Yai could also provide valuable information needed to protect these animals and ensure their long-term survival, both in Khao Yai and elsewhere.

COSTS

Costs include the direct costs paid by the government to develop and manage Khao Yai, as well as the opportunity costs associated with traditional uses that are prohibited and alternative development opportunities forgone. While the direct costs are fairly easy to identify from government budget documents, estimates of opportunity costs must be based on certain assumptions.

Direct Management Costs

Table 5 shows the annual budget for Khao Yai between 1982 and 1987. During this period, the average rate of growth in Khao Yai's budget was 12.5 percent compared to an average growth rate of 10.6 percent for all national parks (NPD, various years). The bulk of this increase in Khao Yai's budget occurred between 1983 and 1984 when five additional park protection offices (guard stations) were opened to supplement the six existing offices. In 1986 a twelfth office was added, and three more guard stations were planned for 1988. This is the largest total number of guard stations at any national park; on a per hectare basis, however, Khao Yai has fewer stations than many other parks. If poaching and encroachment are to be controlled, additional guard stations will be needed. Khao Yai's permanent staff increased from fifty in 1982 to a

Table 5.

Budget (in Baht) for Khao Yai National Park: 1982–1987

Fiscal Year	Wages of Temporaries	General Expenses	Supplies	Total
1982	1,126,400	330,000	420,000	1,876,400
1983	1,130,000	330,000	420,000	1,880,000
1984	1,810,000	538,000	632,000	2,980,000
1985	2,085,000	569,000	677,000	3,331,000
1986	2,185,000	599,000	707,000	3,491,000
1987	2,163,000	559,000	654,000	3,376,000

Note: US$1 = 26 baht.
Source: NPD (various years).

high of seventy-two in 1985 before dropping to sixty-six in 1986. As well, there are approximately 100 temporary guards. In addition to its annual budget, Khao Yai also receives an annual supplement for construction and other capital expenditures. The amount of this supplement fluctuates widely from year to year. Between 1982 and 1987, it ranged from a low of 171,000 baht in 1984 to a high of 1.6 million baht in 1986 and 1987.

In 1988, the Thai government approved the implementation of the Khao Yai Management Plan. If carried out, both Khao Yai's annual budget and its capital budget will be substantially increased. More than 7 million baht were appropriated in 1988 for improvements and construction of guard stations, officers' housing, and workers' housing. Capital expenses to establish and maintain protected areas are substantial and should not be overlooked in analyzing the total budgetary implications of new protected areas.

Opportunity Costs

The opportunity costs of protecting Khao Yai as a national park depend on the alternative uses that would occur if Khao Yai were not protected. Many of these uses can be valued using market prices for various goods and services. Given the scarcity of agricultural land in the region, it is likely that most of Khao Yai would be cleared of its forest and converted to farmland, even if productivity is low. Alternatively it could be declared a reserve forest and used for production of timber and other wood products.

The total volume of timber in Khao Yai is considerable. The Khao Yai Ecosystem Project estimated total biomass and commercial timber volume for each of the three main forest types (Kasetsart University 1982). As of 1982, a rough breakdown of timber resources in Khao Yai was as follows:

Forest Type	% of Total Area	Commercial Timber (m³/ha)	Total Commercial Timber (m³)
Moist evergreen	61	302	41,575,000
Dry evergreen	26	73	4,315,000
Hill evergreen	3	410	2,070,000

Note: About 10 percent of the total area is abandoned or cleared; thus percentages do not sum to 100.

To estimate the value of the timber resource, data on the following points are needed:

- Which areas would be harvested?
- Would clear-felling or selective harvesting be practiced?
- What are the likely extraction costs, transportation costs, and techniques?
- Which species would be harvested and what is their price per cubic meter?
- What would be the average yield per hectare?
- What other related environmental costs or benefits are associated with each scenario?

Data are not available to estimate the potential net economic benefits of timber extraction from Khao Yai. Private benefits may be considerable but so may the social costs. Clear-cutting would destroy the wildlife habitat and lead to major hydrologic damage. Tourism would probably suffer. Selective harvesting, if properly managed, may be less destructive. The main question is whether or not private loggers can be effectively managed; the experience in other areas has not been encouraging.

The experience with adjacent lands that were once forested is instructive. Although much of the land surrounding Khao Yai is officially reserve forest, some of it is currently used for agriculture while other portions are now degraded forest producing little in the way of financial returns (NPD 1986). In the absence of strict protection, the same changes are likely to occur in Khao Yai—gradual encroachment and poaching of valuable timber species that results in little long-term benefit.

Allowing Khao Yai to be used as agricultural land would probably not result in significant benefits. Much of the park cannot sustain successful agriculture due to its topography and soils. In the northern section, soils are of low to medium fertility and many areas are susceptible to erosion. In the west, much of the terrain is steep and the soils are shallow with a low water-holding capacity. The southern part of Khao Yai has deep soil but is poorly drained and highly susceptible to erosion. Soils do not present a barrier to agriculture in the east and central portions, but the steep topography would result in high rates of erosion in many areas. This erosion would increase downstream sedimentation resulting in damage to irrigation systems. Water quality would also deteriorate. Conversion to agriculture would thereby harm downstream agricultural areas and offset the benefits of the new agricultural areas in Khao Yai. The costs of reservoir sedimentation have already been discussed.

Another opportunity cost of maintaining Khao Yai as a national park results from the policy of not allowing villagers to make use of resources within the park. Though park policy forbids hunting of animals, felling of trees, and gathering of plants, all these activities are widespread throughout the park. It is clear that a number of villagers depend on the park for the bulk of their income or as a supplemental source of income. In an NPD survey reported in the Khao Yai Management Plan (NPD 1986), 61 percent of the villagers claimed that their income is not enough to support themselves and therefore must be supplemented by illegal use of the park. Meat from sambar deer and wild pigs is sold in local markets and restaurants, while birds and gibbons are also heavily poached not only for the pet trade but also as subsistence food (NPD 1986).

Cutting of timber and gathering of wild plants are also widespread. *Aquilaria crassna*, the source of *mai hom*, a plant product used to make incense, is increasingly scarce in the park, and collectors are now forced to cut smaller and smaller trees when they can be found at all (Dobias 1985). Orchids, rattans, and medicinal plants are also gathered in large quantities. Yet another illegal use of the park is the collection of insects and butterflies. In 1987 we spoke with a European living near Khao Yai whose primary employment was to pay villagers for gathering these creatures (which he then illegally mailed to Europe for purchase by collectors).

A rough estimate of the gross value of resources extracted from Khao Yai can be gained from data found in the Khao Yai Management Plan (NPD 1986). In a survey of 337 families in a sample of thirteen villages in 1984, the average five-member household had a yearly income of about 27,000 baht or just over $1,000—an average of only $200 per person per year. There are about 130 villages around the park boundaries. If each village has twenty-five households, this means that of some 3,250 families as many as 2,000 may make some use of park resources. (Sixty percent of the respondents indicated a need to use the park to supplement their income.) If the average family receives a quarter of its income from park resources, the total value would be more than 13.5 million baht per year (2,000 × 0.25 × 27,000 baht).

The current opportunity cost in terms of forgone use by villagers would be equal to the value of use in the absence of any regulations minus the value of the current illegal use. If we assume that current enforcement reduces use by two-thirds, then total use in the absence of any enforcement would be worth 40.5 million baht (13.5 × 3). In this case, the opportunity cost of protecting Khao Yai would be 27 million baht per year (40.5 − 13.5). Obviously this figure is only a very rough guesstimate based on assumptions of current use and what use would be in the absence of regulation. Better estimates could be made by undertaking a detailed survey concerning both of these assumptions and finding more accurate values. The values obtained would also have to be evaluated to see if these use levels are sustainable. Given that current uses at the lower, illegal level are already having a detrimental impact on certain species (such as *Aquilaria crassna*), allowing open access is likely to have serious effects on valuable species of both plants and animals.

One effort to reduce illegal use and promote protection of the park by nearby villagers is the wilderness trekking program developed at Ban Sap Tai village. Villagers act as porters and guides for a multiple-day trekking program; the treks combine time spent within the park with village visits. Not only has considerable income, both from wages and donations, accrued to the village but a village-based NGO—the Environmental Protection Society (EPS)—has also been established at Ban Sap Tai to provide technical training, promote village develop-ment, and support conservation measures. Villagers who join the EPS agree not to poach park resources and, in return, are given access to low-interest loans, technical training, and discounted merchandise in a store set up by the project. See Dobias (1985), McNeely (1988), and Dobias and Khontong (1986) for more information on this program.

As a result of these programs, the villagers receive income and are made aware of the park's value as a protected area. The trekking program establishes a link between the benefits of protection and the villagers, who pay part of the protection costs via reduced direct use of park resources. Expansion of the program has been slowed, however, by the difficulty of finding bilingual trek leaders who can interact with villagers and the trekking groups that include a mix of Thai and foreign visitors.

SUMMARY OF BENEFITS AND COSTS

Khao Yai is obviously a valuable resource. Located within easy access from the rapidly growing Bangkok metropolitan area, it provides a variety of recreational and amenity benefits to both Thai and foreign visitors. It also offers important biological and hydrologic benefits. Against these benefits, one must consider the costs of management and various alternative development benefits forgone. In examining these benefits and costs, the real issue is not whether the benefits of Khao Yai justify the continuation of its protected status—that is a given. Thai officials realize that a new Khao Yai could not be created in any similarly accessible area if Khao Yai were lost. Thus the real question is: What level of expenditure on improved management is justified given the benefits that Khao Yai provides?

The direct benefits of Khao Yai have already been detailed: maintenance of biodiversity and ecological processes, watershed protection, and tourism. Research and education benefits may also be important but are harder to value. The principal costs are the direct management costs and the opportunity costs of not logging, hunting, gathering plant products, or developing agricultural lands. First let us consider the principal benefits:

- *Biodiversity/ecological processes.* The richness of Khao Yai as a preserve for flora and fauna has been noted. Although the park is most famous for its elephants, numerous other species contribute to its biological diversity. Apart from the pure "existence value" of species diversity, it also provides a powerful pull for tourists. We are not able, however, to place a monetary value on either the current or the future value of the benefits of maintaining biodiversity. *VALUE:* Undetermined. Research and education related expenditures amount to 1 to 2 million baht per year. Option/existence value is estimated at more than 120 million baht per year.
- *Watershed protection.* Khao Yai provides important watershed benefits in terms of the quantity, quality, and timing of water flows. The reservoirs located downstream depend on Khao Yai's watershed protection function. Substantial investments have been made in these reservoirs, and many people depend on the water they provide. *VALUE:* Can be calculated but undetermined at present.
- *Tourism.* Visits by Thai and foreign tourists are a major and potentially growing use of Khao Yai. As many as 400,000 visitors a year use the park, paying admission and lodging fees totaling more than 3 million baht. Additional millions are spent on transport, food, and other services within the park. *VALUE:* Tourism-related expenditures amount to 100 to 200 million baht per year. Consumer's surplus is estimated at 10 to 25 million baht per year.

The costs associated with protection are both direct and indirect:

- *Management costs.* The present annual budget for Khao Yai is about 3.4 million baht. Implementation of the management plan to meet protection, interpretation, and development goals will result in increased annual budgets and substantial capital expenditures in the next few years. With its large area and closely settled borders, greater effort is needed to support programs that improve the standard of living of nearby residents, thereby reducing their dependence on illegal and unsustainable uses of the park. *COST*: Current government management costs are 3 to 4 million baht per year but will rise significantly over the next few years.

- *Opportunity costs.* A variety of development benefits are lost because of protection—principally water resource development, timber harvesting, and agriculture. The potential economic benefits from these uses are not known but could be estimated with more data. Impacts on tourism, biodiversity, and ecological processes, if these activities were allowed, may be considerable. Another major category of opportunity costs is the loss of income to local villagers due to prohibitions on the gathering and harvesting of plants and animals in the park. These two categories are not additive, however, since development of park resources would also result in a loss of opportunity to collect plants and animals. *COST*: A rough guesstimate of the reduction in villager-derived income from park resources is 27 million baht per year, though this amount would probably not be sustainable and would result in significant damage to highly valued species.

In sum, then, expenditures for the direct benefits (tourism) and direct costs (management) of Khao Yai can be estimated with reasonable accuracy. The nonquantified benefits and development benefits lost may also be large, and rough estimates can be made. It seems clear that greater investment in park management is justified by the strong recreational demand. Moreover, the nonquantified biodiversity/ ecological benefits and watershed protection benefits will all be enhanced if more effective management is undertaken. (This issue is discussed in the following section.)

Khao Yai, therefore, is a good example of a protected area that fits the "socially beneficial" category described in Chapter 1. It provides recreational amenities, wildlife habitat, and watershed benefits that can be measured in physical and (in some cases) economic terms. It also furnishes less tangible benefits in terms of preservation of forest cover and associated biological diversity. Without government intervention, however, such a large area would not be protected privately. Not only are the benefits too diffuse, but the financial returns from preservation would be outweighed by those associated with exploitation of Khao Yai's timber, land, and animal resources.

MANAGEMENT AND POLICY ISSUES

The Khao Yai Management Plan (NPD 1986) contains a number of proposals designed to increase the benefits of Khao Yai and reduce the problems it faces. The plan calls for increased budget and personnel, greater support from all levels of government, and development of programs to increase cooperation with nearby villagers. Further, the plan calls for improvement of visitor services, wildlife management plans, and increases in research and monitoring of park resources. The Royal Thai Government has recognized the value of these suggestions and has begun to implement them.

If Khao Yai's benefits are to be maintained, the key management issue is developing a more effective protection scheme. To do this will require an integrated program of community education, development of alternative sources of supplemental income for villagers (perhaps related to park tourism), modification of park regulations, and stricter enforcement. Only a comprehensive program that addresses the source of the problems will be effective.

One issue that merits close attention is the establishment of new boundaries for the park and the development of buffer zones between settlements and undisturbed areas of the park. Since much of the park's boundary is not marked, villagers often claim they do not know when they are operating within the park. In the west, the provincial government has issued land tenure certificates to villagers in an area that park officials claim was encroached after the park was established. Many other areas near the border have also been put under cultivation.

It may be necessary to establish new park boundaries that reflect the realities of the current situation. Allowing encroached areas to remain in private hands while clearly marking new boundaries with strict penalties for further encroachment may be more effective than attempting to evict settlers. New boundaries might also incorporate areas that were not previously part of the park but would be a valuable addition, such as the 60 square kilometers of forest adjacent to the northwest boundary in Sara Buri province (NPD 1986).

Many areas just inside the park are seriously degraded. These

areas should be made into buffer zones and managed to provide benefits to nearby villagers. Programs should be developed in these areas to
promote production of plants that are currently being poached within
the park or to establish other opportunities to supplement villagers'
incomes. These programs could be at least partially paid for with a
percentage of tourism revenues. Once the buffer zones are established,
penalties for poaching beyond them should be strictly enforced. Limited hunting of certain species could also be allowed in these buffer
zones. Such a policy would have to be accompanied by a clear demarca-
tion of park boundaries. Any hunters caught within these boundaries
should have their weapons confiscated.

A buffer zone program could have a number of beneficial effects.
Making resources available to local communities would reduce the
villagers' need to encroach into the park. At the same time, demarcat-
ing clear boundaries would help protect those areas not yet seriously
degraded and eliminate the villagers' excuse that they do not know
where the boundaries are. Enforcement efforts would also be simplified. Priority should be given to those areas currently suffering the
worst problems.

Improvement of visitor facilities is another important issue. The
visitor center should be upgraded to provide more educational information and should be manned by a person knowledgeable about the park.
Brochures and trail guides are needed in both Thai and English. Hiking
trails should be more clearly marked. More opportunities to view
wildlife should be made available including additional wildlife obser-
vation towers and construction of canopy platforms to observe wildlife
that spends most of its time in the canopy (NPD 1986). Certain tourist
development activities could also have secondary benefits (Durst 1988).
Development of organized multiple-day hikes could provide employment opportunities for local villagers as guides and support staff. One
program of this type has already begun at Ban Sap Tai village under the
auspices of a WWF project. These hikes could also be accompanied by
guards who would patrol forest areas currently not guarded effectively.

In 1987, fees from concessions, accommodations, and entrance
were almost equal to the budget allocated to Khao Yai (3.18 million
baht versus 3.38 million baht respectively). If the NPD were allowed to
take over the TAT facilities, it is likely that Khao Yai could more than pay
for itself with direct revenues from tourism. Because of the substantial
budget increases expected from the adoption of the Khao Yai Management Plan, costs will outpace revenues for the next few years. The
increased tourism that would result from the proposed improvements,
however, should help to offset these costs.

There is also a need to step up tourist promotions for Khao Yai and other national parks. Nature-based recreation is becoming increasingly popular in Western countries and could provide the basis for a more substantial tourist industry (Boo 1989; Whelan 1990). TAT should take the lead in this area and distribute brochures to major tour agencies around the world. An updated version of the now out-of-print *Shell Guide to National Parks of Thailand* (Dobias 1982) is long overdue. Any large increase in tourist numbers, however, may require concomitant upgrading of infrastructure and staffing levels.

The NPD should also consider establishing a two-tier fee system. Current entrance fees, though reasonable for Thais, are extremely low by foreign standards. Indeed, fees could probably be raised to ten times their current level without significantly reducing the number of foreign visitors.

Khao Yai's Management Plan provides the basis for a significant improvement in the park's management and administration. Implementation of the plan will ensure that Khao Yai continues to be one of the premier parks in Thailand and help to protect its valuable resources.

7

Analyzing a Nonhunting Area (Thale Noi) and a Wildlife Sanctuary (Khao Soi Dao)

In the preceding chapter we examined the case of Khao Yai at some length. As Thailand's oldest and most developed national park, Khao Yai has been the focus of a number of studies and considerable data exist—making it easier to analyze the economic benefits and costs associated with such a protected area. Thailand's protected area system, however, is quite diverse and includes a number of other categories. This chapter examines two other Thai protected areas, but not at the same level of detail as in the case of Khao Yai. Thale Noi, a nonhunting area, has a major direct-use component and is therefore less protected than Khao Yai. Khao Soi Dao, on the other hand, is a wildlife sanctuary with very little direct resource or recreational use. In both cases, however, the underlying economic questions are similar to those raised for Khao Yai: What are the benefits and costs associated with protected area status? How can these be measured in monetary and qualitative terms? What policy recommendations emerge from the analysis?

THALE NOI: A NONHUNTING AREA

Thale Noi (literally, "little lake") lies at the northern end of the Songkhla Lake basin in peninsular Thailand (see Figure 10). Located 36 kilometers northeast of the town of Phatthalung, it straddles the junction of three provinces—Phatthalung, Nakhon Si Thammarat, and Songkhla.

Figure 10.
Location of Thale Noi NHA

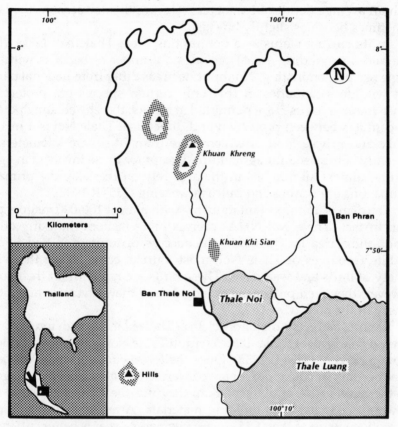

In 1975, the lake and surrounding land were designated as Thailand's first nonhunting area to protect valuable wildlife resources.

Thale Noi Nonhunting Area (NHA) includes the lake and considerable surrounding areas; it has an area of 457 square kilometers (45,700 hectares). Approximately 28 square kilometers of the area (6 percent) is the lake itself. A variety of habitats comprise the remaining area: rice fields (66 square kilometers), grasslands and wet meadows (40 square kilometers), *Melaleuca* forest (42 square kilometers), and varying areas of evergreen and scrub forest, floating vegetation, and other forms of vegetation (TISTR 1982). In addition to these habitats, a small but increasing area, mostly former evergreen and swamp forest, is now being used for rubber plantations and orchards. The freshwater lake itself is approximately 5 kilometers wide and 6 kilometers long with an average depth of 1.2 meters. During the dry season, the lake sometimes becomes slightly brackish.

In its current status as a nonhunting area, Thale Noi NHA (the lake and surrounding areas) provides a number of benefits with no single use predominating. Nonhunting areas differ from national parks and wildlife sanctuaries in that only certain species are protected. Other commercial uses are permitted in NHAs, thereby creating potential conflicts between protection and direct use. Thale Noi is a mix of public and private land of which more than 70 square kilometers is currently being used for agriculture. Except for those involved in agriculture, almost all families in the area rely on the lake; the primary occupations are fishing and bulrush weaving (TISTR 1982).

Tourism is an important industry with almost 100,000 visitors per year. In fact, Thale Noi NHA receives more visitors than any other nonhunting area in Thailand. The success of tourism is tied to the wildlife resources of Thale Noi; most tourists come to see the wide variety of birds and waterfowl. These birds are not without their cost, however; they feed on nearby rice fields and may adversely affect the fishery in the area.

Deforestation is a major problem at Thale Noi. Though forests once covered nearly all of the land area within Thale Noi, they now cover less than 15 percent (TISTR 1982). Once the forests are cut, most of these areas become wet meadows or are converted to wet rice fields. Villagers are the main cause of deforestation; they use the harvested wood for firewood, charcoal, and building materials. A recent estimate of deforestation suggests that 0.25 square kilometer a year is being cut; most of the forests are being replaced by rice fields and wet meadows (TISTR 1982). The following sections elaborate on the financial and economic benefits and costs associated with Thale Noi NHA.

Benefits

The main benefits from Thale Noi are the maintenance of biodiversity and ecological processes, watershed and hydrologic regulation, tourism to the area, and research and education. Only some of these benefits are estimated in monetary terms.

BIODIVERSITY AND ECOLOGICAL PROCESSES. Thale Noi is considered to be one of the most important areas in Thailand for birds and has been categorized as "internationally or nationally significant" in a recent study (John Taylor & Sons and others 1984). This rating is based on a qualitative scale of seven key characteristics including species diversity, habitat, recreational value, environmental conditions, and presence of rare and endangered species. Each category is ranked from 1 to 5, with 5 as the highest possible score; Thale Noi scored 31 out of a possible 35 points.

Thale Noi NHA contains the second largest of the four natural freshwater lakes in Thailand. Freshwater wetlands have become increasingly rare because of the need for more agricultural land, and many have been drained and converted into wet rice fields or land for other field crops. This decline in available wetland areas for wildlife is offset somewhat by artificial lakes and areas created for drainage canals (*khlongs*).

Thale Noi is the only known nesting area for painted storks in Thailand. In addition, ten other endangered bird species are known to use Thale Noi. It is also an important area for migratory waterfowl with sixty-seven species identified (John Taylor & Sons and others 1984). Overall 187 species of birds have been recorded at Thale Noi (TISTR 1982).

Because of its variety of habitats, Thale Noi also has a diverse array of aquatic plants, benthic fauna, and plankton. Plankton are the primary producers in the food chain and also act as an indicator of water quality. The diversity of planktonic species varies seasonally due to changes in salinity and nutrient inputs into the lake and the surrounding marsh. This is also true of the benthic fauna (annelids, mollusks, crustaceans, and insects), whose diversity index is highest during the rainy season and reduced during low rainfall and drought periods (TISTR 1982).

Very little original forest is left in Thale Noi NHA, most having been replaced by pure stands of *Melaleuca leucadendron*, a species commonly found near mangroves. Small areas of evergreen forest remain, but most are now scrub forest. Scattered individual trees of *Alstonia* spp. occur in both types of forests. This is the only tree known to be used as a nesting site by the endangered painted stork.

Threats to the plant and animal life in Thale Noi NHA are mostly of human origin. Deforestation, hunting, and conversion of land to agricultural uses are the primary problems. Though hunting is not legal within the NHA, it is still considered to be a problem. Moreover, collection of birds for markets in Bangkok and other cities puts pressure on the populations of certain species. Another potential threat to

Thale Noi and its wildlife are hydrologic projects including drainage improvements and the development of irrigation facilities.

Pollution may threaten the continued existence of some species. High levels of pesticides including DDT have been recorded in various parts of the nonhunting area (TISTR 1982). Further, domestic sewage and animal wastes from nearby villages have degraded the water quality, especially near Ban Thale Noi (Thale Noi village). Introduction of exotic species is another problem. Water hyacinth (*Eichornia crassipes*), a floating weed, has been spreading over large areas of formerly open water in the lake.

No economic values have been placed on the benefits from maintaining biodiversity. It is clear, though, that Thale Noi is environmentally significant and has a considerable tourism value that is directly dependent on the diversity of wildlife found in the area.

WATERSHED/HYDROLOGY. Unlike the two other Thai protected areas discussed in this book, there are few externalities associated with the hydrologic effects from land use in Thale Noi NHA. It is more likely that the effects of land use outside the nonhunting area will affect Thale Noi rather than the reverse. Changes in land use within Thale Noi NHA itself, however, will affect other parts of the sanctuary.

Though the lake within the sanctuary is basically fresh water, it does become brackish in drought periods. The degree of salinity depends on the saltwater inputs from the lower lake system relative to the freshwater inputs from precipitation and the *khlongs* that empty into the lake. As a result of diversion of water upstream for agriculture, freshwater inputs are diminished, raising the lake's salinity and thereby affecting less salt-tolerant species. Moreover, deforestation within the NHA results in greater erosion in some areas. The main effects of this erosion are increased turbidity and a shallowing of the lake itself. This shallowing allows emergent vegetation to replace open-water areas at the expense of birds that require open water.

Since the watershed and hydrologic effects are mainly confined to the nonhunting area, there is no need to value external effects outside Thale Noi. However, development of any irrigation schemes near Thale Noi or construction of the proposed salinity barrier in Thale Sap must take into account the effects these projects may have on Thale Noi.

TOURISM. Thale Noi's beautiful scenery, along with its abundant and diverse bird life, makes it a natural tourist attraction. Birdwatching is the primary activity, usually done from longtail boats (long, narrow boats powered by large outboard motors) that are available for hire.

Table 6 shows tourist statistics for the last nine years. Tourism reached a maximum of 136,000 visits in 1981 but then showed a decline over the following years, reaching a low in 1984 when visits were at half their 1981 level. April and October are consistently the peak months for visitors. About a quarter of the visitors come in private cars; the remainder arrive in small vans (minibuses) or regular buses. Most of the van or bus visitors are members of organized social and recreational groups. The Wildlife Conservation Division (WCD) maintains facilities for overnight accommodations. Currently there are several small bungalows that can hold a total of approximately fourteen people and larger bungalows that can accommodate groups of up to fifty people.

Because there is no admission charge and no charge for accommodations, nonhunting area authorities receive no direct financial benefit from tourism. Instead of tourism providing needed funds, it is actually a drain on the Thale Noi budget since there are associated construction and maintenance costs. One could estimate potential revenue from admission fees and overnight stays based on prices charged elsewhere in Thailand. Although general visitor statistics are given in Table 6, data on overnight visitors are not available at present.

Tourism does benefit the local communities, however. Many tourists hire boats operated by local residents; the average boat can hold about ten people and charges are from 150 to 200 baht per trip around the lake. Tourists also contribute to the local economy through pur-

Table 6.
Visitor Statistics for Thale Noi NHA: 1979–1987

Year	Visitors
1979	114,477
1980	118,316
1981	136,662
1982	85,296
1983	75,849
1984	68,376
1985	88,034
1986	105,588
1987	83,312

Source: Wildlife Conservation Division (various years).

chase of meals and souvenirs, especially locally made handicrafts such as mats, baskets, and hats. A 1981 study estimates that the total tourist expenditure of Thale Noi visitors was 500 baht per person (TISTR 1982). Of this amount, approximately 50 baht per person was spent in nearby communities. The balance was spent for transportation to and from Thale Noi, food and drink, and other expenses. With some 100,000 visitors per year, the 50 baht per person for local expenditures totals about 5 million baht a year. With a multiplier effect, these expenditures represent a considerable direct economic benefit to the local community. To estimate the consumer's surplus received by Thale Noi visitors (the amount of utility they receive in excess of what they pay for), a travel-cost study would be needed. Such a study has not yet been done for Thale Noi.

Thale Noi has the potential for significant growth in tourism. The Hat Yai/Songkhla area is a major tourist destination for visitors from Malaysia and Singapore. Since birdwatching is increasingly popular in the Western world, an information campaign boosting Thale Noi could result in a large increase in visits from foreigners who currently make up only a small percentage of the NHA's visitors. Development of group tours from Bangkok would make it easier for foreigners to visit the nonhunting area. Such an increase in foreign visitors could make a substantial contribution to the local economy.

RESEARCH AND EDUCATION. Figures are unavailable on the use of Thale Noi as an educational facility. Certainly the availability of group lodging facilities and the resources of the area afford excellent opportunities to acquaint schoolchildren with the beauty of nature and teach them an appreciation of the environment.

Thale Noi also provides many opportunities for research. Many aspects of the ecosystem have been studied including zooplankton (Angsupanich 1983), macrophytes (Bhurintavaraku and Leknim 1983), water quality (Kanatharana 1983; Nachiangmai 1980), captive fishery (Rittbhonbhun and others 1983), plant communities (Tansakul 1983a, 1983b), and bird communities (TISTR 1982). Government agencies such as the National Institute of Coastal Aquaculture, the Songkhla Fishery Station, and the Office of Phatthalung Fishery, as well as many staff members of Prince of Songkhla University, have shown interest in various aspects of Thale Noi. The development of shrimp pens for producing giant freshwater prawn (*Macrobrachium rosenbergii*) is also continuing.

Overall, Thale Noi has a high potential for both research and education. Data collected for Khao Yai indicate that research and education generate expenditures of 1 to 2 million baht a year. Expenditures at Thale Noi NHA are probably less than this amount.

Costs

The costs associated with Thale Noi fall into three main categories: direct budgetary outlays for operation and maintenance of the nonhunting area, indirect costs due to damage to crops and fisheries from birds, and the opportunity cost of not being able to hunt in Thale Noi or develop new aquaculture areas.

DIRECT COSTS. Budget figures for the last six years are shown in Table 7. Over this period the allocated budget grew yearly to reach almost 1.5 million baht in 1986 with a slight decrease in 1987. There was also an increase in staffing levels during this period, rising from fifteen in 1981 to a high of twenty-nine in 1986 before falling back to twenty-six in 1987. In 1986 the staff consisted of three forest technicians; the remainder were guards (TDRI 1987). Many temporary employees are also hired.

Given its size, Thale Noi NHA has enjoyed a relatively large budget. While the average budget per hectare allocated directly to nonhunting areas in 1986 was 18.7 baht, Thale Noi's budget was equal

Table 7.
Budget (in Baht) for Thale Noi NHA: 1982–1987

Fiscal Year	Wages of Temporaries	Compensation, General Expenses, and Supplies	Total
1982	720,000	368,900	1,088,900
1983	864,000	446,000	1,310,000
1984	864,000	456,700	1,320,700
1985	912,000	504,000	1,416,000
1986	918,000	576,000	1,494,000
1987	918,000	546,000	1,464,000

Note: US$1 = 26 baht.
Source: Wildlife Conservation Division (various years).

to 32.7 baht per hectare (Kasetsart University 1987). In absolute terms, Thale Noi received the largest budget of any nonhunting area.

INDIRECT COSTS. Indirect costs are costs associated with the existence of the nonhunting area that are not paid in cash but still affect nearby residents. In this case, the indirect costs include damage to crops and fisheries caused by the bird population at Thale Noi. Large flocks of teals feed on rice grains during the broadcasting and harvesting periods, as well as rice seedlings. Purple gallinules, usually feeding on tubers and root of a local reed, *Scirpus mucronatus*, are also a problem.

In the 1982 TISTR survey of residents near Thale Noi, 69 percent of the respondents stated that birds were sometimes a problem in their rice fields. Using a change-in-productivity approach, the study estimated that the total damage by birds was approximately 500,000 baht per year. Since this figure includes rice fields in the Thale Sap area south of Thale Noi, it may overestimate the damage done by birds from Thale Noi.

Some families take protective measures to reduce crop damage. The cost of these measures, both for materials and time involved, can be considered another indirect cost. This is an example of the preventive-expenditures approach mentioned in Chapter 2. The TISTR survey found that 48 percent of respondents took some kind of precaution against bird damage. Use of netting was the most popular measure, with guarding a close second. A few families used poison bait or scared birds with fireworks. The cost of these protective measures has not been determined. To calculate this, one would have to compute the cost of materials, plus the number of hours involved, multiplied by an appropriate shadow value for labor. Both the cost of lost agricultural production and preventive expenditures are part of the indirect costs of Thale Noi.

A few families (less than 3 percent) also reported damage by birds to fisheries. Egrets and bitterns often forage for shrimp and fish in snares set by residents. No estimates were given of total damage, however. As the captive fishery production increases, this problem may grow.

OPPORTUNITY COSTS. The opportunity costs of managing Thale Noi as a nonhunting area are relatively minor, since regulations allow all uses except hunting of certain species. Thus the main opportunity costs are those associated with the benefits forgone from not being able to hunt selected species. In reality, some hunting does still occur even though it is officially prohibited. In the TISTR study (1982), residents were questioned about their hunting practices. The data cited here are from this study, but the actual incidence of hunting may be higher than reported since people are reluctant to admit engaging in illegal practices.

According to the survey, approximately two-thirds of the respondents (65.3 percent) claim never to have hunted birds. An additional 29 percent claim to have hunted birds in the past but say they no longer do so. Only 1.3 percent admit to hunting birds regularly; another 4.3 percent claim they hunt irregularly. When asked their main objective in bird hunting, almost 95 percent of the hunters claim they only hunt birds for food; an additional 4.7 percent say they hunt partly for food and partly to sell the birds. Only 0.4 percent claim to hunt birds for sale only. Of the primary species of birds hunted, teals account for 60.5 percent, watercock 18.4 percent, and purple gallinules 13.2 percent. Figures vary widely among communities, however.

If we assume that the 29 percent who stopped hunting did so because of the change in hunting regulations, it is these people who have had to pay the opportunity cost associated with making Thale Noi a nonhunting area. Based on the population used in the TISTR study of 36,753 residents (about 6,000 families) in the five *tambons* (subdistricts) in the Thale Noi region, this implies that approximately 1,750 households have been affected by the regulations. (Note that the hunting survey included only three of the five *tambons*; our analysis assumes that statistics are similar for the other two.) To value this opportunity cost, one would need information on the average number and type of bird killed or captured each year, the value of each bird, and the costs associated with hunting. We do not have these data and therefore cannot estimate the total value.

Apart from the forgone benefits of hunting, other opportunity costs are associated with alternative land uses that could be undertaken in Thale Noi. Primarily this would be agricultural use (mostly for rice and rubber) or expansion of aquaculture areas. In terms of agriculture, much of the most valuable land has already been converted. Of the remaining land, some areas of wet meadow or tropical rain forest could possibly be converted to rice fields. These areas, however, especially the remaining rain forest, are critical nesting and feeding areas for many species of birds. Moreover, the agricultural potential of these swampy areas is limited. Thus agriculture does not seem to be an efficient alternative use.

Expansion of aquaculture is another matter. In the late 1970s, the Thailand Fishery Department received a loan of 700 million baht from the Asian Development Bank to develop an aquaculture project in the Songkhla Lake basin. The primary species involved was the giant freshwater prawn, *Macrobrachium rosenbergii*, which was to be grown in submerged baskets. Another study is examining production of certain freshwater fish that feed on aquatic plants. This project would increase fish production and the fish, in turn, would feed on the aquatic vegetation that obstructs certain areas of the lake.

There does seem to be some potential for increasing aquaculture in Thale Noi, though there may be conflicts. Areas used for aquaculture may diminish the habitat available for birds (IUCN 1979). On the other hand, increasing the income of local families may result in less poaching of the natural resources of the area. Some expansion of aquaculture, limited to areas where it would least affect bird populations, may be worthwhile. A more detailed study of the cost and benefits, including the environmental and wildlife impacts, would be necessary to determine the opportunity costs of aquaculture.

Summary of Benefits and Costs

Thale Noi is one of the few protected wetlands in Thailand. It harbors a great variety of birds and waterfowl that are valuable both for their inherent value and as an attraction for tourists. The main benefits of Thale Noi can be summarized as follows:

- *Biodiversity.* Almost 200 species of birds, including 11 endangered species, can be found at Thale Noi. There is also a wide variety of aquatic plants, benthic fauna, and valuable areas of freshwater swamp forest that are now rare in Thailand. These living resources are valuable to local residents and important to continued growth in tourism. *VALUE:* Considerable but undetermined.
- *Tourism.* With approximately 100,000 tourists per year and good prospects for growth in the industry, tourism provides valuable benefits to the local community and Thailand as a whole. Using the 1982 TISTR estimate of 50 baht per person of direct expenditures in the immediate area, tourism at Thale Noi adds 5 million baht to the local economy each year. This estimate seems low, however, if one considers potential expenditures for boats (for birdwatching), meals, and the renowned handicrafts of the area, especially mats and baskets. Given the increasing popularity of birdwatching, Thale Noi has the potential to attract a large number of both local and foreign tourists. Because there is no charge for entry or accommodation, considerable amounts of potential revenue are forgone.

Even at a very low entry fee of 10 baht per person, receipts would be 1 million baht. Foreigners could probably be charged ten times this much without reducing attendance significantly. *VALUE*: Expenditures by tourists range from 5 million baht in the local communities to more than 50 million baht in total.

• *Direct use.* Fishing and bulrush weaving from Thale Noi's resources are major sources of income. Even if portions of the area were closed to direct use, these activities could continue in the remaining area without significant losses. The value of legal and illegal hunting of birds is not currently known but could be estimated with more data. *VALUE*: Substantial but undetermined.

The main costs of Thale Noi are the following:

• *Direct costs.* Thale Noi receives a yearly management budget of almost 1.5 million baht. If tourists were charged entry and accommodation fees, this amount could easily be recouped or even exceeded. With improved management, larger numbers of visitors could be accommodated. *COST*: Government management costs about 1.5 million baht per year.

• *Indirect costs.* The TISTR study (1982) estimates that damages to crops are approximately 500,000 baht per year, an amount approximately equal to one-tenth of the estimated direct expenditures by tourists in the nearby villages. (Of course, the people who benefit from the expenditures are not always those who bear the costs.) There are also additional costs in time and materials spent by villagers to protect their crops. If residents are forbidden to kill birds, they should be compensated for their losses—by establishing entry fees for visitors, for example, and allocating a portion of these fees to those adversely affected by the birds. *COST*: Undetermined but probably between 0.5 and 1.5 million baht.

• *Opportunity costs.* Draining and using Thale Noi for agriculture would not result in substantial benefits and would cause large losses. The forgone benefits from hunting may be substantial, but more information is needed to determine the magnitude. This amount could be reduced if hunting of certain species were allowed outside the NHA. *COST*: Value of forgone agriculture is probably small; value of forgone hunting has not been determined.

Overall, the direct benefits of protecting Thale Noi seem to outweigh the costs. This reckoning does not even include the substantial benefits gained from protecting the diversity of species that inhabit Thale Noi.

Thus Thale Noi falls into the "socially beneficial" category described in Chapter 1.

In sum, then, Thale Noi NHA is a valuable resource for both tourism and wildlife protection. The habitat it contains, especially its freshwater swamp, is considered to be one of the most underrepresented habitats in Thailand's protected area system (Round 1985; MacKinnon and MacKinnon 1986; Kasetsart University 1987). The area's many different resources are heavily used by local residents. By careful management of the entire system, the various needs served by Thale Noi NHA can continue to be met. The continued protection of Thale Noi NHA therefore merits a high priority.

KHAO SOI DAO: A WILDLIFE SANCTUARY

Khao Soi Dao (KSD) Wildlife Sanctuary, located in Chanthaburi province in southeastern Thailand (see Figure 11), was established in 1972 as one of Thailand's first wildlife sanctuaries. Unlike national parks or nonhunting areas, wildlife sanctuaries are strict reserves with very limited direct use. Khao Soi Dao has 74,000 hectares, mostly evergreen and semievergreen forests on hilly slopes. These hills form the western end of the Cardamom Mountains and the sanctuary includes two prominent peaks—Khao Soi Dao (1,670 meters) and Khao Soi Dao Nua (1,556 meters). The sanctuary lies in a high-rainfall region with an annual precipitation of more than 2,000 millimeters a year.

Like much of Thailand, the southeastern region has seen large-scale deforestation over the past few decades. In 1961 the region was 56 percent forested, but by 1985 forest area had declined to approximately 20 percent (ONEB 1986). Figures for Chanthaburi province follow this trend with a decrease in forest area from 62 percent to 30 percent during the same period. Currently KSD contains almost one-third of the province's remaining forests. Though most of the northern forests in the sanctuary appear to have been logged extensively in the past, the southern, more mountainous area is less disturbed (IUCN 1985a). Overall, however, deforestation within the sanctuary's boundaries has been increasing steadily. At the time of its establishment in 1972, KSD was 98 percent forested; in 1985, less than 75 percent was still under forest cover (RFD 1986).

A primary benefit of Khao Soi Dao is its role in maintaining biodiversity and evolutionary processes. KSD is the largest protected area in southeastern Thailand and is crucial for the long-term survival

Figure 11.
Location of Khao Soi Dao Wildlife Sanctuary

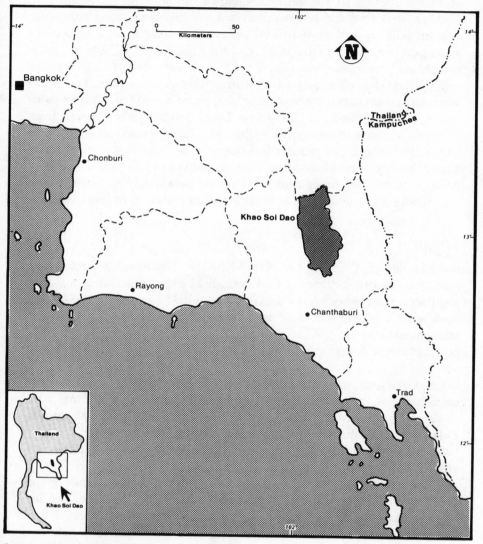

Source: Santiapillai and others (1987).

of many species in the region. Clearing of land for agriculture in southeastern Thailand has resulted in a steadily decreasing area available for wildlife and undisturbed vegetation communities. KSD plays an important role in the hydrology of the region, as well, and provides watershed protection benefits. Tourism, though restricted to a small area around the headquarters, also affords modest benefits. The ongoing research on captive breeding taking place at KSD may prove valuable to local residents in the future. Local residents also benefit from growing *klapwan* (cardamom) within sanctuary boundaries. Though technically illegal, this practice has been going on for many years and is a fairly benign form of land use. The main costs of KSD are the costs of protecting the sanctuary and the forgone benefits from forestry and agriculture. Now let us look at these benefits and costs in greater detail.

Benefits

As at Thale Noi, the main benefits of Khao Soi Dao are its key role in the maintenance of biodiversity and ecological processes and as a watershed area with associated hydrologic benefits. Tourism to the area is somewhat limited, but there is potential for expanded research and educational uses of the sanctuary. Only some of these benefits have been quantified, and even less is known about their monetary value.

BIODIVERSITY AND ECOLOGICAL PROCESSES. Southeastern Thailand was once home to large numbers of mammals including elephant, wild cattle, deer, rhinoceros, and tigers. Some of these species, for example Eld's deer and kouprey, no longer survive in the region while others have been reduced to small relict populations, mostly within protected areas (ONEB 1986).

There are five national parks and three wildlife sanctuaries in the southeastern region. Of these, only four still support the larger species of mammals: Khao Soi Dao, Khao Kitchakut National Park, Khao Chamao National Park, and Khao Ang Rua Nai Wildlife Sanctuary. KSD, together with the much smaller Khao Kitchakut National Park which borders it, is believed to offer the best possibility for the long-term survival of wild elephants and other large mammals in the southeastern region (ONEB 1986).

Among the notable species found within KSD are elephant, gaur, tiger, clouded leopard, wild dog, and silvered leaf monkey. Moreover, KSD's rain forests harbor the most dense and extensive population of pileated gibbon in Thailand (Jintanugool and others 1982). Round (1985) reports that more than 200 species of resident and migrant birds are known to exist in KSD. This number includes four species of montane or submontane birds whose Thai range is restricted to KSD and Khao Sabup National Park. One of these, *Arborophila cambodiana*, is considered to be in great danger of extinction.

As for vegetation communities, the sanctuary has dry and moist evergreen forest in the northern part and relatively undisturbed wet evergreen rain forest in the southern portion. This latter subtype of forest is considered to have the highest diversity of plant and animal species in the country (Sriburi 1986). There are also small areas of mixed deciduous forest, though most accessible areas have been logged. The few remaining stands of giant dipterocarps are subject to poaching pressure.

Almost all the hill evergreen forest in the southeastern region of Thailand is located within the boundary of KSD since this vegetation community is limited to areas above 1,000 meters. The margins of the sanctuary contain small areas of lowland valley bottom habitat along streamsides; protected habitat of this type is relatively rare in Thailand (MacKinnon and MacKinnon 1986).

The submontane areas of the sanctuary are considered to be of botanical interest (IUCN 1985a), but no extensive surveys of the vegetation have been undertaken. There are, however, several endemic species within the sanctuary. Economically valuable plants include *Scaphium lichnophorum* (samlong fruit), *Aquilaria crassna* (eaglewood, known locally as *mai hom*, used to make incense), and *Amomum krevanh* (cardamom, known locally as *klapwan*, used as a spice).

MacKinnon and MacKinnon (1986) rate KSD as a protected area of global importance—their highest-priority category. As the largest remaining forested area in southeastern Thailand, KSD offers the best hope for the survival of many species in this area. Directly measuring the economic value of benefits from maintenance of biodiversity is not generally possible. One can, however, measure the economic benefits gained from other uses associated with species and habitat protection: the value of drugs or other products derived from unique species found in the area, off-site benefits of maintaining forest ecosystems, and economic benefits from tourism, among others.

WATERSHED/HYDROLOGY. There have not been any studies on the sanctuary's water resources and hydrologic role, nor have there been any erosion studies. Nevertheless, studies performed in other parts of the southeastern region can be used to make some general observations of KSD's probable hydrologic role.

Much of KSD is steeply sloped. It is also a high-rainfall area (more than 2,000 millimeters a year) receiving almost all its rainfall between May and October. These combined factors mean that deforestation will have a great impact on many hydrologic variables. Clearing of forests has long been a problem in many protected areas, including KSD, though the rate of deforestation in KSD is substantially lower than that of Chanthaburi province as a whole. The annual deforestation rate in Chanthaburi between 1973 and 1982 was approximately 5.5 percent, for example, while in KSD the rate was approximately 1.1 percent (RFD, various years). Wholesale clearing usually stems from expansion of agriculture to forested areas. Timber poaching also reduces forest cover, though it usually does not involve clear-cutting. Timber poaching, however, is often followed by agricultural clearing.

Preservation of forest cover has beneficial effects on infiltration, runoff, and streamflows. It also reduces the erosion rate and the amount of sediment and nutrients in streams. The extent of these impacts depends on how much of the forest cover is maintained. In the higher portions of KSD, the effects of erosion control may be greater due to the generally steeper slopes, but the hydrologic effects may be different. High-elevation forests frequently enshrouded by clouds may condense atmospheric moisture, thus increasing the effective moisture received by an area. This added moisture, known as occult precipitation, may be substantial. If forested portions of these areas are cut or converted to other uses, this moisture is lost and may result in lower stream discharges, especially in the dry season. No experimental results are available to quantify this change (Hamilton 1983).

Most of KSD's water drains into the Chanthaburi River, eventually reaching the Gulf of Thailand. Downstream effects of maintaining forest cover, though difficult to quantify, probably include more moderate streamflows during the rainy season and reduced turbidity due to erosion. Streamflows may be greater during the dry season due to increased infiltration and less runoff during the wet season.

Given the data available, it is not possible to value the benefits of maintaining KSD as a protected area and preserving its forest cover. As at Khao Yai, a number of benefits could be estimated if data were available. These include the following:

- Irrigation benefits may derive from improved dry-season streamflow as compared to the situation after extensive deforestation. The appropriate measure would be the change in productivity of agricultural fields dependent on KSD waters. To estimate this value, one would need data on present use of water for irrigation and the likely impact on streamflows with a major change in land use in KSD. One would then estimate agricultural production under the new hydrologic regime and compare the net returns under both situations.

- Sediment control benefits from the present pattern of land use in KSD could be estimated by examining the costs of increased sediment delivery under a changed pattern of land use. These costs may include increased reservoir sedimentation, sediment removal from irrigation systems, and increased water treatment costs for downstream users.

- Changed streamflow patterns may also result in more rapid runoff resulting in increased flood damage or increased expenditures for preventive measures.

TOURISM. Though the southeastern region is a major tourist destination, the bulk of tourist activity revolves around coastal recreation on the Gulf of Thailand, especially at Pattaya. The people who frequent this region would provide a large pool of potential visitors to KSD if tourism were actively encouraged, but there are both benefits and costs of increasing tourist numbers at KSD. The sanctuary's importance as a refuge for wildlife should continue to be its top priority. Since the major management problems at KSD are poaching and encroachment, carefully controlled tourism may help by increasing awareness of its importance and resulting in a greater management presence.

Tourism at KSD has in fact been increasing, especially with improved road access in the early 1980s. Though early records are often incomplete, WCD visitor statistics show that tourism nearly doubled between 1984 and 1987 (see Table 8). In 1987, more than 32,000 visitors were counted at KSD. Most of these visits were limited to areas near the park headquarters, including nearby waterfalls. Some visitors arrived in private cars, but most came in organized groups by van or bus.

Another wildlife sanctuary in the southeast, Khao Khieo in Chonburi province, contains a nature and wildlife education center. This center serves both recreational and educational functions. Since it is also located closer to the main tourist facilities in the region, Khao Khieo has a higher potential for attracting increased numbers of tourists. KSD's role as a tourist destination will probably remain limited to local residents and tourists passing through the area on their way to other destinations.

The economic impact of tourism can be measured in several ways. At the most basic level, one can estimate the income generated by

Table 8.

Visitor Statistics for Khao Sol Dao Wildlife Sanctuary: 1978–1987

Month	1978	1979	1980	1981	1982	1983	1984	1985	1986	1987	Total
January	—	655	664	749	3,455	993	1,474	1,890	2,200	4,974	17,054
February	—	431	1,436	1,274	2,486	1,798	1,410	3,257	3,605	2,108	17,805
March	—	359	386	593	—	—	1,150	1,321	1,567	3,017	8,393
April	—	909	2,136	2,007	—	—	1,430	5,265	5,837	5,822	23,406
May	—	332	461	621	—	—	940	1,504	1,517	2,352	7,727
June	—	161	60	180	—	—	655	2,059	1,572	2,282	6,969
July	—	221	195	585	—	—	1,922	2,088	1,428	1,099	7,538
August	—	222	343	—	—	—	1,740	2,062	2,085	2,899	9,351
September	—	151	1,176	343	—	—	1,180	1,497	1,886	1,313	7,546
October	—	332	279	1,010	—	1,036	1,517	1,555	3,006	2,935	11,670
November	—	304	478	288	—	1,155	1,295	1,821	1,973	1,504	8,818
December	178	266	720	558	—	1,810	2,302	1,140	2,422	1,758	11,154
TOTAL	178	4,343	8,334	8,208	5,941	6,792	17,015	25,459	29,098	32,063	137,431

Note: Dashes signify that data were not reported.
Source: Wildlife Conservation Division (various years).

visitors coming to KSD. Whether expenditures are for transport, food, or other services, these expenditures generate local revenues. No data are available for KSD, but studies in other areas of Thailand report visitor expenditures in the range of 200 to 500 baht per person per day, including transportation. Since most visitors probably come from areas relatively close to KSD, this range may be a little high. If we conservatively assume a total expenditure of 150 baht per person with 50 baht spent in or around KSD (food, drinks, guides), this would represent a total yearly expenditure of 4.8 million baht with 1.6 million spent directly at the park. Although these numbers should be verified, they indicate the already sizable economic contribution of KSD to the economy. A more accurate economic estimate would be based on the consumer's surplus enjoyed by visitors to KSD. This would require a travel-cost study to estimate the social benefit associated with park use. Such a study has been carried out in Thailand in the case of Lumpinee Park (Eutrirak and Grandstaff 1986).

Both measures (total expenditures and consumer's surplus) will grow in value with increases in the number of total visitors and foreign tourists. Since tourism, properly managed, can be a nonconsumptive use of the wildlife sanctuary, its growth could be a positive force for enhanced management and protection.

RESEARCH AND EDUCATION. Though KSD does receive groups of schoolchildren, Khao Khieo plays a much more important educational role. Nevertheless, KSD provides a number of significant research opportunities on a variety of species including pileated gibbons, which have been studied by Brockelman (1975) and Srikosamatara (1980). Of great potential importance is the wildlife captive breeding program established at KSD under the patronship of the king and partially supported by FAO. If captive breeding of native wildlife could be profitably undertaken, this would provide a means of reducing the hunting pressures in protected areas. As in the case of tourism, the size of research and education expenditures can be calculated (as was done for Khao Yai in Chapter 6).

Costs

The main costs of Khao Soi Dao are the government outlays for management and the forgone potential benefits from commercial exploitation of timber and other resources in the area. There is agricultural potential, as well, in some of the flatter, lower-elevation areas in Khao Soi Dao.

DIRECT COSTS. Table 9 shows the budget allocations for KSD between 1982 and 1987. Over this period budgets have increased at an annual rate of approximately 10 percent. The present level of about 1.6 million baht is fairly modest compared to the tourism benefits described earlier. During this period, the number of staff increased from twenty in 1982 to twenty-six in 1986 before falling to twenty-three in 1987 (Wildlife Conservation Division, various years). In 1987, six of the employees were government officers (foresters and technicians); the rest were guards. An unknown number of temporary employees was also hired. KSD has four permanent guard stations around the sanctuary and one temporary station.

OPPORTUNITY COSTS. The opportunity costs of protecting KSD as a wildlife sanctuary must be gauged against some alternative use. One possibility is to consider keeping KSD protected but as a national park rather than a wildlife sanctuary. This step would generate increased benefits from tourism but would have to be weighed against possible disturbance to wildlife. As mentioned earlier, a carefully regulated tourism program may improve park management and yield wildlife benefits in terms of reduced levels of poaching. Given KSD's location and the other recreational opportunities available in the region, however, the potential of increased tourism may be limited.

A more likely alternative would be to remove KSD's protected status and allow commercial timber harvesting, followed either by a return to forest or conversion to agricultural land. Though it is impossible to estimate the precise value of such changes in land use, a number of effects could be expected. It is unlikely that any timber harvesting would be allowed in the higher-elevation areas. Most of these areas are steeply sloped and timber harvesting would cause severe erosion. As well, the hill evergreen areas on the higher slopes (above 1,000 meters) have little timber of commercial value compared to the lower-elevation, dipterocarp-dominated evergreen rain forests (Sriburi 1986). The hill evergreen areas account for approximately 5 percent of KSD's area (CMC 1986). Just below these areas in elevation, there are more than 14,400 hectares of dry and moist evergreen forest between the 600- and 1,000-meter levels. These areas too have relatively steep slopes and, if logged, would also result in severe erosion problems. Another 11 percent of KSD (8,150 hectares) is listed as secondary growth (CMC 1986). These areas have been extensively logged and would have little value as commercial forest in their current condition.

Table 9.

Budget (in Baht) for Khao Soi Dao Wildlife Sanctuary: 1982–1987

Fiscal Year	Wages of Temporaries	Compensation, General Expenses, and Supplies	Total
1982	612,000	408,900	1,020,900
1983	612,000	494,500	1,106,500
1984	612,000	519,800	1,131,800
1985	708,000	528,000	1,236,000
1986	858,000	644,000	1,502,000
1987	990,000	632,000	1,622,000
Average annual growth rate	10.10%	9.10%	9.70%

Note: US$1 = 26 baht.
Source: Wildlife Conservation Division (various years).

The bulk of KSD, 48,220 hectares (65 percent), is evergreen forest between sea level and 600 meters. Many of the most accessible areas in this category have already been selectively logged within the past few decades, so the remaining commercial value is of variable quality. To estimate the economic costs of logging benefits lost because of protection, the following data are required: areas suitable for commercial logging, volume of commercial species in each area, estimated average value of timber, and total harvesting and transportation costs. With this information it is possible to estimate the net economic rent or profit that could be earned by commercial logging. Note that profit is not equal to the total value of timber products; all costs must be deducted to determine the net profit from timber harvesting. This net profit/ economic rent is the true opportunity cost to society of not harvesting these trees.

Because unused agricultural land in the southeast is now scarce, most of the land with good potential would probably be converted to agricultural use. The flat, lowland areas might be used as rice fields or for field crops such as cassava and various vegetable crops. The foothill areas could be planted in fruit trees or rubber trees but might require conservation measures to reduce erosion during the early years of establishment. As in the case of timber extraction, the correct measure of the opportunity cost of not using KSD for agriculture is the economic rent that could be earned by converting protected lands to agricultural fields.

Conversion to agriculture is not without costs, of course. Since most of the animal species in the area are forest dwellers, most of them would be eliminated. The loss of vegetation communities—especially the hill evergreen and the wet evergreen rain forest, which are not found in many other areas in the southeastern region—may also result in the extinction of species. The conversion process would also bring severe erosion, and the hydrology of the downstream areas would be drastically changed. Increased population would also be likely to result in increased poaching in the remaining forested areas.

Another opportunity cost of KSD's protected status is its loss to the community as a source of animal and plant products. Theoretically such uses are not supposed to occur at all in a wildlife sanctuary. In reality, though, hunting of animals, both for food and for profit, still goes on within the sanctuary. In the absence of protection, however, many of the larger animal species would probably be hunted to extinction. Even at the current level of protection, long-term survival of these larger animals beyond thirty to fifty years is considered uncertain (ONEB 1986).

Summary of Benefits and Costs

Since KSD is a wildlife sanctuary, direct use of the area is designed to be limited. Nevertheless, a number of important benefits are associated with KSD; some are direct-use benefits while others arise from ecological and biodiversity values. Against these benefits one must consider the costs involved in maintaining KSD as a wildlife sanctuary. The main benefits, and their relative importance, are the following:

- *Biodiversity.* KSD is the main habitat in this region of Thailand for a number of endangered and important species. Without protection, many of these species would no longer exist in southeastern Thailand. Protected vegetation communities include a small area of lowland forest habitat that is now rare in Thailand and the only hill evergreen forest in this portion of the country. A number of endemic plants are also found in the sanctuary. *VALUE*: Undetermined but substantial.
- *Hydrologic value.* As a protected watershed, KSD provides hydrologic benefits to downstream areas. Further research is needed to

quantify these benefits and the impacts that would result if KSD were no longer protected. *VALUE*: Undetermined but potentially important.

- *Production of cardamom and minor forest products.* Present production on the fringes of KSD benefits a number of people. More data are needed, however, to estimate the annual gross value of production. *VALUE*: Can be determined with additional data; potentially substantial.
- *Tourism.* Tourism is not encouraged in wildlife sanctuaries, but KSD does receive more than 30,000 visitors annually, generating expenditures of 1.6 million baht or more in the area. Given the increases in tourism at KSD over the past few years, this number will probably continue to grow. Instituting an admission fee would provide a source of revenue to help offset management costs. Studies are needed to determine how much tourism can increase without adversely affecting wildlife. *VALUE*: Total expenditures range from 3 to 10 million baht, only part of which is spent in the sanctuary itself.

Against these benefits one has to weigh the costs of protection. The main costs are direct administrative and management costs and forgone development benefits (opportunity costs):

- *Direct management costs.* The present budget from the WCD is approximately 1.6 million baht per year. *COST*: Government management costs of about 1.6 million baht per year.
- *Timber extraction.* Opportunity costs in terms of forgone timber revenues are probably fairly low. Many of the more accessible areas have already been selectively logged. Less accessible areas are on more steeply sloping lands where logging costs would be higher and erosion potential substantial. *COST*: Can be estimated with additional data.
- *Agriculture.* Since much of the land is steeply sloped, its agricultural potential is limited. More data are needed to estimate the potential value of agriculture and thus the forgone benefits. *COST*: Calculable but perhaps declining over time.
- *Hunting.* Though some species may be able to tolerate low levels of hunting, many species would be adversely affected if hunting were allowed. Data are not available on the amount and value of illegal hunting or the potential value of hunting in the absence of protection. *COST*: More data are needed.

Given the uncertainty about various factors associated with Khao Soi Dao, it falls into the "undetermined benefits" category. Additional research and data are required to assess the exact benefits and costs of protection.

MANAGEMENT AND POLICY ISSUES

Thale Noi and Khao Soi Dao are quite different types of protected areas and illustrate the "socially beneficial" and "undetermined benefits" categories. As our analysis has shown, it becomes more difficult to estimate many of the benefits from protection when the degree of direct use declines (as in Khao Soi Dao). This is not surprising; economic analysis is easiest when markets operate and goods or services are bought and sold. Nevertheless, as the Khao Soi Dao example also shows, estimates can still be made of economic benefits and costs, especially when there are measurable off-site effects or direct on-site expenditures within the protected area.

Thale Noi

The key management issue with respect to Thale Noi is its protected status. As Thale Noi is one of most important bird sanctuaries in Thailand, upgrading its status to national park or wildlife sanctuary are both possible options. The degree of direct use allowed under either option is less than under its present NHA status. It has also been suggested that Thale Noi could be included in the list of wetlands of international importance set up under the Ramsar Convention on wetlands of international importance, especially as waterfowl habitat (Kasetsart University 1987). Thailand, however, is not yet a signatory of the Ramsar Convention.

Upgrading the entire area to either a national park or wildlife sanctuary would have substantial opportunity costs. Currently almost the entire population of the area depends on Thale Noi NHA for agricultural land, fishing, or materials for bulrush weaving. Moreover, much of the land within the NHA boundaries is privately owned. Relocating all the current residents who live within the boundaries of the nonhunting area would be difficult.

Upgrading the entire area to wildlife sanctuary status would normally mean eliminating most tourism, another source of substantial benefits. Though this would benefit the bird populations, the high cost makes it unlikely that such a change would be worthwhile. Upgrading a *portion* of the area, however, might bring about greater benefits at much less cost. For example, IUCN (1979) suggests upgrading the marsh area between Thale Noi and Thale Sap plus the *Melaleuca* forest north of the lake. This would leave most of the heavily used regions of Thale Noi unaffected and thus reduce the opportunity costs of the upgrade to only a fraction of those that would occur if the whole area were upgraded. The upgraded area should be primarily for wildlife use; tourism can be restricted to the remaining part of the nonhunting area. In fact, since entry into wildlife sanctuaries is restricted, this would also help protect the remaining forestland. Moreover, the potentially upgraded area is far smaller than the recommended minimum for national parks.

Limited hunting of a few species within Thale Noi might have an overall beneficial effect. Whistling teal and purple gallinule are both present in Thale Noi in large numbers and are responsible for much of the crop damage attributable to birds. With proper regulation, limited hunting of these species could reduce crop damage while providing a food source.

Another issue that requires attention is the control of pollution in Thale Noi. Because of its proximity to residential and agricultural areas, pollution from these sources is adversely affecting both wildlife and water quality. Domestic and animal wastes have resulted in higher nutrient levels in the lake, and residues of dangerous chemicals including DDT, heptachlor, and dieldrin have been found in water, soil, and fish in Thale Noi (TISTR 1982). These are persistent chemicals that can become more concentrated as they move up the food chain.

Khao Soi Dao

Maintaining Khao Soi Dao as a wildlife sanctuary seems to be the best policy option. MacKinnon and MacKinnon (1986) give KSD top priority for protection, a status given only to seven of the more than eighty major protected areas in Thailand. Round (1985) considers KSD to be a key site for the preservation of forest birds.

KSD is a good example of the dichotomy frequently found between the incidence of costs and benefits of protection. The primary costs (other than government budget allocations for management) are disproportionately borne by local people who are prevented from using and exploiting the resources in KSD. Benefits, especially from biodiversity and downstream hydrologic impacts, occur at some distance. In such a situation, a natural tension develops between those trying to protect the area and nearby residents who would like to make use of its resources.

Deforestation and animal poaching continue to be serious problems. Though increased funding for protection would probably help alleviate such problems, it must be supplemented with other measures. The wildlife captive breeding project, if successful, could provide a source of income to residents involved in the project as well as a low-cost source of protein to local residents. Even if some subsidization is required, this might be more cost-effective than relying solely on protective measures.

Another possible means of protecting the important habitats and species of the forest would be to establish buffer zones around the perimeter of the park that could be used by local residents. If these zones could be developed to grow fuelwood and other plant products currently being poached within the sanctuary, this might reduce the pressures on the sanctuary. Establishment of a buffer zone, combined with an education campaign and stiff penalties, might be beneficial to both local residents and the sanctuary itself.

8

Analyzing Selected National Parks

We have considered the case of Thailand in some detail to illustrate how economic analysis can be applied to different types of protected areas with varying degrees of direct and indirect use. The approaches used in the Thai analysis can also be applied in other countries. There exists a fairly extensive literature, both published and unpublished, that examines various economic dimensions of protected areas. In this and the following chapter we report on some of these studies. No attempt has been made to be comprehensive; studies were selected because they illustrate certain points about applying economic analysis to the values associated with protected areas and the benefits and costs of protection. Most of the studies are presented here in abbreviated form. The interested reader is directed to the original references for more details.

The studies reported on in this chapter are fairly complete: the Virgin Islands National Park; Kangaroo Island, Australia; and Korup National Park, Cameroon. The Virgin Islands and Australian studies benefit from being done in developed countries with relatively abundant data. The analysis of the Korup National Park project in Cameroon, Central Africa, is a social-economic study of a protected area in a developing country with limited data. Throughout we focus on the economic measures of goods and services, both tangible and intangible, that have commonly been left unvalued when assessing the main policy question: What are the benefits of protection worth?

VIRGIN ISLANDS NATIONAL PARK

The Virgin Islands National Park (VINP), created in 1956 and later expanded through land purchases and donations, is principally located on the island of St. John, the smallest of the three major islands comprising the U.S. Virgin Islands (Figure 12). In 1962, major offshore acreage was added to the VINP. Of St. John's 20 square miles (12,600 acres), 55 percent (6,968 acres) is administered by the National Park Service as the VINP. There are two main urban centers, Cruz Bay and Coral Bay; in 1980 the permanent population was about 2,400. The island economy is based on resorts and tourism; the principal attractions are the beautiful scenery and underwater attractions.

In what has become a frequently cited example of recreational valuation in a tropical setting, the Island Resources Foundation study of the Virgin Islands National Park (Posner and others 1981) examined the economic impact of the VINP on tourism in St. Thomas and St. John. The study focused on the direct economic benefits associated with tourism and recreational use of VINP: visitor expenditures; increased land values attributable to VINP; employment; and sales by local merchants and park concessionaires. No attempt was made to quantify benefits from preservation of natural scenery, historical preservation, aesthetic and cultural benefits, and, surprisingly, "provision of recreational opportunities." The latter, of course, is a major draw for the visitors that generated most of the measured expenditures.

There are three major resort areas (one luxury resort hotel and two campgrounds) associated with the park, and virtually all visitors come by boat. (St. Thomas is less than 2 miles away to the west.) Cruise ships also regularly visit St. John, and recreational boaters come from other parts of the U.S. Virgin Islands as well as Puerto Rico and other Caribbean islands. In 1980 there were a total of 445,500 visitor-days recorded in VINP. Shuttle boat (ferry) users totaled about 300,000 passengers and some 65,000 visitors came by cruise ship.

Economic Analysis

The economic study of VINP relied on secondary data on the St. John economy and survey results obtained from visitors and local businesses. There is a wide variation in the level of per person expenditure. Many of the shuttle boat passengers were one-day visitors (about 47 percent of the total, half of them Virgin Island residents). The average expenditure of the shuttle boat passengers surveyed was $36.60. Ex-

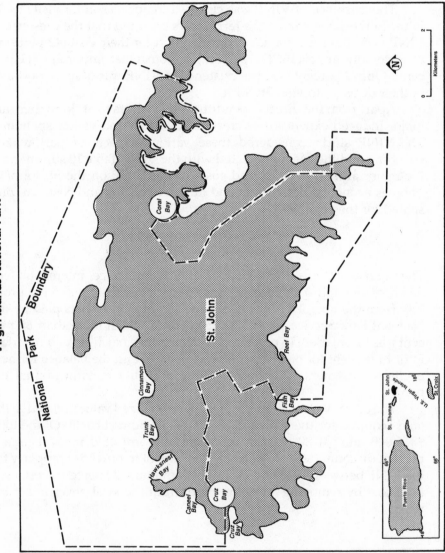

Figure 12.
Virgin Islands National Park

penditures by overnight visitors were much higher. Visitors at the deluxe Caneel Bay Plantation reported spending an average of $210 per adult per day, while guests at the two campgrounds spent from $48 to $61 per adult per day. These amounts include food and lodging.

The existence of VINP was clearly a major reason for visits to St. John. In the same survey the ferry users reported that the presence of VINP was either the primary consideration for their visit (42 percent), considerably important (36 percent) or somewhat important (11 percent). Only 2 percent said the existence of VINP was of no importance in their decision to visit St. John.

Apart from the direct expenditures by visitors to St. John there are major induced expenditures created by tourist and visitor spending. The VINP study considered these various aspects of park-related spending and the costs associated with the VINP. Table 10 summarizes the major annual benefits and costs of the VINP on the St. John/St. Thomas economy. Both direct and indirect benefits and costs are presented for the year 1980.

Costs

The main cost items are operations and maintenance, interest on federal investment in VINP property, and taxes lost from removing property from the tax rolls. Operations and maintenance costs paid by the National Park Service totaled $1,250,000, of which more than 66 percent was for salaries, 16 percent for maintenance (such as road resurfacing), 14 percent for other operating expenses, and the balance for new capital (equipment) purchases. These are all recurring annual expenses.

The other two cost items represent annualized values related to the land acquired for the park and are listed as indirect costs. Of the total $846,000, almost 80 percent represents the imputed interest (at a 6 percent discount rate) on the $11 million spent to purchase property for the VINP between 1956 and 1980. The remaining 20 percent represents taxes lost by removing VINP property from the local government tax rolls.

Benefits

Against the total annual costs of $2,096,000, the study identified benefits more than ten times larger: $23,391,000 ($3,330,000 in direct benefits and $20,061,000 in indirect benefits). Most of the direct benefits cited in the study are from outlays by VINP concessionaires in the local

Table 10.

Economic Impact of VINP on the St. Thomas/St. John Economy: 1980

Costs and Benefits	Direct	Indirect	Total
COSTS			
Operation and maintenance of VINP	$1,250,000		
Interest on federal investment in VINP properties		$ 670,000	
Taxes lost on property removed from local government tax rolls		$ 176,000	
TOTAL	$1,250,000	$ 846,000	$ 2,096,000
BENEFITS			
Outlays of VINP in local economy	$ 830,000		
Outlays of VINP concessionaires in local economy	$2,500,000		
Imputed benefits from VINP's impact on tourism		$12,061,000	
Imputed benefits from VINP's impact on boat industry		$ 3,000,000	
Imputed benefits from VINP's impact on increased land values on St. John as an indicator of economic growth		$ 5,000,000	
TOTAL	$3,330,000	$20,061,000	$23,391,000

Note: All figures in U.S. dollars.
Source: Posner and others (1981: table 5).

economy—largely the payroll, taxes, and local purchases made by the resorts operating on St. John. As mentioned earlier, about half of the visitors reported that the existence of VINP was "very important" or "important" to their decision to come. Thus the concessionaire expenditures were adjusted by 50 percent to reflect the importance of the

VINP in attracting resort visitors, and a ballpark figure of $2,500,000 per year was arrived at. An additional $830,000 per year was attributed to the local purchases by VINP and its staff. (There is some double-counting here since these same salaries are included in the costs as well as in the benefit category.)

The major benefits, however, were labeled as indirect and included the multifaceted expenditures by visitors ($12 million per year), the VINP impact on demand for boat charters and the boat industry ($3 million per year), plus increased land values attributed to the exist-ence of VINP ($5 million per year). These numbers are based on the results of surveys of visitors to St. John and island businessmen.

The estimate of tourism expenditures attributable to the existence of the VINP ($12 million) is based on a series of assumptions (Table 11). The total number of visitors in each of six categories was multiplied by their average expenditure per day. This value, in turn, was multiplied by a factor representing the importance of VINP on the decision to visit. The resulting "imputed value of VINP influence" was further adjusted by a multiplier (from 0.55 to 0.70) to represent the impact of these expenditures on the local economy. (The high import content of tourist-related purchases meant that considerable revenue from tour-ism expenditures flows outside the Virgin Islands to pay for imported goods.) As a result of these calculations, the total expenditures of $32.6 million result in net economic benefits imputed to VINP of $12 million.

The VINP's impact on the charter boat industry was calculated in a similar manner. The total annual income of the industry ($17.5 million) was adjusted by the share of all boats operating within VINP waters (70 percent) and the percentage of their total charter time actually spent in VINP waters (about 50 percent). This value is further adjusted by a multiplier factor (about 0.55) and other factors to derive an "order of magnitude" estimate of economic benefits from the boating industry attributable to the VINP of about $3 million per year.

Similarly, the estimated benefits of the VINP on land values were based on tax records of changes in land value on St. John between 1961 and 1980. Land values obviously depend on a number of factors, but the presence of VINP (and associated resort development) is definitely significant. The authors of the study decide on a conservative impact of $5 million per year. This is a large number, and one can question some of the assumptions made. In particular, one needs to examine how much the tourist industry would be affected by some alternative use of the VINP land. One could envisage a scenario where other private development patterns could lead to even greater visitor use and higher

Table 11.

Estimated Economic Impact of VINP-Related Tourism Expenditures: 1980

Tourist Expenditures	1 No. of VINP Visitor-Days in 1980	2 Expenditure per Day	3 Influence of VINP	4 (1 × 2 × 3) Imputed Value of VINP Influence	5 Multiplier	6 (4 × 5) Net Economic Benefit Imputed to VINP
Cruise ship visitors	65,000	$ 84.00	78%	$4,259,000	0.55	$ 2,342,000
Tourists visiting VINP on vacation[a]	114,500	$ 86.00	78%	$7,681,000	0.55	$ 4,224,000
U.S. Virgin Island residents visiting VINP on vacation	68,000	$ 27.67	79%	$1,486,000	0.70	$ 1,040,000
Guests on St. John						
Caneel Bay	100,000	$101.48[b]	44%	$4,435,000	0.55	$ 2,439,000
Cinnamon Bay Campground	56,000	$ 48.17	73%	$1,959,000	0.55	$ 1,077,000
Maho Bay Campground	42,000	$ 61.14	67%	$1,708,000	0.55	$ 939,000
TOTAL	445,500					$12,061,000

Note: These figures do not include the impact on the boating industry.
[a] Other than U.S. Virgin Island residents and guests residing on St. John.
[b] Expenditures for Caneel Bay guests do not include room charges.
Source: Posner and others (1981, table 3).

land values. Such a with-and-without-project analysis is necessary to determine the true impact of VINP on the economy. To be a complete analysis it is also necessary to assess the impact of alternative development scenarios on the marine and terrestrial ecosystems and, in turn, these effects on tourism.

Comments on the Study

Clearly the existence of the park has helped create a sizable tourist industry revolving around the VINP and its natural attractions. If the analysis were to be redone, however, a number of changes could be made:

- Within the context of a social-economic analysis of the park, labor costs should be included only as costs, not as a benefit via local expenditures adjusted by a multiplier.
- Land acquisition costs can be handled as capital expenditures in the year they occur.
- Lost property tax revenues are lost transfer payments and should not be included in an economic analysis. Instead, the net productive value of the land uses before protection or the value of any potential alternative land uses should be included as a cost.
- An analysis of the impacts of tourism and recreational expenditures should be based on a with-and-without VINP scenario. There are sizable benefits from having the park as a natural attraction, but much of the visitor industry might still exist even in the absence of VINP. The answer depends on what form alternative developments might take. Similar questions must be raised about the boat industry benefits.
- The property-value approach is valid in theory but may have limited use here. It has been noted that property values on St. Thomas, where there is no park, increased just as rapidly. Similarly, the fact that the park removed so much of the island from private use probably drove up property prices.

In sum, then, the VINP study provides a useful guide to answering some of the financial questions associated with a protected area and intensive resort development. It documents the importance of recreational and tourism expenditures to the local economy, but it does not prove that an alternative development scenario would not provide similar benefits. (In fact, VINP could well be an example of a "privately beneficial" protected area if one could acquire the land before prices skyrocketed.) To carry out a proper economic analysis of the VINP, one would need to consider a wider range of issues—an examination of the ecological or environmental impact of alternative land uses, a careful study to measure consumer's surplus of park visitors (via a travel-cost or CVM study), and a fuller assessment of alternative development scenarios.

VINP Update

The previous section was based on a 1981 study of the VINP. More recent data further support the importance of the national park to the local economy. The number of visitors has almost doubled, reaching 750,000 in 1986. A new luxury hotel has been built at Great Cruz Bay, and the established Caneel Bay resort reported 1986 gross revenues of $120,000 per hotel room per year. With an occupancy rate of about 80 percent, this is equal to $400 of gross revenue per room per day. This is among the highest revenues reported by any resort in the United States and reflects the premium the resort can charge because of its location next to the VINP.

A multiyear collaborative study by the Virgin Islands Resource Management Cooperative produced a series of twenty-nine reports as part of their Biosphere Reserve Research Project. These reports examine the VINP and associated Biosphere Reserve in great detail. Report 24 by Rogers, McLain, and Zullo (1988) examines the recreational uses of the marine resources in the VINP. The trends in use, both by individuals and by boats, are all strongly upward, indicating the growing demand for these protected resources. Although these recent studies have not examined the VINP's economic impact on the local economy, such a study would no doubt show a major increase in economic benefits when compared to the results of the 1981 study.

KANGAROO ISLAND

Located halfway around the world from St. John in the Virgin Islands is Kangaroo Island, the largest island in South Australia. The small resident population is dependent on agriculture and tourism. Agriculture, although the dominant form of land use at present, is a declining industry and future income growth is constrained by available area for farming, salinity problems, and restrictions on land clearance. Still, in 1982–1983 the gross value of agricultural production on the island was A$26–27 million—more than twice the A$7–12 million contribution of the tourism industry.

Situated 13 kilometers from the Fleurieu Peninsula of South Australia and about 100 kilometers from the capital of Adelaide, Kangaroo Island is large (140 by 55 kilometers) and relatively accessible to major population centers in South Australia (Figure 13). The relatively small resident population of about 4,000 people in 1984 plays host to 60,000 to 70,000 visitors per year.

Of the sixteen parks on the island, the largest and most popular is the Flinders Chase National Park, which contains 75 percent of the entire protected area. The remaining parks are all conservation parks and most are smaller than 1,000 hectares in size. In general, the parks are on land that is not attractive for agricultural development because of unsuitable soil or topography. The relative isolation of the parks themselves and the distance from the mainland to Kangaroo Island results in these protected areas retaining a high degree of their natural state and native flora and fauna. Still, plans to expand the park system meet with resistance from local agricultural interests.

This study (Touche Ross 1984) examined the economics of tourism and the overall impact of the sixteen parks located on the island. The parks range in size from 10 to 74,000 hectares and cover about one-quarter of the island's total area of 435,000 hectares. (By way of comparison, the VINP covers over 55 percent of St. John's land area.) The goal of the study was to determine the economic costs of the parks and their tourism-associated benefits. Its focus was somewhat broader than the VINP study. In addition to examining the economic and recreational benefits of the parks, the study also cited a number of other key factors including the opportunity cost of alternative sustainable land uses and the costs that parks impose on adjacent landowners (economic externalities). Thus the Kangaroo Island study illustrates a number of the points raised in Part I of this book.

Costs

The study examined a number of direct and indirect costs of the Kangaroo Island parks. Three major cost items were identified: direct costs met by government funding, indirect costs (economic externalities) imposed on adjacent landowners, and the potential opportunity cost of alternative uses for park resources.

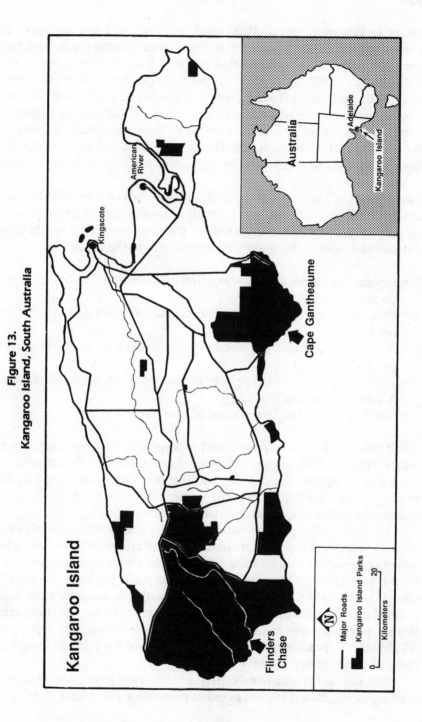

Figure 13.
Kangaroo Island, South Australia

DIRECT GOVERNMENT COSTS. Park establishment and management includes capital expenditures related to visitor management and park management. These costs totaled A$215,000 in the three-year period 1980–81 to 1982–83; yearly expenditures thus averaged about A$75,000. Annual operating costs average about A$206,000—74 percent for salaries and related labor costs and the balance for materials, supplies, and other recurrent expenses. Total yearly direct costs are therefore about A$281,000. (No charges are included for land acquisition; most land was acquired by the government at little or no cost.)

INDIRECT COSTS. There are, in addition, sizable external costs of the park system. These costs are paid for by adjacent landowners and are largely caused by the movement of park animals into neighboring agricultural fields. The main cost items include the following:

- Grazing of native animals on private agricultural lands and loss of productivity
- Fencing costs to keep park animals out of developed agricultural lands
- Ammunition and time needed to cull park animals on private property
- Possible restrictions on private development on land immediately adjacent to the parks
- Fire hazards from fires started in park lands

All of these cost items impose direct expenses on adjacent landowners, either from a loss in productivity (measured by the change-in-productivity approach), fencing and hunting costs (measured by the preventive-expenditure approach), or restrictions on land development (measured by the opportunity-cost approach).

The productivity losses stem from the park's native animals (wallabies, kangaroos) feeding on outside pasture and thereby reducing the carrying capacity of these adjacent lands. Based on an estimated 6,400 hectares of affected pasture and a loss of carrying capacity of 1.25 sheep per hectare (a 12.5 percent reduction), the equivalent of 8,000 fewer sheep can be raised because of the existence of the national parks. With a yearly income value of about A$15 per sheep, this represents A$120,000. This amount is about 0.5 percent of the island's total agricultural productivity.

Fencing costs come from construction of new fences and repairs to existing ones. Based on expected replacement costs and sharing of expenses with the government, private landowners pay about A$30,000 per year to maintain their fences as a result of damage by native animals.

Animal culling is allowed by private landowners to reduce their productivity losses. Based on costs of ammunition (about A$9,000 per year) and the time spent hunting (based on an average gross farm return of A$25 per hour), calculations give an annual culling cost of around A$47,000 per year. (This assumes that the hunters do not receive any benefits from the process of hunting.)

The numbers turn out to be sizable: external productivity costs of A$120,000 per year, fencing costs of A$30,000 per year, and animal culling expenditures of A$47,000 per year. Thus the total external costs of A$197,000 are almost as large as the annual operating expenditures. Most of the external costs are estimated by using market prices for changes in production or direct expenditures for goods and services or time. The total of direct and indirect costs comes to A$478,000 per year.

OPPORTUNITY COSTS OF ALTERNATIVES. The opportunity costs of protection (alternative development options forgone) was also considered. The main alternatives involved agricultural activities, but most park areas did not appear suited for sustainable agriculture. (One should note that the present protected areas were the areas left after the greater part of the island had been developed.) Based on discussions with land users and government officials, it was concluded that there are no alternative land uses that can be sustained without degradation. The opportunity cost of the park lands is therefore zero.

Benefits

The study carefully examined the extent and pattern of recreational and tourism development on Kangaroo Island and the role of the park system within it. It cited a number of benefits from the park system:

- Tourism industry benefits and associated recreational benefits
- Future values (option value, existence value, and bequest value) from the retention of natural resources
- Local and regional multiplier effects
- Conservation benefits

Since the main focus of the study was on tourism-related benefits, the patterns and reason for tourism and recreational visiting were analyzed. Visitor totals were expected to grow at an annual rate of about 6 percent per year from the 60,000 to 70,000 visitors in the base year (1983–84). Most visitors cited the existence of various protected areas as a primary attraction; many visited a number of sites.

Total tourism expenditures on the island are about A$6.5 to $7.5 million per year (excluding transportation costs paid to nonisland operators). Using an approach similar to the VINP study, the authors estimated that about 50 percent of holiday visitor expenditures can be directly related to the park. (Some visitors would still come even without the parks.) Therefore, at least A$3 to $4 million per year in direct tourism expenditures can be attributed to the existence of the various parks.

The study correctly pointed out that a willingness-to-pay survey would be required to estimate consumer's surplus and thus the true benefits derived from the park. (The observed values on actual expenditures are not a true measure of the economic benefits to the individual. Net benefits to an individual are correctly measured by the value of total enjoyment or benefits received minus actual expenditures.)

The study also examined the local and regional impact of tourism. Capital invested in tourism-related facilities is about A$9 to $10 million, with planned investment of an additional A$3 million. Operating expenses averaged A$4 to $5 million per year. If the same 50 percent rule applies as for total tourism expenditures, the variety of protected areas on Kangaroo Island has contributed up to A$5 million in capital investment and A$2 to $25 million per year in operating expenditures. Although a benefit to Kangaroo Island, these same expenditures might have gone elsewhere if they had not been made on Kangaroo Island.

The Kangaroo Island study also considered various other economic impacts related to the wider economy as well as beneficial externalities from the parks (windbreak effects, aesthetic benefits, insect control, and others). These are not valued here. Conservation benefits consisted, in part, of existence, option, and bequest values, but no monetary values were assigned.

Benefits Versus Costs

The analysts carried out a simplified benefit/cost analysis of park-related benefits and costs over a twenty-year period. Based on the results presented earlier—and the estimate that half of park-related expenditures represent value added in local profit and labor (the rest being supply inputs and other expenditures)—the total value added in the local tourism industry due to the existence of the park system is estimated to be a minimum of A$1.5 to $2.0 million per year, or an average value of A$1.75 million. By way of contrast, direct and indirect costs come to about A$500,000 per year (Table 12).

Table 12.
Annual Benefits and Costs of Kangaroo Island Protected Areas

BENEFITS	A$1,750,000
COSTS	
Park operating expenditures	A$206,000
Average capital expenditures	A$75,000
External productivity cost	A$120,000
External fencing cost	A$30,000
External animal culling expenditure	A$47,000
TOTAL	A$478,000

Note: Tourism income accruing to Kangaroo Island because of the park system is about A$3–4 million. Adjusting for labor and profit to derive value added attributable to parks leaves A$1.5–2.0 million. Average annual value is thus estimated at A$1.75 million.
Source: Touche Ross (1984).

Net benefits are obviously considerable. Annual net benefits, with constant revenues and costs, are A$1,250,000 per year—a sizable number which indicates that the park has a positive net present value. Clearly the protected areas on Kangaroo Island yield major economic benefits to the local economy and produce considerable enjoyment.

Note that this study attempted to value external costs of parks but failed to measure consumer's surplus of users. The net benefit estimates are very much minimum values, moreover, and depend heavily on value-added estimates for park-dependent tourism expenditures. Still, the careful consideration of various benefit and cost factors, including the opportunity costs of the protected areas and various future values, makes this a useful model.

KORUP NATIONAL PARK

Korup National Park, located along the border with Nigeria in the southwestern part of Cameroon, is the only park in the evergreen forests of Central Africa (Figure 14). The park covers 126,000 hectares and is unique in terms of species richness. It contains more than 400 species of trees and a large number of rare mammals and birds, some of which are found only in Korup (WWF 1987). Korup's large mammal fauna are very diverse, for example, and Korup is an exceptionally important shelter for primates. Due to fairly infertile soils, Korup has never been logged and is little affected by shifting agriculture. Population density within Korup is low, about one person per 1.2 square kilometers.

The pristine state of Korup is under threat from human uses of the forest that are unsustainable. Both hunting and shifting agriculture are placing pressure on the area's resources. The Korup Project was proposed to develop both the national park and an additional 300,000-hectare buffer zone outside the park (WWF 1987). As the project paper states, "by developing and disseminating sustainable uses of the forest in the project area [the national park and surrounding buffer zone], it is hoped to reduce pressures on the forest and reverse the process of degradation. . . . It is essential to involve and motivate the local people so that their own living conditions can be improved from their own means."

A social benefit/cost analysis was undertaken of the Korup Project at the request of the government of Cameroon and WWF–UK (World Wide Fund for Nature–UK). In an excellent study the consultant (Ruitenbeek 1989) considered both social costs and social benefits to the project site and to Cameroon as a whole.

As explained in the report, the analyst used conventional techniques, valuing outputs at world prices for traded goods and using shadow prices where appropriate. The analysis ignores sunk costs (pre-1989) and includes those incremental costs specifically enumerated in the August 1989 draft of the Korup Project master plan. Based on consultations with the Cameroon government, a social discount rate of 5 percent was used and labor costs were set at 35 percent of the "market" rate (implying that the official wage rate is inflated and does not represent a true equilibrium wage rate). For the base case, however, somewhat more restrictive criteria were selected: a shadow wage rate of 50 percent of the market rate and a discount rate of 8 percent. Sur-

Figure 14.
Korup National Park, Cameroon

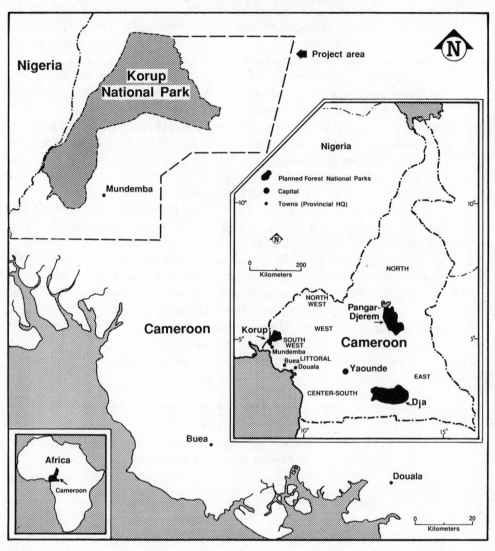

prisingly the analyst used an infinite time horizon and implicitly assumed no major changes in annualized benefits or costs. (With an 8 percent discount rate, any values that occur after sixty years in the future are worth very little today in a benefit/cost analysis.)

An alternative development scenario was chosen to carry out a with-and-without-project analysis: the nonpark alternative assumed normal exploitation of biological and forest resources in the area with most of the forest being logged between the years 2010 and 2040. Since no distributional considerations were incorporated into the analysis, there is an implicit assumption that the government placed the same welfare weights on benefits and costs accruing to people within the project areas as they did in the rest of the economy.

A summary of the base case results is given in Table 13. All figures are in constant 1989 terms discounted at 8 percent to the base year 1989. Total benefits, both to the project and to the country, are clearly larger than total costs. The net benefits of the project are over £1 million when measured from the project perspective and £7.5 million when measured from the perspective of Cameroon. This is equivalent to an internal rate of return to the project of about 8.3 percent and to Cameroon of 13.4 percent. The project's benefit/cost ratio is just above 1 while Cameroon's social benefit/cost ratio is 1.94.

As reported by Ruitenbeek (1989), the base case results were based

---

Table 13.

Summary of Base Case Results for Korup National Park (8 Percent Discount Rate): 1989

Costs and Benefits	Net Present Value (£'000)
DIRECT COSTS	−11,913
Total capital costs excluding roads (1989–1995)	−7,697
Total capital cost of roads	−1,859
Total long-term operating costs (post-1995)	−4,761
Labor credit	2,404
OPPORTUNITY COSTS	−3,326
Lost stumpage value	−706
Lost forest use	−2,620
TOTAL COSTS	−15,239

Costs and Benefits	Net Present Value (£'000)
DIRECT BENEFITS	11,995
Sustained forest use	3,291
Replaced subsistence production	997
Tourism	1,360
Genetic value	481
Watershed protection of fisheries	3,776
Control of flood risk	1,578
Soil fertility maintenance	532
INDUCED BENEFITS	4,328
Agricultural productivity increase	905
Induced forestry	207
Induced cash crops	3,216
TOTAL BENEFITS	16,323
NET BENEFIT (PROJECT)	1,084
Social benefit/cost ratio	1.07
Internal rate of return	8.3%
ADJUSTMENTS	6,462
External trade credit	7,246
Uncaptured genetic value	−433
Uncaptured watershed benefits	−351
NET BENEFIT (CAMEROON)	7,546
Social benefit/cost ratio	1.94
Internal rate of return	13.4%

Source: Ruitenbeek (1989).

on various assumptions concerning direct and opportunity costs as well as direct and induced benefits. (The following discussion closely follows Ruitenbeek 1989.) The direct costs reflect direct expenditures by external and domestic funding appropriately shadow-priced:

- *Total capital costs excluding roads.* These costs reflect anticipated required capital and operating expenditures by direct foreign and domestic investment in the project over the period 1989–1995, the period for which detailed budgets are given in the Korup master plan. It excludes any costs for compensation for resettlement. These costs are regarded as transfer payments (costs to one element of society are benefits to another element of the same society) and thus do not enter into the project cash flows. The construction costs associated with resettlement are included in project costs.

- *Total capital costs of roads.* This cost reflects anticipated required capital expenditures for roads and airstrips as defined in the Korup master plan. In the base case, only 33 percent of the cost of these investments is regarded as incrementally attributable to this project for social valuation purposes. Here the assumption is that some of the investment would be required in any event for other national initiatives involving the general provision of services for improving welfare. The level of 33 percent was taken as the proportion necessary to accommodate specific resettlement requirements and minimize the negative environmental impact of this infrastructure.
- *Total operating costs.* These costs, which reflect the labor and other operating costs of the project from 1995 onward, are about £560,000 annually.
- *Labor credit.* This cost reflects an adjustment for the shadow wage rate in the operating and capital costs incurred by the government of Cameroon.

The opportunity costs reflect social value lost in various sectors of the economy due to the establishment of the park:

- *Lost stumpage value.* In the base case, this assumes that the forest would otherwise have been exploited for timber from the year 2010 to 2040. The net stumpage value was estimated to be about £8.8 million at that time, which assumes current world timber prices and a shadow wage rate of 50 percent of market rates.
- *Lost forest use.* The resettlement program that is recommended for the park involves resettling six villages over the period 1992–1995. This activity causes a loss in productive output from the park by those resettled.

The direct benefits reflect social value gained as a direct result of establishment of the park:

- *Sustained forest use.* By the same token that the resettlement causes some direct loss in productive output from the villages in the park, the establishment of the park ensures that benefits can accrue to the entire area beyond the year 2010 (when the forest would otherwise start to disappear). This recovered forest use reflects that component and includes local use of forest products. Although it affects almost 30,000 people, it is a relatively small amount due to the discounting process: these benefits do not incrementally start to accrue until 2010 since the forest products will be available to locals until that year whatever the ultimate fate of the forest.

- *Replaced subsistence production.* The resettlement program is assumed to require about 7,500 hectares of land for the six villages. The subsistence food production from this area is included here.
- *Tourism.* This calculation reflects a rather conservative estimate that the park will attract visitors at an escalating rate, reaching a plateau at 1,000 visits per year by 2000.
- *Genetic value.* This component reflects a minimum expected genetic value of resources for the purposes of pharmaceuticals, chemicals, or agricultural crop improvements. While most observers claim that the genetic value of these resources is tremendous, we are more concerned with what proportion of this genetic value might eventually be captured or embodied in a form that a local government can extract some rent from it. The methodology adopted here relies on using patent values for expected gains from research into such commodities. Even given the vast benefits that might be afforded human welfare from these resources, implicit patented values seem quite low; they provide expected rents on the order of £5,000 per discovery.
- *Watershed protection of fisheries.* This component estimates the value of watershed protection of Korup forest to Nigerian and Cameroonian fisheries. Although the value of the total fisheries has been placed as high as £100 million annually by some studies, estimates conducted for this study—using two different methods—place the value closer to £10 million annually for fisheries that will be directly affected by this watershed. The net present value of this fishery protection is, as indicated, estimated to be £3.8 million—assuming that the protection benefits will only gradually start to accrue in 2010 and will continue in perpetuity beyond then.
- *Control of flood risk.* This calculation reflects the expected value of losses from flooding if the Korup forest were to disappear over the period 2010–2040. The risk is proportional to the amount of forest left at any time and is assumed to potentially affect 20,000 people in the catchment area. Flood risk is conservatively assumed to destroy

50 percent of local production once every five years. The expected value loss by 2040 is about £1.6 million per year.

- *Soil fertility maintenance.* This component reflects a 10 percent soil fertility loss in 25 percent of the output from the project area commencing in the year 2010 and coming into full effect by 2040. After deforestation of the Korup forest, the soil fertility loss in output corresponds to about £530,000 per year.

The induced benefits reflect social values gained as a result of the economic development initiatives undertaken by the project in the buffer zone:

- *Agricultural productivity increase.* This calculation reflects the increase in agricultural productivity experienced in the current food and cash crop sector in the project area as a result of expenditures under the project's program. It is equivalent to a modest increase in productivity of 5 percent achieved by the year 1997.
- *Induced forestry and cash crops.* The project plans to initiate new forestry or crop production on new land. It is assumed that one-third of the resettlement area will be dedicated to cash crop production and 3 percent to long-term forestry for wood production. The cash crop is assumed to be cocoa. Forestry production is marginal, yielding only a 10 percent return at current market prices. Under our assumptions of 8 percent discount rates and 50 percent shadow wage rates, however, wood production on a plantation basis is profitable. The constraint to its adoption is primarily the long period between investment and harvest (thirty-five years).

The sum of the preceding costs and benefits provides the net social benefit for the project. In addition, the following adjustments are necessary to calculate the net social benefit from Cameroon's perspective:

- *External trade credit.* This component reflects external direct funding of the project that is regarded to be a benefit to Cameroon. Since the shadow value of foreign exchange is taken as the current exchange rate, no premium is placed on it. For the purposes of this analysis, it is assumed that Cameroon will fund long-term (post-1995) costs as well as the infrastructure development (for roads and airstrips). If external funding is secured for the infrastructure, the net present value of the project would increase commensurately.

- *Uncaptured genetic value.* This adjustment reflects the assumption that Cameroon will be able to capture only 10 percent of the total value of genetic benefits; therefore 90 percent of the total genetic value of £481,000 is lost.
- *Uncaptured watershed benefits.* This adjustment accounts for the estimated Nigerian share of the watershed protection benefits. In theory this amount could be recaptured by Cameroon if it uses it as a lever for other trade policies, although in practice no such recapture is assumed.

Detailed sensitivity analyses were undertaken of the social discount rate and shadow wage rate. It was established that net benefits were positive from the Cameroonian perspective over a range of discount rates and with labor valued at market prices. Further sensitivity tests established that the project remained beneficial under a wide range of assumptions regarding the alternative development scenario. Although the base case assumed that deforestation started in the year 2010, the benefits of the project to Cameroon were still positive even if this deforestation were delayed ten years.

An analysis was also undertaken to determine the impact if no shadow pricing of roads or labor occurred. If 100 percent of the road costs budgeted in the master plan is included in the analysis and all labor is valued at market rates, the (financial) rate of return for the project becomes 6.4 percent and for Cameroon it becomes 7.8 percent. The corresponding net present values (at an 8 percent discount rate) are therefore negative:

> Project: (£7.1 million)
> Cameroon: (£0.6 million)

Finally, a separate analysis was undertaken to reflect the Cameroon planning assumption of a shadow wage rate of 35 percent and a discount rate of 5 percent. The resulting net present value is larger than the base case results:

> Project: £2.3 million
> Cameroon: £8.7 million

This study illustrates in capsule form many of the factors that can be considered in a social benefit/cost analysis of a proposed protected area. Both direct and indirect costs are considered, and a wide range of project-related benefits are evaluated. Shadow prices are used for labor, and border prices are used for internationally traded goods. Sensitivity analysis is carried out on key variables such as labor costs and the discount rate.

The analysis also shows how several off-site benefits from the park (such as fisheries, induced cash crops, and agricultural productivity increases) can be substantial and help make a convincing economic argument for protection. The project is profitable by itself (positive NPV of more than £1 million) and even more profitable from a national perspective when the external trade credit (reflecting foreign exchange inflows to support the project) is included. Korup National Park thus falls in the "socially beneficial" category, as was also true of Khao Yai.

9

Analyzing
Specific Benefits

In the previous chapter we looked at examples of analyses for national parks or, in the case of Kangaroo Island, a system of parks on one island. Apart from these full analyses, a number of studies have examined selected economic dimensions of protected areas or activities frequently associated with parks and other protected areas. The most common examples of these analyses relate to tourism and recreational use of protected natural resources: trekking in Nepal, sun-seekers and divers in the Caribbean, big-game photo safaris in Africa, and visitors to the Galápagos Islands of Ecuador. Moreover, useful work has been done on determining the value of selected environmental resources in protected areas.

This chapter reviews a number of these cases to illustrate specific applications of various economic techniques. Although none of these examples attempts to assign monetary values to all the diverse goods and services produced by a protected area, they do illustrate key components of a comprehensive analysis.

TOURISM AND RECREATION

Tourist expenditures were important items in both the Virgin Islands National Park and the Kangaroo Island studies. Tourism has become a major industry worldwide and is expected to show continued strong growth. According to the World Tourism Organization, international tourism generated some $150 billion in expenditures in 1987 and domestic tourism was worth more than ten times this amount. Travel and tourism now constitute one of the largest industries in the world and directly or indirectly support over 65 million jobs (Kutay 1989).

Tourism can be divided into a number of categories; one useful distinction is between mass tourism and special-interest tourism— sport, nature, and cultural tourism, for example. Whereas overall tourism revenue is expected to grow at 8 percent per year from 1990 to 1995, estimates of special-interest travel growth are in the 10 to 15 percent range (Vickland 1989). In the Caribbean, Mediterranean, and other seaside areas, mass tourism predominates. This is commonly called "sun and sand" tourism. But special-interest tourism is becoming increasingly important. Natural areas are major attractions and there is growing worldwide interest in what is commonly called "nature tourism" or "ecotourism." Ecotourism includes recreational uses of the natural environment in ways that do not require extensive associated development but at the same time, provide economic gains to nearby communities. In this way, both recreation and nature preservation coexist.

Two types of ecotourism are highlighted here: marine-based tourism (as found in the Caribbean) and big-game/safari tourism. It is important to note, however, that the figures presented here are indicative of the total economic impact of tourism and recreational expenditures; they are not measures of the *economic value* of the protected areas, which is usually larger for reasons explained in Part I of this book.

In many cases the existence of protected areas increases visitor satisfaction and, by protecting an ecosystem, provides the goods or services that attract tourists. This is more true for special-interest tourism than it is for mass tourism. Miami Beach and Waikiki contain no protected areas, for example, but have very high use rates and generate considerable economic benefits. They are major examples of mass tourism. Similarly, private development of presently undeveloped or even presently protected areas can lead to greater visitor use, especially in the case of certain coastal or marine areas. Nevertheless, the numbers do indicate the strong demand for both sun-and-sand tourism and specialized ocean-oriented uses such as diving. On the other hand, big-game viewing and safaris may require a higher degree of protected status to ensure continued consumer satisfaction.

Marine and Coastal Tourism in the Caribbean

Tourism is the largest industry in the Caribbean, and most of it is due to beaches, diving, and the weather. It combines both mass tourism and special-interest tourism. In addition to beaches, shopping, resorts, and nightlife, marine resources are a major attraction. A recent inventory of Caribbean marine and coastal protected areas (OAS/NPS 1988) noted some 135 legally established marine and coastal protected areas in the Greater Caribbean Basin. Most were classified as either park-like or wildlife-reserve-like areas. The thirty-three countries and territories in the inventory had from as little as 6 hectares (Montserrat) to as much as 1 million hectares protected (United States, Venezuela, Cuba).

Total tourist arrivals number in the millions and generate billions of dollars worth of expenditures for transportation, food, lodging, services, and local purchases. In 1985, Caribbean tourism was estimated to generate visitor expenditures of more than $5 billion (Blommestein 1985). By 1988 total expenditures were over $7.2 billion; the largest amounts came from the Bahamas ($1.1 billion), Puerto Rico ($1 billion), the Dominican Republic ($616 million), the Netherlands Antilles ($608 million), and Jamaica ($525 million) (McElroy and Albuquerque 1989). Divers and other special-interest tourists may account for one-fifth or more of the total.

Tourism expenditures as a contribution to gross domestic product (GDP) varied widely depending on the size of the economy and level of expenditures. Puerto Rico and the Bahamas, for example, had similar levels of tourism expenditures but their percentage of GDP was 6 percent in Puerto Rico and 50 percent in the Bahamas. Many Caribbean states had tourism shares of between 15 to 30 percent. The total number of tourism-related jobs in the Caribbean was estimated at 314,000 (Blommestein 1985). A large share of tourism expenditures leaks out to other countries, but a substantial share stays within the region in the form of salaries, purchases of local food, handicrafts, and services, and returns to local capital investment.

It is hard to say what share of total tourism expenditures can be directly attributed to the existence of marine and coastal protected areas. Even special-interest groups like divers choose vacation spots according to a number of different criteria. But even if only a share of all tourism is entirely attributable to the existence of protected areas, these areas are still part of the bundle of goods and services being bought by vacationers. Moreover, narrowly defined nature tourism (birdwatchers, hikers) may be largely attributable to the existence of protected areas.

In any case, the aggregate numbers are impressive. Table 14, drawn from the marine and coastal area inventory, lists twenty protected areas and the estimated cash income and annual visitation rates for each. There is a wide variation in intensity of use. Some of the parks had very large visitation rates: over 2 million people per year in the

Table 14.
Monetary Value of Tourism in Marine and Coastal Protected Areas in the Caribbean

Area	Cash Income Generated/Year	Visitations/Year
Bahamas	Divers spent $80–90 million; percentage attributable to parks unknown (estimated 1985)	
Biscayne National Park, Florida		578,000 visitors
Bonaire Marine Park, Netherlands Antilles	Divers spent $30 million (estimated 1985)	85,000 dives/year (1976–1985)
British Virgin Islands parks		45,000 divers in Wreck of the Rhone Park
Buck Island National Monument, St. Croix	$14 million	50,000 visitors
Buckoo Reef/Bon Accord Lagoon, Tobago	$510,000	12,000 visitors
Cahuita National Park, Costa Rica		100,000 visitors (1979)
Caroni Swamp National Park, Trinidad	$2 million (1974)	
Cayman Islands marine protected areas	Divers spent $53.2 million (estimated 1985)	168,000 divers and snorkelers
Cozumel and Chankannaab Parks, Mexico		400–500 visitors/day in cruise-ship season

Park		
Curaçao Underwater Park, Netherlands Antilles		2,196 divers, 4,060 dives; 30–40% in park (1986)
Everglades National Park, Florida		760,000 visitors
Key Largo National Marine Sanctuary, Florida		1 million visitors
Montego Bay National Park, Jamaica	$395,000 (projected)	96,000 visitors (projected)
Morrocoy National Park, Venezuela		1.5 million visitors (estimated)
Pennekamp Coral Reef State Park, Florida		1.5 million visitors
Pitons National Park, St. Lucia	$534,000 (projected)	116,000 visitors (projected)
Saba Marine Park, Netherlands Antilles	$16,500 (1988)	2,100 divers; 10,000 dives (estimated 1988)
Tobago Cays National Park, St. Vincent	$350,000 (projected)	50,000 visitors (projected)
Virgin Islands National Park, St. John	$23.4 million (1980)	750,000 visitors

Source: OAS/NPS (1988: table 6).

largely marine Pennekamp Coral Reef State Park and associated Key Largo National Marine Sanctuary in Florida; 1.5 million visitors to Morrocoy National Park, Venezuela; over 100,000 yearly visitors to parks in Costa Rica, Cayman Islands, St. Lucia, and Jamaica. Expenditures per visitor are also large: in 1985, divers alone were estimated to spend over $30 million for activities associated with Bonaire Marine Park, Netherlands Antilles, and more than $50 million for similar activities in the Cayman Islands. Nondivers used the protected areas for swimming, sunning, and exploring as well.

Sport divers are willing to spend considerable amounts of money in connection with their hobby. In a 1987 survey of readers of a leading sport diving magazine (*Skin Diver* 1987) it was found that divers are relatively well educated and have sizable incomes (an average of $48,500). Divers frequently travel abroad for diving, and the Caribbean is the most popular destination. Of those who traveled abroad (60 percent of the total), the average trip lasted one week and cost about $1,400 per person. Moreover, the percentage of readers reporting taking diving trips abroad has doubled in the past ten years. The most important criterion given for selecting a vacation site was the quality of the diving (73 percent)—far ahead of other factors such as destination image (19 percent) or even price (11 percent). One increasingly sees ads for diving trips to Asia, the Pacific, and the Indian Ocean. Obviously divers travel and are willing to pay a premium for environmental quality and good diving (clear water, healthy reefs, abundant fish life). Marine parks and reserves—such as Key Largo in Florida, the Virgin Islands National Park, or the Saba Marine Park—are all important attractions.

SABA MARINE PARK, NETHERLANDS ANTILLES. Established in 1987, the Saba Marine Park includes all of Saba's offshore waters. To help cover management costs, the park has implemented a three-pronged fundraising effort based on user fees, souvenir sales, and donations. User fees come from the fee of $1 per dive collected by dive operators. In 1988, some $10,000 was collected in this way from the 2,100 divers using the park's waters. Diver use is projected to increase to 5,000 visitors making a total of 30,000 dives by 1994. Sales of souvenirs and guidebooks also generate revenue, and a Friends of Saba Marine Park organization has been set up to solicit private donations.

In its first year of existence, the park was able to raise half its operational revenue from these three sources. The park is expected to become self-financing within the next few years. Although operating costs are low because of the modest visitation rate and lack of management problems, Saba Marine Park illustrates what can be done to generate revenues from users to help support a marine protected area (Caribbean Conservation Association 1989; van't Hof 1989).

A conservative estimate of total expenditures in the local economy by the 2,100 divers recorded in 1988 is probably between $1 and $1.5 million. Given the projected growth in diver tourism, there is a considerable economic incentive to provide effective protection of the marine resource.

TOBAGO CAYS NATIONAL PARK, ST. VINCENT. In a study examining the proposed establishment of a national park in the Tobago Cays area of the Grenadine Islands (part of the St. Vincent Grenadines), Heyman and others (1988) examined the financial and economic benefits and costs of establishing and maintaining the proposed park. The park would cover 49.5 square kilometers including the cays, adjacent coral reefs, and the island of Mayreau.

The study estimated that 33,000 to 37,000 people a year visit the area for an estimated total of 44,000 to 48,000 visitor-days. If the park is established, the number of visitors is projected to increase to 82,000 over a ten-year period. Without the park, the estimated number of visitors will only reach 46,000.

The costs of the marine park are estimated at US$1 million or $2.7 million Eastern Caribbean (EC) dollars. Annual operating costs are estimated at US$161,000. No land acquisition is included. (Since the government will acquire it through a land swap, its value is not included in the analysis although it represents an important in-kind contribution from the government.) The main source of income to the park will be fees paid by users and their expenditures in the area— yacht and cruise ship visitor fees, facility entrance fees (to an aquarium, for example), and souvenir sales.

Both financial and economic analyses were carried out on the project—the establishment of the marine park. Over a ten-year period the economic analysis showed a positive net present value of about US$111,500, or an internal rate of return of 14 percent. The financial rate of return was slightly lower, about 10 percent.

Although the study focuses on a narrow set of concerns—costs of establishing and operating the protected area and ways to capture revenues to pay those costs—it provides useful information for the government's decision makers. The broad economic impact of tourism in the area (with a gross value in 1986 of about US$6 million) has not been discussed here nor the park's potential benefits to the local fishing industry.

Above all, the Tobago Cays and other protected areas ensure long-term conservation of these fragile ecosystems. In turn, this protection allows continuing use of the resources by both local residents and foreign visitors, thereby ensuring a flow of revenues and economic benefits for both groups. Since many of the uses of marine protected areas are nonconsumptive (such as diving, snorkeling, and sailing), these resources can be "sold" over and over again.

Considerable work remains to be done on the economics of marine tourism and its interaction with protected areas. For more information see van't Hof (1985) and Goodwin and Wilson (1986).

Wildlife Parks in East Africa

Another major type of natural area/protected area tourism centers on the wildlife parks of East Africa, particularly in Kenya and Tanzania. Although both countries have spectacular scenery including mountains (Kilimanjaro, Mount Kenya), the Great Rift Valley, and a tropical coast, it is the game parks and the animals they support that attract visitors from all over the world.

Tourism is big business. In Kenya it is worth an estimated $350–400 million per year and involves a great deal of indirect demand for a wide variety of goods and services produced by the economy. Wildlife parks are huge but often occupy land that is semiarid and has only limited alternative uses—usually grazing of livestock. A number of studies have been made comparing the benefits from protection (and tourism) compared to extensive agricultural use (grazing or crops). In one study the estimated tourism value of protecting an area to maintain a big-animal population (lions, elephants, and the like) was over US$40 per hectare versus $0.80 per hectare under "optimistic" agricultural returns (Western and Thresher 1973). Even if these numbers are somewhat questionable, the point is that many areas yield much more under protection with their subsequent attraction for tourists than they would under marginal agricultural development.

Some analysts have attempted to ascertain game park visitor patterns and time spent searching for and viewing selected animals. These activities are the principal tourist attraction in a number of countries. Although international opinion frequently stresses the conservation of protected areas, one should not lose sight of the profit motive where appropriate. As outlined earlier, many protected areas fall in the "socially beneficial" category (and a few are even "privately beneficial"). Many of the East African parks are clearly "socially beneficial." Western and Henry (1979) estimated the gross worth of lions in Amboseli National Park in Kenya, in terms of generating tourism revenues, to be $27,000 each per year—an elephant herd was worth $610,000 per year! And yet a poacher will kill an animal to earn a few hundred dollars.

In a provocative note, Thresher (1981) considered "the economics of a lion" in Amboseli National Park in Kenya. Using survey results, he determined that the average visitor to Amboseli spent seventy minutes looking for and then viewing lions—which amounts to 30 percent of the average of four hours spent viewing wildlife per visit. Through a series of assumptions about Amboseli's lion population, the number of adult maned lions, and average success rate in viewing one, Thresher determined that an individual lion will draw $515,000 in foreign exchange receipts over a fifteen-year period (with a 10 percent discount rate). The value of a lion as a tourist attraction can be compared to the lion as a hunting resource: a 21-day lion hunt costs a nonresident hunter about $8,500. The lowest value for a lion was the retail price for a well-cured skin: somewhere between $960 and $1,325 (Thresher 1981).

This example illustrates one approach to estimating the varying direct values of the lion as a natural resource. Tourism is clearly the most efficient use of the lion: it generates a sizable amount of foreign exchange and does not require the death of the animal. The lion is much less valuable as a quarry or as a cured skin. (In many cases the two are additive: lion hunts often result in lion skins.) The parallels with elephants are very close. In national terms, they are much more valuable as a tourism attraction than for their ivory. The reverse is obviously true for an individual poacher.

Although these numbers have to be viewed with great caution, there is no doubt that the protected area/game park system in East Africa is both a major tourist attraction and generator of foreign exchange—and under considerable pressure from animal poaching and encroachment. The major challenge to management is to find ways to include those who live adjacent to the parks in the economic benefits generated by tourism. This form of community involvement and development is essential if the current pressures on resource use are to be reduced.

Animal poachers frequently come from some distance outside the area and are difficult to regulate. Efforts are needed both on the demand side (reducing worldwide demand for and trade in poached products and thereby reducing their price) and on the supply side (controlled harvesting of desired products on a sustainable basis). International agreements such as the Convention on International Trade in Endangered Species of Wild Fauna and Flora (CITES) have helped reduce trade in endangered species, but in many cases local regulation and police enforcement are also needed to control the killing of these animals.

The recent worldwide attention given to the international trade in ivory is resulting in trade restrictions or outright bans. Such changes can cut both ways, however. Several southern African countries that have practiced sustained-yield production of elephants are protesting that they are losing a valuable export market. Nevertheless, since ivory is a fairly homogeneous product, illegally harvested ivory will always find its way into the market (and hence the killing will continue) if some exports are legally allowed. An international solution is needed that recognizes differing legitimate viewpoints. In some cases compensation may have to be paid to those suffering losses.

SUSTAINABLE HARVEST OF FOREST PRODUCTS

Whereas tourism expenditures in protected areas are easily measured, many of the other benefits, even those associated with direct use, are often overlooked. This is especially true of tropical rain forests where pressures for logging or conversion to other uses are high. In Part I of the book we discussed the many benefits provided by natural forest ecosystems. These include such difficult to value aspects as preservation of biological diversity and genetic stock, the known but hard to measure hydrologic and climatic effects, and the values of nontimber (so-called minor) forest products.

A number of researchers have begun to focus on more thorough valuation of the resources found in tropical forests. Dixon and Burbridge (1984) have studied the valuation problems associated with mangroves, a unique tropical forest ecosystem. Farnworth and colleagues (1983) have considered the valuation of tropical moist forests by using a combined ecological/economic approach. Applying a three-part typology (Value I goods use market prices, Value II goods use quasi-market or surrogate market prices, and Value III goods are non-marketed intangibles) developed earlier (Farnworth and others 1981), these analysts discuss the various values and attempt some rough estimates of benefits for rain forests in general. This approach can be used to quantify some of the varied benefits from tropical forest ecosystems.

Most financial analyses of tropical forests focus on timber resources (sawlogs and pulpwood) while ignoring the potential market benefits of nonwood products such as edible fruits, oils, latex, fiber, and medicines. Based on this narrow perspective, it is commonly shown that since the net revenues from forestry in a particular area are small, logging followed by conversion to alternative uses is justified. Deforestation frequently results, with the loss of both wood and non-wood products as well as a host of biological and genetic benefits.

In a recent study Peters, Gentry, and Mendelsohn (1989) examined one particular hectare of species-rich Amazon forest located in Peru and estimated the economic returns from both commercial tree species and nonwood resources. Their surprising result is that the actual market benefits of timber are small when compared to nonwood resources and that "the total net revenues generated by the sustainable exploitation of 'minor' forest products are two to three times higher than those resulting from forest conversion" (p. 655).

The analysis considered just three major products: merchantable timber, forest fruits, and latex (rubber). Based on estimates of tree density and productivity, as well as local market prices, 1 hectare of forest produced fruit worth almost $650 per year and latex worth another $50. Deducting collection and transportation costs reduced annual revenues to $400 and $22 respectively for the two products, a total of $422 per hectare. These are *yearly* returns; the net present value of all future collection of fruit and latex (at a 5 percent discount rate) is $8,440. Assuming that a quarter of the fruit crop is left for regeneration, the net present value is reduced to $6,330 per hectare.

Forestry, in comparison, is expected to yield a net revenue of $1,000 per hectare if all merchantable timber is extracted and delivered to a sawmill. Such massive cutting will effectively eliminate fruit and latex production. If selective harvesting is practiced (thereby allowing continued fruit and latex collection), a net revenue of $310 per cutting cycle is anticipated. With the appropriate regeneration period, the net present value of selective harvesting per hectare is about $490 for timber.

The options are rather stark: clear-cutting for all commercial timber yielding a net revenue of about $1,000 per hectare (with a very long and uncertain regeneration period) or fruit and latex collection alone yielding a net present value of $6,330 per hectare. If sustainable selective timber harvesting is also practiced, the net present value increases to $6,820 per hectare ($6,330 plus $490). Selective cutting, however, may damage the residual stand and thereby reduce the benefits of fruit and latex collection somewhat.

Given these numbers, why is forest conversion usually considered so attractive? As Peters and colleagues point out, tropical timber is sold in the international market and generates foreign exchange; nonwood products are collected and sold locally and are therefore usually ignored. Another possible reason is that timber companies often have far greater political power than local villagers.

One hastens to add that this analysis is dependent on local market conditions and may not be valid if fruit from 100,000 hectares, as opposed to 1 hectare, enters the market. Nevertheless, the approach illustrates how data can be collected on directly consumed and marketed products and this information used to present a complete economic analysis of the economic benefits of a natural area. The social dimensions are also important: although timber extraction generates some local employment, fruit and latex collection involve a much larger number of people and are income-earning activities that can continue year after year.

QUALITATIVE STUDIES

In addition to the financial and economic analyses of entire national parks presented in Chapter 8 and the analyses of specific resources just examined, a number of qualitative studies indicate the types of benefits, economic and otherwise, to be obtained from protected areas. Although they do not contain monetary estimates, these studies provide valuable guidance on identifying benefits and costs. Using the techniques presented in Part I of the book, many of these aspects can be monetized with additional work. Here we highlight two of these studies—one on national parks in Indonesia, the other on nature tourism in Latin America and the Caribbean.

Linking Development and Parks in Indonesia

Indonesia has a protected area system that includes six main categories: national parks, nature reserves, game reserves, recreation parks, hunting reserves, and protection forests. Many of these protected areas are under pressure from expansion of agricultural lands, illegal hunting, fuelwood collection, and uncontrolled burning. These threats tend to concentrate in those areas with direct access by outside groups—that is, along park boundaries, on the borders of settled enclaves along access roads, and beside rivers.

A recent report prepared for the World Bank (Wells 1989) examines several such threatened areas and the potential role for integrated conservation and development projects (ICDPs) in promoting the economic development of communities living adjacent to park boundaries and thereby reducing degradation within the parks. Wells examines three parks: Dumoga–Bone in North Sulawesi, Kerinci–Seblat in Western Sumatra, and Gunung Leuser in Northern Sumatra. Here we consider the case of Dumoga–Bone in North Sulawesi.

Dumoga–Bone National Park includes three former wildlife and nature reserves within its 300,000 hectares. Established in 1982–1984, Dumoga–Bone consists primarily of closed-canopy rain forest set in rugged mountains. The establishment and management of the park are closely linked to several irrigation projects in the Dumoga Valley funded by the World Bank (Figure 15). In addition to conservation of its important flora and fauna, the park has a more direct economic rationale—to protect the upper watershed of the Dumoga River and ensure the continued functioning of the river-dependent irrigation system that covers 11,000 hectares of rice fields cultivated by some 8,500 farmers.

The irrigation schemes have been quite successful and have resulted in major gains in rice production; the increased rice output has helped to convert North Sulawesi from a net rice importer to a net exporter. Whereas progress on successful irrigation was previously spotty due to uncertain water supply (in part due to deforestation in the catchment area), the new integrated conservation and development program has been much more successful.

Although the report does not offer an economic analysis of the linked irrigation/national park projects, some interesting data on costs and benefits are available. More than 400 farmers were evicted from the park in 1983; of these one-third were resettled on 2-hectare lots for a total cost of $240,000. Other costs included extension campaigns, law enforcement, and court cases. There were also considerable social costs incurred by local inhabitants who were forced to leave the park area. Substantial benefits were also derived. Large areas of moist tropical forest were protected, and the new irrigation areas were successfully implemented. Whereas average annual farmer income in the valley was reported to be $340 in 1980 ($600 in irrigated areas), average incomes doubled or tripled over the following six years as the irrigation schemes were completed.

Future possibilities for better protection and limited direct use of the national park (rattan harvesting, for example, and buffer strips of fast-growing fuelwood trees) are discussed in more detail in Wells's report. Although no quantitative estimates are offered, the link between successful management of both the irrigation systems and the national park is clear. Continuing pressures on the park come from nearby resi-

Figure 15.
Dumoga–Bone National Park, Indonesia

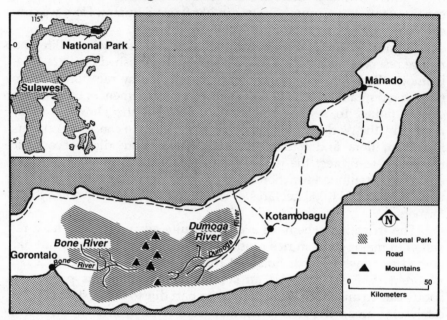

dents, and efforts are needed to find ways to meet their legitimate economic needs while ensuring effective protection of the park. In turn, the park preserves a valuable natural area and provides continuing off-site benefits via ensured water inputs into the irrigation system.

Ecotourism in Latin America

One promising avenue for promoting both protection and economic development goals is the growth of what has been called ecotourism or nature tourism. As mentioned earlier, this is a form of tourism that relies on the natural aspects of protected areas as an attraction and, as such, is a common feature in many national parks and reserves. Perhaps the distinguishing characteristic of ecotourism (as opposed to traditional tourism and recreational uses of protected areas) is the attempt to support protected areas in a relatively undeveloped state—not merely as a site within which to carry out profitable recreation activities such as skiing or camping or as a location for resort facilities.

Ecotourism is receiving increased attention now as a result of two major trends. One is the growing demand for "off the beaten track" destinations. The second trend is the shift by park managers to find innovative ways to increase support (both political and financial) for protected area management by integrating economic components into conservation activities. In a recent report prepared by World Wildlife Fund/US for U.S.A.I.D. (Boo 1990), the status and impacts of nature tourism, both national and international, in Belize, Costa Rica, Dominica, Ecuador, and Mexico are examined. Two park sites in each country were covered in the analysis.

The WWF report cited the benefits and costs associated with nature tourism (and tourism more generally). On the benefit side it noted that tourism is a growth industry, it is relatively "unprotected" (entry to the market is fairly open), it can help diversify an economy, and it may spur economic development of peripheral or under-developed areas. The study found that demand for ecotourism is large but not yet fully met by the managers of protected areas. Significant opportunities are being missed to bring money into the area, provide local employment, and offer environmental education to visitors.

There are also dangers and costs. Tourism is a discretionary expenditure and therefore unstable (in times of economic turndowns or uncertainty, tourism expenditures may drop sharply); certain sites may lose their appeal and their tourists; congestion may reduce the attractiveness of many areas ("tourism destroys tourism"); tourism may lead to various social and cultural problems; a large percentage of tourist revenues may leave the country; and tourism is frequently seasonal. Moreover, there is a need to ensure that part of the money generated by nature tourism stays in the park area, especially with local residents.

Of the five countries studied, only Ecuador has an internationally known protected-area destination that is a clear example of a nature tourism site: the Galápagos Islands. Ecuador receives about 260,000 visitors annually and the Galápagos from 30,000 to 45,000 visitors, of which about half are Ecuadorians and the rest from abroad. Mexico has numerous historical sites that are also well known, but its large tourist industry (more than 5 million visitors per year) is driven by a diverse mix of attractions—beaches, weather, ruins, food, and an attractive culture. Costa Rica has a relatively small tourism industry (about 260,000 visitors per year), but a sizable share come because of Costa Rica's natural attractions. Just because a country's protected areas are not widely known does not necessarily mean that specialized groups (members of the Sierra Club or Audubon Society, for example) may not have considerable knowledge of a site and constitute a sizable potential market.

Although the WWF survey did not quantify the economic benefits produced by nature tourism, the study did highlight the importance placed on access to natural areas by many visitors. As economic growth and development proceed, the number of such "wild places" will decline and their attractiveness will increase. As part of a mixed bundle of attractions, nature tourism can play an increasingly useful role as various countries seek to differentiate their "product" in the world market. Just as Kenya and Tanzania (and now Rwanda) have already done, many countries in the Americas and Asia can profitably promote unique aspects of their protected areas.

The WWF study also highlighted a small but important development in protected area management: the private provision of protected areas. The study identified a number of privately beneficial sites in the sample of five countries. These sites include the Community Baboon Sanctuary in Belize; Trafalgar Falls in Dominica; the Monteverde, La Selva Biological Station, and Marenco sites in Costa Rica; and Tinalandia in Ecuador. These areas tend to be small, they have simple accommodations, and they are managed by highly motivated people. Costa Rica, with several of these sites, is a leader in this field. There are also economic benefits. An economic analysis of the impact of research and nature tourism expenditures induced by the field stations of the Organization for Tropical Studies, Inc. (OTS) in Costa Rica was carried out by Laarman and Perdue (1988). OTS, which operates La Selva and other sites, was responsible for generating from $2.9 to $10.2 million worth of transactions per year. A maximum of $3.4 million represents direct foreign exchange spending; the balance is secondary spending via an economic multiplier. This figure represents 2 to 3 percent of Costa Rica's annual tourist receipts. These private efforts also create important qualitative benefits both within the country and abroad. Awareness of the value—and fragility—of these resources is heightened, thereby building the political case for greater support.

When countries are fortunate enough to have especially unique or spectacular natural areas or resources (the Galápagos, big game in East Africa, the Great Barrier Reef), this alone may provide sufficient attraction to draw international tourists. In most cases, however, nature tourism is more realistically promoted as part of a series of attractions to a country or region. Either way, the economic impact can still be considerable and serve as a valuable source of income for both domestic development and improved management of protected areas.

10

Conclusions and Implications

This book has focused on the economic issues associated with protected areas. For various economic reasons that economists call "market failures," the benefits of protection are only partly accounted for whereas the costs of protection receive thorough coverage. As a result, fewer areas are protected than is socially desirable. And because governments find it difficult to capture these benefits, budget allocations for management of protected areas are frequently inadequate.

Benefits are undervalued for a number of reasons. Some benefits, such as maintenance of biodiversity and ecological processes, are hard to express in monetary terms. Other benefits, such as those from watershed protection, are dispersed over the landscape at large and are not confined to the protected area itself. A final reason is that users of protected areas are usually charged only a nominal fee (if any fee at all) and hence do not express their true valuation of the area's benefits in the marketplace.

Part I of the book covered the general issues involved in determining monetary values, as well as the role of economic analysis in the establishment and management of protected areas. Part II examined the situation in a number of countries—fairly detailed analyses of three protected areas in Thailand as well as brief analyses of protected areas and their benefits in other parts of the world. From these analyses a number of conclusions can be drawn.

CONCLUSIONS

CONCLUSION 1. *Economic analysis offers valuable insights into the process of establishing and managing protected areas, but data may be difficult to obtain.* The studies reported here highlight the important role that economic analysis can play in promoting the establishment and improved management of protected areas. Once the associated benefits and costs have been identified, the economist must translate these values, to the extent possible, into monetary terms. Data limitations are sometimes formidable but, as shown in the following findings and conclusions, economic analysis can often provide valuable information about the benefits and costs associated with protected areas.

CONCLUSION 2. *Few protected areas are "privately beneficial" and thereby protected and managed by individuals.* Because of the wide range of benefits from protection—some on-site, others off-site, some with market prices, others without clearly identifiable prices—most protected areas fall in the "socially beneficial" or "undetermined benefits" category. The immediate implication of this is that many potentially valuable protected areas will be degraded or converted to other uses if there is no formal (usually governmental) intervention. This finding is very clear in the Thai case: there is heavy pressure for private development of selected resources in both existing and proposed protected areas. The results of such development are usually degradation and loss of integrity of these areas. Active outside intervention is therefore required to identify, establish, and manage important protected areas.

CONCLUSION 3. *Establishment of protected areas does not ensure that these areas will be effectively protected.* There are two crucial steps in protecting important natural areas. First, protected areas must be established through some administrative and legal process. Second, it is essential to design and implement management practices that will effectively protect the resources in the area. Although an increasing number of countries have established impressive protected-area systems, far fewer have allocated sufficient resources to manage these areas properly.

Economic analysis of benefits and costs can be a valuable tool in both steps of this process. It can help to justify the establishment of protected areas and can also play a critical role in helping protected area authorities fight for larger budget allocations to improve their management capabilities. Unless establishment and management are both given sufficient attention, areas will not be effectively protected.

CONCLUSION 4. *The costs and benefits of protection are often not distributed equally, thereby leading to management problems.* In many cases a major "cost" of protection is the loss of opportunity to use the resources within the protected area for direct consumption. These costs are largely paid by local villagers and other nearby residents. Traditional uses such as harvesting of timber and other forest products, capturing of animals, or clearing of new agricultural land are often prohibited. The "benefits" of protection, however, may not be readily apparent to the villagers. When costs loom large and the benefits are seen as either small, distant, or received by others, pressures for illegal use of the area's resources result. This is certainly true in the case of Khao Yai National Park, in other protected areas in Thailand, and in many of the wildlife parks in Africa. In other cases, the establishment of protected areas imposes costs on resource-extraction firms (timber or mining companies, for example). Although these groups may be politically powerful, they are usually easier to monitor than individual villagers. (The presence of powerful vested interests may, however, prevent the establishment of a protected area in the first place.)

Effective management, therefore, requires that this divergence between those who lose and those who benefit be recognized and addressed. The use of an exclusionary policy relying on guards or police is usually an inadequate and unsatisfactory response. The creation of buffer zones and programs outside the protected area's boundaries may be necessary.

CONCLUSION 5. *Economic values can be placed on many, but not all, benefits of protection.* The examples given in Part II of this book demonstrate that monetary values can be placed on a number of benefits associated with protection. Some of the benefits are measured in financial terms (valued at their actual dollar prices) while others are economic (or social welfare) values.

The most difficult issue for valuation is that of biodiversity and habitat preservation. Conservation of biological resources and habitats is a fundamental reason for establishing protected areas, but it is exceedingly hard to value directly. One can, however, place monetary values on many of the direct and indirect benefits that accompany protection. These benefits include the following:

- Tourism
- Recreation
- Sustainable harvest of flora and fauna
- Education and research expenditures
- Water quantity and quality
- Downstream effects on various types of infrastructure

    With appropriate planning before an analysis is begun, data can be collected to place monetary values on many of these benefits. Not all of the quantities estimated are true "economic measures." Some estimates—such as gross expenditures by tourists—are measures of income generation in one locale but do not measure the consumer's surplus received by park users. Others—such as downstream costs for replacement of structures or maintenance that is not needed because the protected area reduces soil erosion—are measures of social benefits. Nevertheless, the sums involved for all benefits can be substantial, particularly when compared to government budget allocations for management.

CONCLUSION 6. *Estimates of tourism/recreational benefits yield useful information for protected areas with a large direct-use component.* Examination of the three sites in Thailand shows that in at least two of the areas tourism and recreational expenditures (and benefits) are large. The studies from Australia and the Virgin Islands in Chapter 8 yield similar results. Direct use of protected areas is important for a number of reasons:

- Tourism and recreational use increase the public's—and the government's—awareness of the value of protected areas.
- Tourism can provide jobs and income opportunities to replace income lost from restrictions on allowable uses in protected areas.
- Increased recreational use may reduce the level of illegal use of the resource (poaching, agricultural expansion).
- Reliable methods of measuring and valuing recreational use have now been established.

    This line of reasoning does not mean that areas which are inaccessible or closed to public use have no value. There may be valid reasons (fragile topography, sensitive habitats) for protecting certain areas and not permitting any direct use. In these cases, other approaches must be used to assess the magnitude of benefits. Sometimes the benefits will be quantifiable; in other cases they may be assessed only in a qualitative manner. Protected areas that fall into the "undetermined benefits" category are often examples of this situation.

CONCLUSION 7. *The opportunity costs of not developing the resources in a protected area may vary, but they can usually be calculated.* One valuable piece of information is the actual opportunity cost of not developing or exploiting the resources in the protected area. This "cost" of protection can usually be calculated and must measure the *net* benefit lost by forgoing development. The opportunity cost of not logging a forest area, for example, is not the value of the total amount of timber on the site but the net return after all processing and harvesting costs are taken into account. A similar analysis can be done for mineral resources. In the case of hydropower development, the appropriate measure is the difference in cost of supplying the same amount of energy by the next best alternative means.

The opportunity-cost approach indicates what society has to pay to ensure protection. If the sum is very large, protection may be found to be too costly. When the sum is smaller (or even negative as in the case of some water projects), the case for preservation and protection may be easy to make.

POLICY IMPLICATIONS

Although the focus of this book has been on economic issues concerning protected areas and ways in which market failures can be overcome, it is also abundantly clear that there are serious management and developmental issues that go beyond merely "getting your prices right" to correct market failures. In particular, two topics must be considered when assessing programs for improving management of protected areas. The first topic, the way in which people living next to a protected area are treated, is largely a developing-country problem. The second topic, increasing government revenues from protected areas, is important in all countries.

Villager Involvement and Buffer Zones

One of the major threats to protected areas in almost all developing countries is the depletion or degradation of resources caused by encroachment and poaching. This is as true in Thailand as it is in East Africa or Central America. The problems have similar causes: poverty, population pressure, and limited options. Once an area is given protected status, villagers often are prohibited from continuing many traditional (even if illegal) uses of its resources—for example, collection of plants, animals, and other products is banned in many national parks and wildlife sanctuaries. On the other hand, villagers receive few of the benefits from protection.

Direct regulation and police measures have not been very successful in curtailing this pattern of use. The villagers are commonly quite poor and cannot easily afford to give up this income. But if left uncontrolled, many traditional uses would eventually threaten the resources within the protected area. Proper attention to local needs can reduce the potential for conflict. Some suggestions follow.

First, local residents should be included in the planning process before the protected area is established. Although they rarely have veto power, their voice may be essential in minimizing future conflicts and various accommodations can be made by the authorities to meet their needs. Where a limited amount of a certain use would not threaten the protected area, for example, an agreement can be arranged detailing allowable levels of use.

Second, wherever feasible, nearby residents should receive preference for jobs generated within and by the park. Local residents often have detailed knowledge of the area and its resources and can be valuable in park protection and research. Park maintenance also provides job opportunities. When tourist development is undertaken, local residents should be hired to the greatest extent possible. If necessary, training should be provided to increase opportunities for local residents to fill the available positions.

Third, it may be necessary to establish a buffer zone around the protected area where "illegal" uses are permitted, even if only informally. This compromise recognizes that local villagers are being asked to pay a substantial price in terms of lost access to resources within the protected area. It also acknowledges that a policy which relies solely on strict enforcement is not possible without unacceptably high social costs (that have even included deaths of villagers and guards). Ideally, a clearly identified buffer zone should be designated just within or beyond the protected area's boundary. The size of the zone will depend on the requirements of nearby residents. Planning, development, and management of the buffer zone should be performed in close consultation with local residents to ensure that it will serve its intended purpose. A number of potentially appropriate activities for buffer zones were discussed in Chapter 4. Management of buffer zones is also discussed in McNeely (1988), MacKinnon and others (1986), Oldfield (1988), and McNeely and Miller (1984).

Increasing Revenues from Protected Areas

Our examination of Thailand's protected area system illustrates the problem of capturing the benefits from protection: admission fees, accommodation charges, and other revenues are very small when compared to the sizable benefits enjoyed by those using certain protected areas. In many cases admission fees are either nonexistent or so low that they are not considered in individual decision making about the use of protected areas. Many protected areas provide important habitat, research, or hydrologic benefits, none of which are compensated for and thus are often not reflected in management budgets.

Budget allocations, however, are a reflection of the policymakers' perception of the importance of the protected area. Since protected areas generate little in the way of revenue, they are considered a drain on financial resources, especially when compared to "productive" resource uses like logging or mining. Improved understanding of the economic importance of the wide range of social benefits provided by protected areas is one step in the process of justifying increased budget allocations for protection. Another important step, if only for psychological reasons, is increasing the revenue from direct (and indirect) uses of protected areas. Some possibilities for revenue enhancement are obvious; others are more controversial but still worthy of study.

Promotion of greater nonconsumptive use of protected areas, such as tourism and research, should be encouraged and admission fees or gate charges either established or increased. Although one would not want to directly link budget allocations to a protected area's ability to generate revenue, it may be desirable to develop some mechanism whereby those areas that generate large revenues receive credit for their contribution. This could be done by allowing a protected area to keep a portion of any fees it collects, including entrance and accommodation fees, concession charges, and fines. The difficult part is to provide adequate levels of management support to all protected areas, including those without a commercially successful component, while still encouraging increased revenue generation.

When gate fees are charged at all, they tend to be very low and are the same for all visitors. It may be desirable to develop some form of differential pricing whereby those who are better able to pay are charged more. This could be done via a differential charge for foreign as opposed to domestic visitors or by higher fees for private vehicles and tourist coaches.

Budget and fiscal changes are never easy to implement. It is quite possible, however, to increase gate fees and admission charges and to charge for accommodations. Instituting a multilevel admission system may be more difficult. The partial linking of revenue generation with enhanced budget support will be administratively difficult but is an idea well worth pursuing. Certain popular protected areas will generate a "surplus" that can be used to help support other areas. The goal, therefore, is to reward those areas that have a large direct-use component without penalizing inaccessible areas or those that cannot support direct public use.

A GLOBAL PERSPECTIVE

Economic analysis can be fairly precise at the level of the individual project and can yield valuable insights at the national or macro level. This book has examined how these analyses can be improved. But many of the benefits from protected areas, particularly those relating to biological diversity and environmental processes, are international in scope and their loss would have global impacts. Economics does not deal well with this problem.

While implementing the ideas discussed in this volume will improve decision making at the local and national levels, the international nature of protected area benefits calls for international action. The need for international assistance is particularly important when one considers that developed countries benefit a great deal from the continued existence of natural areas while some of the richest, most diverse areas are located in some of the world's poorest countries. These countries, for reasons given earlier, are least able to make the investments required for protection and back up their decisions with effective management.

Given that the developed world stands to lose a great deal if natural areas are not effectively protected, there is good reason to compensate countries who must sacrifice the use of resources to maintain these benefits. International compensation in the form of bilateral and multilateral aid, debt-for-nature swaps, transfer of technology, and provision of training and supplies are all necessary. In this way, the world community will share more fairly the cost of maintaining its natural heritage.

Glossary

Benefit/cost analysis (BCA). A project analysis technique based on welfare economics theory that examines the present value of the stream of economic benefits and costs of an activity or project over some defined period of time (the time horizon) using some predetermined discount rate. A boundary of analysis is also defined in order to indicate what effects are included in the analysis. The results of a BCA are usually presented in terms of a net present value (NPV), a benefit/cost ratio (B/C ratio), or an internal rate of return (IRR). A benefit/cost analysis uses economic scarcity values (shadow prices) as opposed to the market prices used in a financial analysis.

Benefit/cost ratio. An index of project worth in a BCA based on the ratio of the discounted benefits of a project to the discounted costs of the project. If the ratio is 1 or greater, the present value of benefits is greater than the present value of costs—that is, the project generates net benefits (or is profitable). If the B/C ratio is less than 1, the project produces a net loss. The formula for the B/C ratio is

$$\text{B/C ratio} = \frac{\sum_{i=1}^{n} \frac{B_i}{(1+r)^i}}{\sum_{i=1}^{n} \frac{C_i}{(1+r)^i}}$$

Bequest value. The personal or social benefit received by the present generation from leaving a resource for future generations to enjoy or use. Bequest values are one of the reasons why present generations protect natural areas or species for future generations. See also *future values*.

201

Bidding games. A set of contingent valuation techniques that rely on the creation of a hypothetical market for some good or service. In a single-bid game the respondents are asked to give a single bid equal to their willingness to pay or willingness to accept compensation for the environmental good or service described. In an iterative-bid game the respondents are given a variety of bids to determine at what price they are indifferent between receiving (or paying) the bid or receiving (or losing) the environmental good at issue.

Biodiversity. Also known as biological diversity, biodiversity is the variability of the stock of genetic material found in the flora and fauna of any location, much of which may not yet be fully identified and cataloged.

Change-in-productivity approach. A valuation technique based on the difference in the value of production with a proposed project and without the project. This is a form of *with-and-without-project analysis.*

Compensating variation. In measuring changes in an individual's social well-being, compensating variation is the amount of additional money that would be required to keep a person at the initial utility level (state of well-being) after there has been an increase in the price of one of the goods the person consumes. This is the same as the willingness-to-pay measure. See also *equivalent variation.*

Congestible. Congestible goods or services are public goods such as parks or other public places that can become crowded. Up to some point, increasing use of the resource by additional people does not affect the enjoyment received by each user; after congestion sets in, increased use results in diminishing enjoyment and benefits for each person.

Consumer's surplus (CS). An estimate of total economic benefits from consuming a good or service consists of the market value of the good or service (the price paid) plus consumer's surplus. Consumer's surplus is measured by the maximum willingness to pay over and above the actual cash cost of consumption. For goods or services with a very low (or free) market price such as a national park or clean air, the consumer's surplus may be very large.

Consumptive benefits. Benefits received by individuals or society from directly using or consuming a good or service. These tangible benefits are in contrast to nonconsumptive benefits whereby the resource in question is not consumed and is still available for others to enjoy. Hunting and killing an animal produces consumptive benefits whereas receiving a sense of well-being from merely knowing that the animal exists (or viewing, photographing, or reading about it) is an example of a nonconsumptive benefit.

Contingent valuation. Analytic survey techniques that rely on hypothetical situations to place a monetary value on goods or services. This approach is commonly used when normal markets do not exist. Most survey-based techniques are examples of contingent valuation methods (CVM). Contingent valuation frequently elicits information on willingness to pay (WTP) or willingness to accept compensation (WTAC) for an increase or decrease in some (usually nonmarketed) good or service. Thus these techniques are related to the concepts of compensating variation and equivalent variation.

Cost-effectiveness analysis. A technique of project analysis that makes no attempt to estimate benefits and focuses on the least-cost means of reaching a goal. This approach is commonly used for social or environmental projects in which the benefits of reaching a goal are difficult to value (immunization of all children under the age of five, for example, or providing six years of education to all children) or hard to identify (for example, protecting biodiversity in endangered habitats).

Costless-choice method. A contingent valuation technique whereby people are asked to choose between several hypothetical bundles of goods to determine their implicit valuation of an environmental good or service. Since no monetary figures are involved, this approach may be more useful in settings where barter and subsistence production are common.

Debt-for-nature swaps. An agreement between an organization and a national government whereby a certain amount of foreign debt is exchanged for guarantees by the national government to establish and protect endangered natural areas. The sponsoring organization usually buys the debt at a discount and exchanges it for a commitment in local currency. This approach is increasingly being used to help protect endangered tropical forests and other ecosystems in poor, debt-ridden countries.

Delphi technique. A variant of the survey-based techniques wherein experts, rather than consumers, are interviewed. These experts place values on a good or service through an iterative process with feedback among the group between each iteration. This expert-based approach may be useful when valuing very esoteric resources.

Direct costs. In project analysis, direct costs are the out-of-pocket expenditures associated with an activity. These include costs of land acquisition, capital, and labor, as well as operations, maintenance, and replacement (OM&R). Indirect costs, by way of contrast, are costs associated with a project that do not involve financial outlays. Indirect costs often occur offsite or later in time and are not included in a traditional financial analysis of a project.

Discount rate. The interest rate used in project analysis to reduce future benefits and costs to their present-day equivalent. The discount rate is a percentage; the higher the discount rate, the less any future benefit or cost is worth today. A zero discount rate implies complete indifference to the timing of receipt of any benefit or cost.

Ecological processes. The functioning of a natural ecosystem and the interactions between its various components. The interactions between land and water in a watershed or a coastal area are examples of ecological processes, as is nutrient cycling or natural cleansing of air and water.

Economic analysis. In a narrow sense, the analysis of an activity using social-welfare values as distinguished from financial values. Distortions in prices are eliminated via means of shadow prices, and transfer payments are usually excluded. In a broader sense, economic analysis can refer to both private (financial) and public analyses of a project, policy, or activity.

Equivalent variation. In measuring changes in an individual's social well-being when there has been a price increase, equivalent variation is the amount of income loss that would leave a person at the same welfare (well-being) level before the price change as after. Whereas compensating variation measures money transfers needed to keep a person at the same utility level as in the initial situation, equivalent variation measures the monetary equivalent of the change in welfare based on the utility levels after the change has occurred. This is the same as the willingness-to-accept-compensation measure. See also *compensating variation.*

Excludability. Attribute of a good or service that allows one to exclude users and thereby ration use. Most goods are excludable; if one person owns a car, for example, someone else cannot own the same one. A number of environmental and public goods are nonexcludable. Examples include sunshine, rain, beautiful views, national defense, and most radio and TV transmissions.

Existence value. The benefit an individual or society receives from merely knowing that a good or service exists. This is a nonconsumptive, nonexcludable benefit. Existence values may be important reasons for protecting wildlife.

Externalities. In the economic sense, externalities are impacts of an activity that affect others outside the activity. Externalities may be benefits or costs. Economic externalities include the impact of smoke and ash produced by a powerplant, downstream effects of eroded soil or fertilizer runoff, or effects of mangrove destruction on a coastal fishery.

Financial analysis. An analysis of a project or activity based on the private individual's or firm's perspective. It uses market prices and market interest rates, includes transfer payments (taxes, duties, subsidies), and does not normally include economic externalities. The alternative to financial or private analysis is public analysis, also referred to as social-welfare or economic analysis.

Foreign exchange. Any monetary resource from a country that is convertible and tradable on international markets. When goods or services are exported, they earn foreign exchange just as imports cost foreign exchange. If a national currency is not freely convertible and traded, shadow prices may be necessary to indicate the true domestic value of imports or exports. Foreign exchange can be used to settle accounts (pay debts) or pay for imports.

Free rider. Any individual or group that receives a benefit which it values but does not pay for. Free rider problems occur with nonexcludable public goods such as national defense or air pollution control; as a result, these services are usually paid for by taxation. The benefits from habitat preservation and biodiversity also share many of these characteristics. Once a habitat is preserved or a species is protected, the benefits are received whether or not individuals have helped pay for them.

Future values. Benefits from preserving a species or ecosystem that will be received at some time in the future. These include option values and bequest values as well as consumptive and nonconsumptive use benefits by future generations.

Goods and services. Those things produced by humans or nature that yield benefits or increase our well-being. They may be tangible (forestry products, recreation sites, food, industrial products, haircuts) or intangible (the value received from knowing of the continued existence of whales, a view of a distant landscape). Goods are usually tangible; services can be either tangible or intangible. Many natural ecosystems produce valuable services by maintaining species diversity, the integrity of hydrologic cycles, or the level of air or water quality.

Gross national product (GNP). The value of finished goods and services produced by a society but excluding intermediate goods (goods used up in the production of other goods, such as wood used in furniture or steel used in an automobile). GNP takes into account net payments (positive or negative) abroad. Another measure, gross domestic product (GDP), represents the total final output of goods and services produced within the country's borders—that is, by residents and nonresidents—regardless of whether ownership is by domestic or foreign claimants.

Indirect costs. Costs not directly accounted for in the analysis of a project. Direct project costs include land, labor, and capital; indirect costs derive from economic externalities. A financial analysis usually ignores indirect costs; such costs, however, should be included in a social-welfare analysis.

Intergenerational equity. Fairness from generation to generation; a concern for the resources and opportunities left for future generations. Causing extinction of a species or destroying an ecosystem may cause substantial losses in social welfare to future generations and thus would be considered inequitable in an intergenerational sense unless compensated for by social-welfare benefits to future generations.

Internal rate of return (IRR). An evaluation criterion used in project analysis. The IRR is the discount rate at which the present value of benefits exactly equals the present value of costs. If the IRR is higher than the cost of capital or a predetermined rate of interest, the project is profitable and accepted. Commonly used by banks for both financial and economic analyses of projects. The formula is as follows: The internal rate of return equals the interest rate (r) such that

$$\sum_{i=1}^{n} \frac{B_i}{(1+r)^i} = \sum_{i=1}^{n} \frac{C_i}{(1+r)^i}$$

Land-value approaches. A set of valuation techniques that relies on differences in the market value of different parcels of land to infer the monetary value of various levels of environmental quality. This surrogate market approach is closely linked to the *property-value approach.*

Loss-of-earnings approach. A valuation technique that uses changes in human productivity to value the effect of a change in environmental conditions. Commonly used when environmental factors cause illness and lost workdays or reduced productivity.

Market failure. Market failure occurs when prices do not completely reflect true social costs or benefits. In such cases, a market solution results in an inefficient or socially undesirable allocation of resources. If the benefits of protected areas are underestimated, for example, a smaller amount of area will be protected than is socially desirable. If the social costs of an activity (such as downstream effects of soil erosion) are not included, the level of soil-conserving measures undertaken will be lower than is socially desirable.

Mitigation-cost approach. A valuation technique that examines the cost of mitigating or reversing damages associated with a project or activity. This is a cost-based approach that relies on data on potential expenditures. See also *preventive-expenditure method*.

Multiplier. A factor that reflects the total impact of an initial expenditure in an economy. Usually larger than 1, the multiplier indicates the additional economic activity generated as the recipients of an expenditure use it in turn to buy other goods and services. In some cases, as with expenditures on imported goods, the multiplier can be less than 1.

Natural areas. Areas that remain relatively undisturbed by humans and are close to their natural state. They provide a wide variety of benefits including maintenance of biodiversity and ecological processes as well as other consumptive and nonconsumptive benefits.

Net present value (NPV). A criterion used in project analysis. The NPV is the present-day value of the benefits and costs of a project that occur over a defined time horizon. A discount rate is used to reduce future benefits or costs to their present equivalent. A commonly used measure of project worth, NPV is expressed in monetary terms and indicates the magnitude of net benefits generated by a project over time. An NPV greater than zero implies positive net benefits. The formula is

$$\text{NPV} = \sum_{i=1}^{n} \frac{B_i}{(1+r)^i} - \sum_{i=1}^{n} \frac{C_i}{(1+r)^i}$$

Nonconsumptive benefits. Benefits to an individual or society that do not require consumption or direct use of a good or resource. Examples include knowledge of the existence of an endangered species or habitat and viewing a beautiful vista. Nonconsumptive benefits are also nonrival and usually nonexcludable.

Opportunity costs. The economic or financial value of opportunities that must be given up when making one use of a resource as opposed to another. The opportunity cost of protecting a natural area, for example, includes the commercial development options that are denied or the value of timber that could have been harvested.

Option value. The benefit received by retaining the possibility (the option) of using a resource in the future by protecting or preserving it today. For protected areas, option values reflect the value of potential future use, even if the individual is uncertain whether he or she will ever use the resource.

Preventive-expenditure method. A cost-based valuation technique that uses data on actual expenditures made to alleviate an environmental problem (such as countermeasures to deal with polluted water or air). It gives a minimum estimate of a person's valuation of reducing or eliminating the environmental problem. The *mitigation-cost approach* relies on estimates of potential expenditures.

Property-value approach. A surrogate market technique used to place monetary values on different levels of environmental quality. The approach uses data on market prices for homes and other real estate to estimate consumers' willingness to pay for improved levels of environmental quality (air, noise, views).

Public goods. Goods or services that are usually nonexcludable and nonrival in consumption and hence commonly provided by governments and financed by tax revenues. Examples include national defense, clean air and water, and the benefits from preservation of endangered species or habitats. Because of exclusion and pricing problems, the private sector does not normally supply enough public goods (that is, market failures occur).

Quasi-option value. The benefit associated with preserving a resource in the present in the expectation that additional information will be forthcoming about the value of benefits or costs associated with the resource. Quasi-option value is the value to an individual or society of avoiding irreversible decisions today—such as destroying a natural ecosystem of unknown genetic value.

Relocation-cost approach. A cost-based technique used to estimate the monetary value of environmental damages based on the potential costs of relocating a physical facility that would be damaged by a change in environmental quality. This technique relies on data on potential expenditures. See also *replacement-cost approach*.

Replacement-cost approach. A cost-based technique that measures the potential expenditures that would be required to replace or restore a productive asset that would be damaged by some project or development. These costs are then compared to the costs of preventing the damage from occurring to determine which is more efficient.

Rival/nonrival goods. Rival goods concern the consumption or use of the good by an individual (an apple, a shirt) that prevents its use by someone else. Markets help allocate rival goods by setting prices for exchange of goods for money. Nonrival goods can be used by one or many people at the same time. Clean air, national defense, open views, benefits from a species' existence or protection are largely nonrival goods. Some nonrival goods can be affected by crowding (as in public parks); see *congestible*.

Safe minimum standard (SMS). A proposition developed by S. V. Ciriacy-Wantrup which states that an endangered species or habitat should be protected at some minimum level sufficient to ensure its existence at a very high level of probability unless the social costs of doing so are "unacceptably large." The SMS is an argument for conservation when contemplating irreversible actions.

Shadow prices. In economic or social-welfare analysis, shadow prices are prices used in lieu of market prices for goods or services when market prices are distorted or no market prices exist. Sometimes referred to as accounting prices, shadow prices are supposed to reflect the true social value of a benefit or cost.

Shadow project. A variant of the replacement-cost approach that examines the potential costs of replacing a lost or damaged asset with an identical one in an alternative location. The shadow project, therefore, physically replaces the lost resource.

Social benefits/costs. Benefits or costs received by members of society at large or in the aggregate. As opposed to private or financial benefits and costs—which only include those benefits and costs directly affecting the individual decision maker or firm—social benefits and costs include all the impacts of a project or activity. Economic externalities are examples of social benefits or costs. Social values may be affected by income distribution and intergenerational concerns.

Surrogate markets. When no market exists for a good or service (and therefore no market price is observed), surrogate (or substitute) markets can be used to derive information on values. For example, travel-cost information can be used to estimate value for visits to a recreational area; property value data are used to estimate values for nonmarketed environmental attributes such as view, location, or noise levels.

Sustainable development. Sustainable development implies ability to maintain the production of goods and services from a system over time. In this way, present-day needs are met without foreclosing future options for meeting future needs. Associated with the scale and style of resource use over time.

Take-it-or-leave-it experiment. One of the class of survey-based techniques wherein the respondent is given a single monetary value and must decide whether or not to accept it in exchange for some environmental good or service. The respondent may answer either yes or no. In contrast, *bidding games* elicit information on how much money the respondent will offer for some environmental good or service.

Time horizon. The period of time included in an economic or financial analysis. The time horizon may be fairly short and defined by the expected life of any capital invested (for example, ten to twenty years for a factory), or it may be very long or even infinite for certain renewable resource projects. Discounting, however, results in an effective time horizon beyond which the present values of benefits or costs are effectively zero.

Trade-off game. A variant of the bidding game wherein respondents are asked to choose between two different bundles of goods. Each bundle might, for example, include a different sum of money plus varying levels of an environmental resource. The choices indicate a person's willingness to trade money for an increased level of an environmental good. When no money is involved, the approach is similar to the *costless-choice technique.*

Transboundary effects. An impact that occurs outside the boundary defined for a project. Off-site effects are common examples of these effects: fertilizer or pesticide pollution in irrigation return flows, agricultural losses from wildlife ranging beyond a protected area, or long-range air quality impacts. Many economic externalities of projects are caused by transboundary effects.

Transfer payments. Payments such as taxes, subsidies, and duties made between individuals, firms, and governments that do not represent payments for real resource allocation. Transfer payments are monetary and therefore represent a transfer of a *claim* on resources but do not reflect productive decisions such as payment for land, labor, or capital. Transfer payments are included in private financial analyses but are not included in public, social-welfare economic analyses.

Travel-cost approach. A widely used surrogate market approach that relies on information on time and travel costs to derive a demand curve for a recreational site. This curve is in turn used to estimate the consumer's surplus or "value" of the site to all users. This approach is widely used to value the recreational benefits of public parks and other natural areas.

Triage. A decision-making technique that can be used in an emergency when limited resources preclude undertaking all desirable or feasible actions. Originally a medical concept, triage involves the classification of resources (or individuals) into three categories: those in no danger at present; those that are irrevocably lost; and those that can be preserved (or saved) with additional time and money. The resources available are primarily applied to the third category.

Unsustainable. Using renewable resources in a manner that reduces the stock available over time (such as overfishing or harvesting trees at a rate higher than natural regeneration rates). Nonrenewable resources such as minerals and petroleum are, by definition, used in an unsustainable manner. Effectively nonrenewable resources such as soils can also be said to be used in an unsustainable manner if use causes their productive powers to decline over time.

Valuation (monetary). The process of placing monetary value on goods or services that do not have accepted prices or where market prices are distorted. Many environmental goods or services (such as clean air and biodiversity) do not enter the market and therefore have no commonly accepted market price.

Wage-differential approach. A surrogate market approach that uses information on differences in wage rates for similar jobs in different areas to estimate monetary values for different levels of environmental quality. This approach has been used to estimate values for such environmental variables as different levels of congestion, air pollution, and aesthetics.

Welfare. In economics, welfare is the level of well-being of an individual or a society. Social welfare refers to the general level of well-being of a society and includes both tangible (food, housing, cars) and intangible elements (national security, existence of natural areas, stress levels).

Willingness to accept compensation (WTAC). A measure of what an individual would have to be given to cause him or her to accept a loss in welfare caused by, for example, a decline in the level of resources or environmental quality. The WTAC measure indicates the monetary equivalent that would be necessary to compensate for the welfare loss from the change. See also *equivalent variation.*

Willingness to pay (WTP). A measure used in survey-based valuation techniques (also known as contingent valuation methods) that indicates an individual's willingness to pay money to obtain some desired level of a good or service (an improved environment, for example, or greater species diversity). The WTP measure is used when market prices do not exist. See also *compensating variation.*

With-and-without-project analysis. An analytic approach that always considers at least two alternatives in assessing a proposed project: what is expected to happen with the project and what would have happened without the project. It is not the same as before-and-after-project analysis, which assumes simply a continuation of current conditions in the future.

References

Angsupanich, S. 1983. *Zooplankton Community in Thale Noi*. Songkhla: Faculty of Natural Resources, Prince of Songkhla University.

Arrow, K. J., and A. C. Fisher. 1974. "Environmental Preservation, Uncertainty and Irreversibility." *Quarterly Journal of Economics* 88:312–319.

ASEAN. 1982. *Asian Heritage Parks and Reserves*. Bangkok: ASEAN Experts Group on the Environment. Mimeo.

Bhurintavaraku, C., and V. Leknim. 1983. *Seasonal Appearance of Macrophytes in Thale Noi*. Songkhla: Faculty of Science, Prince of Songkhla University.

Bishop, R. C. 1978. "Endangered Species and Uncertainty: The Economics of a Safe Minimum Standard." *American Journal of Agricultural Economics* 60:10–18.

Blommestein, E. 1985. *Tourism and Environment: An Overview of the Eastern Caribbean*. Port of Spain, Trinidad and Tobago: Economic Commission for Latin America and the Caribbean.

Blower, J. 1984. "National Parks for Developing Countries." In J. A. McNeely and K. R. Miller (eds.), *National Parks, Conservation and Development*. Washington, D.C.: Smithsonian Institution Press.

Boardman, R. 1981. *International Organization and the Conservation of Nature*. Bloomington: Indiana University Press.

Boo, E. 1990. *Ecotourism: The Potentials and Pitfalls*. Washington, D.C.: World Wildlife Fund.

Brockelman, W. Y. 1975. "Gibbon Populations and Their Conservation in Thailand." *Natural History Bulletin of the Siam Society* 26:133–157.

Caribbean Conservation Association. 1989. "Innovative Funding Strategies for Protected Areas." *Park and Protected Area News* 2(2):3.

Child, G.F.T. 1984. "Managing Wildlife for People in Zimbabwe." In

J. A. McNeely and K. R. Miller (eds.), *National Parks, Conservation and Development*. Washington, D.C.: Smithsonian Institution Press.

Chunkao, K., and K. Pricha. 1976. *Sediment Yields and Surface Runoff from Small Plots of Four Types, Mae-Huad Forest, Lampong, Thailand.* Bangkok: Kasetsart University. Mimeo. (In Thai.)

Chunkao, K., and others. 1983. *Research on Hydrological Evaluation of Land Use Factors Related to Water Yields in the Highlands.* Bangkok: Kasetsart University.

Ciriacy-Wantrup, S. V. 1952. *Resource Conservation.* Berkeley: University of California Press.

CMC. 1986. *Khao Soi Dao Wildlife Sanctuary.* Bangkok: Conservation Monitoring Center for Thailand, Department of Biology, Mahidol University.

Commission on National Parks and Protected Areas (CNPPA). 1984. *Threatened Protected Areas of the World.* Gland, Switzerland: IUCN.

Conrad, J. 1980. "Quasi-Option Value and the Expected Value of Information." *Quarterly Journal of Economics* 92:813–819.

Cumberlege, P. F., and V.M.S. Cumberlege. 1964. "A Preliminary List of the Orchids of Khao Yai National Park." *Natural History Bulletin of the Siam Society* 20: 183–204.

Cummings, R., and V. Norton. 1974. "The Economics of Environmental Preservation: Comment." *American Economic Review* 64:1021–1024.

Cummings, R. G., D. Brookshire, and W. Schulze. 1986. *Valuing Environmental Goods: An Assessment of the Contingent Valuation Method.* Savage, Md.: Rowman & Littlefield Publishers.

Dixon, J. A., and J. P. Bojö. 1988. "Economic Analysis and the Environment." Report to the African Development Bank based on a workshop held 7–9 June 1988 in Abidjan, Côte d'Ivoire.

Dixon, J. A., and P. R. Burbridge. 1984. "Economic Considerations in Mangrove Management." In L. S. Hamilton and S. C. Snedaker (eds.), *Handbook for Mangrove Area Management.* Honolulu: East-West Center.

Dixon, J. A., R. A. Carpenter, L. A. Fallon, P. B. Sherman, and S. Manopimoke. 1988. *Economic Analysis of the Environmental Impacts of Development Projects.* London: Earthscan Publications.

Dixon, J. A., L. M. Talbot, and G. J. Le Moigne. 1989. *Dams and the Environment: Considerations in World Bank Projects.* Washington, D.C.: World Bank.

Dixon, J. A., and M. M. Hufschmidt, eds. 1986. *Economic Valuation Techniques for the Environment: A Case Study Workbook.* Baltimore: Johns Hopkins University Press.

Dobias, R. J. 1982. *The Shell Guide to National Parks in Thailand.* Bangkok: Shell Company of Thailand.

————. 1985. *Elephant Conservation and Protected Area Management.* WWF/IUCN Project 3001 Final Report. Bangkok: WWF Thailand. Mimeo.

————. 1988. *Influencing Decision Makers About Providing Enhanced Support for Protected Areas in Thailand (Beneficial Use Project).* WWF Contract 3757 Interim Report. Bangkok: WWF Thailand. Mimeo.

Dobias, R. J., and C. Khontong. 1986. "Integrating Conservation and Rural Development in Thailand." *Tigerpaper* 13(4):1–4.

Dobias, R. J., V. Wangwacharakul, and N. Sangswang. 1988. *Beneficial Use Quantifications of Khao Yai National Park: Executive Summary and Main Report.* Bangkok: Thorani Tech for World Wide Fund for Nature.

Durst, P. B. 1988. "Nature Tourism: Opportunities for Promoting Conservation and Economic Development." Paper presented at the International Symposium on Nature Conservation and Tourism Development, 22–26 August 1988, Surat Thani, Thailand.

Eutrirak, S., and S. Grandstaff. 1986. "Evaluation of Lumpinee Public Park in Bangkok, Thailand." In J. A. Dixon and M. M. Hufschmidt (eds.), *Economic Valuation Techniques for the Environment.* Baltimore: Johns Hopkins University Press.

FAO. 1985. *Tropical Forestry Action Plan.* Rome: Food and Agriculture Organization of the United Nations.

Farnworth, E. G., T. H. Tidrick, C. F. Jordan, and W. M. Smathers, Jr. 1981. "The Value of Natural Ecosystems: An Economic and Ecological Framework." *Environmental Conservation* 8(4):275–282.

Farnworth, E. G., T. H. Tidrick, W. M. Smathers, Jr., and C. F. Jordan. 1983. "A Synthesis of Ecological and Economic Theory Toward More Complete Valuation of Tropical Moist Forests." *International Journal of Environmental Studies* 21:11–28.

Fisher, A. C., J. V. Krutilla, and C. J. Cicchetti. 1974. "The Economics of Environmental Preservation: Further Discussion." *American Economic Review* 64:1030–1039.

Freeman, A. M., III. 1979. *The Benefits of Environmental Improvement.* Baltimore: Johns Hopkins University Press.

_____. 1984. "The Quasi-Option Value of Irreversible Development." *Journal of Environmental Economics and Management* 11:292–295.

Goodwin, M., and M. Wilson, eds. 1986. *Caribbean Marine Resources: Opportunities for Economic Development and Management.* Washington, D.C.: U.S.A.I.D. and NOAA.

Hamilton, L. S. (with P. N. King). 1983. *Tropical Forested Watersheds: Hydrologic and Soil Response to Major Uses or Conversions.* Boulder: Westview Press.

Hansen, S. 1988. *Debt for Nature Swaps: Overview and Discussion of Key Issues.* Environment Department Working Paper no. 1. Washington, D.C.: World Bank.

Heyman, A. M., T. J. Riegert, A. Smith, T. Shallow, and J. R. Clark. 1988. "Project Proposal: Development of the Tobago Cays National Park." Washington, D.C.: Government of St. Vincent and the Grenadines and Organization of American States.

Hodgson, G., and J. A. Dixon. 1988. *Logging versus Fisheries and Tourism in Palawan: An Environmental and Economic Analysis.* EAPI Occasional Paper no. 7. Honolulu: East-West Center.

Hoskins, W. G. 1970. *The Making of the English Landscape*. Harmondsworth: Pelican.

Hufschmidt, M. M., D. E. James, A. D. Meister, B. T. Bower, and J. A. Dixon. 1983. *Environment, Natural Systems and Development: An Economic Valuation Guide*. Baltimore: Johns Hopkins University Press.

Ingram, C. D., and P. B. Durst. 1987. *Marketing Nature-Oriented Tourism for Rural Development and Wildlands Management in Developing Countries: A Bibliography*. Asheville, N.C.: Southeastern Forest Experiment Station.

IUCN. 1978. *Categories, Objectives, and Criteria for Protected Areas*. Gland, Switzerland: IUCN.

———. 1979. *Conservation for Thailand—Policy Guidelines*. Vols. 1 and 2. Morges, Switzerland: IUCN.

———. 1980. *World Conservation Strategy*. Gland, Switzerland: IUCN/UNEP/WWF.

———. 1982. *Species Conservation Priorities in the Tropical Forests of Southeast Asia*. Proceedings of a symposium held at the 58th meeting of the IUCN Species Survival Commission. Gland, Switzerland: IUCN/WWF/UNEP.

———. 1984. "Categories, Objectives and Criteria for Protected Areas." In J. A. McNeely and K. R. Miller (eds.), *National Parks, Conservation and Development*. Washington, D.C.: Smithsonian Institution Press.

———. 1985a. *Directory of Indomalayan Protected Areas—Thailand*. Protected Areas Data Unit, Conservation Monitoring Center. Gland, Switzerland: IUCN.

———. 1985b. *United Nations List of National Parks and Protected Areas*. Gland, Switzerland: IUCN.

Jakobsson, K. M., and A. K. Dragun. 1989. "The Economics of Species Preservation: Theory and Methodology." Paper presented at the Australian Agricultural Economics Society conference, Lincoln College, 6–9 February 1989.

Jintanugool, J., A. A. Eudey, and W. Y. Brockelman. 1982. "Species Conservation Priorities in Thailand." In R. A. Mittermeier and W. R. Konstant (eds.), *Species Conservation Priorities in the Tropical Forests of Southeast Asia*. IUCN Species Survival Commission, Occasional Paper no. 1. Gland, Switzerland: IUCN.

John Taylor & Sons, Redecon Australia Pty. Ltd., Asian Engineering Consultants Corp. Ltd., Roger Tym and Partners. 1984. *Songkhla Lake Basin Planning Study*. Bangkok: NESDB.

Jordan, C. F. 1986. "Local Effects of Tropical Deforestation." In M. E. Soule (ed.), *Conservation Biology: The Science of Scarcity and Diversity*. Sunderland, Mass.: Sinauer Associates.

Kaeochada, C. 1984. "Effects of Topography and Land-Use on Water Balance of Khao Yai National Park." M.S. thesis, Kasetsart University, Bangkok. (In Thai.)

Kanatharana, P. 1983. *Analysis of Water Quality*. Songkhla: Faculty of Science, Prince of Songkhla University.

Kasetsart University. 1982. *Khao Yai Ecosystem Project.* Vol. 1: *Surface Water Hydrology* and Vol. 3: *Soil and Vegetation.* Bangkok: Kasetsart University.

_____. 1985. *Tourist Development in Nakhorn Ratchasima Province.* Report to the Tourism Authority of Thailand. Bangkok: Kasetsart University.

_____. 1987. *Assessment of National Parks, Wildlife Sanctuaries and Other Preserves Development in Thailand.* Bangkok: Kasetsart University.

Kellert, S. R. 1984. "Assessing Wildlife and Environmental Values in Cost-Benefit Analysis." *Journal of Environmental Management* 18:355–363.

Khomkris, T. 1965. *Forestry in Thailand.* Bangkok: Faculty of Forestry, Kasetsart University.

Kim, S., and J. A. Dixon. 1986. "Economic Valuation of Environmental Quality Aspects of Upland Agricultural Projects in Korea." In J. A. Dixon and M. M. Hufschmidt (eds.), *Economic Valuation Techniques for the Environment.* Baltimore: Johns Hopkins University Press.

Knetsch, J. L., and J. A. Sinden. 1987. "The Persistence of the Valuation Disparity." *Quarterly Journal of Economics* 102:691–695.

Krutilla, J. V., and A. C. Fisher. 1985. *The Economics of Natural Environments: Studies in the Valuation of Commodity and Amenity Resources.* 2nd ed. Washington, D.C.: Resources for the Future.

Kutay, K. 1989. "The New Ethics in Adventure Travel." *Buzzworm* 1(4):31–36.

Laarman, J. G., and R. R. Perdue. 1988. *Tropical Science as Economic Activity: OTS in Costa Rica.* Forestry Private Enterprise Initiative Working Paper no. 33. Research Triangle Park, N.C.: Southeastern Center for Forest Economics Research.

Lausche, B. J. 1980. *Guidelines for Protected Areas Legislation.* Gland, Switzerland: IUCN.

Ledec, G., and R. Goodland. 1988. *Wildlands: Their Protection and Management in Economic Development.* Washington, D.C.: World Bank.

Loomis, J. B., and R. G. Walsh. 1986. "Assessing Wildlife and Environmental Values in Cost-Benefit Analysis: State of the Art." *Journal of Environmental Management* 22:125–131.

Machlis, G. E., and D. L. Tichnell. 1985. *The State of the World's Parks.* Boulder and London: Westview Press.

_____. 1987. "Economic Development and Threats to National Parks: A Preliminary Analysis." *Environmental Conservation* 14(2):151–156.

MacKinnon, J., and K. MacKinnon. 1986. *Review of the Protected Area System in the Indo-Malayan Realm.* Gland, Switzerland: IUCN.

MacKinnon, J., K. Mackinnon, G. Child, and J. Thorsell. 1986. *Managing Protected Areas in the Tropics.* Gland, Switzerland: IUCN.

Malik, A. 1984. "Protected Areas and Political Reality." In J. A. McNeely and K. R. Miller (eds.), *National Parks, Conservation and Development.* Washington, D.C.: Smithsonian Institution Press.

McElroy, J., and K. de Albuquerque. 1989. "Tourism Styles and Policy Responses in the Open Economy–Closed Environment Context." Paper presented at the Caribbean Conservation Association Conference on Economics and the Environment, 6–8 November 1989, Barbados.

McNeely, J. A. 1984. "Protected Areas Are Adapting to Reality." In J. A. McNeely and K. R. Miller (eds.), *National Parks, Conservation and Development*. Washington, D.C.: Smithsonian Institution Press.

_____. 1988. *Economics and Biological Diversity: Developing and Using Economic Incentives to Conserve Biological Resources*. Gland, Switzerland: IUCN.

McNeely, J. A., and K. R. Miller, eds. 1984. *National Parks, Conservation and Development: The Role of Protected Areas in Sustaining Society*. Washington, D.C.: Smithsonian Institution Press.

McNeely, J. A., and J. W. Thorsell, eds. 1985. *People and Protected Areas in the Hindu Kush Himalaya*. Kathmandu: ICIMOD.

McNeely, J. A., K. R. Miller, and J. W. Thorsell. 1987. "Objectives, Selection and Management of Protected Areas in Tropical Forest Habitats." In C. W. Marsh and R. A. Mittermeier (eds.), *Primate Conservation in the Tropical Rain Forest*. New York: Alan R. Liss.

Messerli, B. 1978. "Climatological, Pedological and Geomorphological Process in Tropical Mountain Ecosystems." In *Proceedings of Workshop on Agro-Forestry and Highland-Lowland Interactive Systems*, 13–17 November, Chiangmai, Thailand. NRTS-3/UNDP-77. Tokyo: United Nations University.

Miller, J. R., and F. Lad. 1984. "Flexibility, Learning and Irreversibility in Environmental Decisions: A Bayesian Approach." *Journal of Environmental Economics and Management* 11:161–172.

Miller, K. R. 1978. *Planning National Parks for Ecodevelopment*. Ann Arbor: University of Michigan.

Mitchell, R. C., and R. T. Carson. 1989. *Using Surveys to Value Public Goods: The Contingent Valuation Method*. Washington, D.C.: Resources for the Future.

Moore, A. W. 1984. *Operations Manual for a Protected Area System*. FAO Conservation Guide no. 9. Rome: FAO.

Myers, N. 1981. "The Exhausted Earth." *Foreign Policy* 42:141–155.

_____. 1983. *A Wealth of Wild Species*. Boulder: Westview Press.

Nachiangmai, N. 1980. *Annual Report on Water Quality of Inner Lake Songkhla*. Bangkok: Office of the National Environment Board.

National Parks Division (NPD). 1986. *Khao Yai National Park Management Plan 1987–1991*. Bangkok: National Parks Division, Royal Forest Department.

_____. Various years. *Statistics*. Bangkok: Royal Forest Department.

OAS/NPS. 1988. *Inventory of Caribbean Marine and Coastal Protected Areas*. Washington, D.C.: Organization of American States/National Park Service.

Oldfield, S. 1988. "Buffer Zone Management in Tropical Moist Forests." *IUCN Tropical Forest Papers* 5:1–49.

ONEB. 1986. *Eastern Seaboard—Regional Environmental Management Plan*. Bangkok: Office of the National Environment Board.

Palca, J. 1987. "High Finance Approach to Protecting Tropical Forests." *Nature* 328:373.

Pearce, D. W. 1983. "Ethics, Irreversibility, Future Generations and the Social Rate of Discount." *Journal of Environmental Studies* 22:67–86.

Peters, C. M., A. H. Gentry, and R. O. Mendelsohn. 1989. "Valuation of an Amazonian Rainforest." *Nature* 339:655–656.

Peterson, G. L., and A. Randall, eds. 1984. *Valuation of Wildlands Resource Benefits*. Boulder: Westview Press.

Posner, B., C. Cuthbertson, E. Towle, and C. Reeder. 1981. *Economic Impact Analysis for the Virgin Islands National Park*. St. Thomas: Island Resources Foundation.

Randall, A. 1983. "The Problem of Market Failure." *National Resources Journal* 23(1):131–148.

———. 1986. "Human Preferences, Economics, and the Preservation of Species." In B. Norton (ed.), *The Preservation of Species: The Value of Biological Diversity*. Princeton: Princeton University Press.

Randall, A., and G. L. Peterson. 1984. "The Valuation of Wildland Benefits: An Overview." In G. L. Peterson and A. Randall (eds.), *Valuation of Wildlands Resource Benefits*. Boulder: Westview Press.

Repetto, R. C. 1988. *The Forest for the Trees? Government Policy and the Misuse of Forest Resources*. Washington, D.C.: World Resources Institute.

RFD. 1986. *Forest Area of Thailand from LANDSAT Imagery in 1986*. Bangkok: Royal Forest Department.

———. Various years. *Forestry Statistics of Thailand*. Bangkok: Planning Division, Royal Forest Department.

Rittbhonbhun, N., and others. 1983. *Yield of Capture Fishery in Thale Noi*. Songkhla: Prince of Songkhla University.

Rogers, C. S., L. McLain, and E. S. Zullo. 1988. "Recreational Uses of Marine Resources in the Virgin Islands National Park and Biosphere Reserve: Trends and Consequences." Biosphere Reserve Research Report no. 24. St. Thomas: VINP.

Round, P. D. 1985. *The Status and Conservation of Resident Forest Birds in Thailand*. Bangkok: Association for the Conservation of Wildlife.

Royal Irrigation Department. 1985. *Sediment Survey of Lam Takhong Reservoir*. Hydrology Report no. 698/85. Bangkok: Division of Hydrology, Royal Irrigation Department. (In Thai.)

Ruitenbeek, H. J. 1989. *Social Cost-Benefit Analysis of the Korup Project, Cameroon*. London: World Wide Fund for Nature.

Runte, A. 1979. *National Parks: The American Experience*. Lincoln: University of Nebraska Press.

Samuelson, P. A. 1954. "The Pure Theory of Public Expenditure." *Review of Economics and Statistics* 36:387–389.

———. 1955. "Diagrammatic Exposition of a Theory of Public Expenditure." *Review of Economics and Statistics* 37:550–556.

Santiapillai, C., M. Soekarno, and W. Sukohadi. 1987. "Management of Elephants in Thailand." *Tigerpaper* 14(2):7–14.

Schankerman, M., and A. Pakes. 1986. "Estimates of the Value of Patent Rights in European Countries During the Post–1950 Period." *Economic Journal* 96:1052–1076.

Schonewald-Cox, C., and others. 1983. *Genetics and Conservation: A Reference for Managing Wild Animal and Plant Populations*. Menlo Park, Calif.: Benjamin/Cummings.

Sedjo, R. A. 1988. "Property Rights and the Protection of Plant Genetic Resources." In J. R. Kloppenburg (ed.), *Seeds and Sovereignty: The Use and Control of Plant Genetic Resources*. Durham, N.C.: Duke University Press.

Sherman, P. B. 1988. "The Economics of Protected Areas in Developing Countries." Unpublished manuscript, University of Hawaii.

Sherman, P. B., and J. A. Dixon. 1989. *Economics of Protected Areas in Developing Countries: General Issues and Examples from Thailand*. Honolulu: East-West Center, Environment and Policy Institute.

Sherpa, L. N. 1988. *Conserving and Managing Biological Resources in Sagarmatha (Mt. Everest) National Park, Nepal*. EAPI Working Paper no. 8. Honolulu: East-West Center, Environment and Policy Institute.

Skin Diver. 1987. 1987 Subscriber Survey.

Smith, V. K., and J. V. Krutilla. 1979. "Endangered Species, Irreversibilities, and Uncertainty: A Comment." *American Journal of Agricultural Economics* 61:371–375.

Sriburi, T. 1986. "Forest Resources Crisis in Thailand." In *Proceedings of the Conference on Forest Resources Crisis in the Third World*, 6–8 September, Penang, Malaysia. Penang: Sahabat Alam Malaysia.

Srikosamatara, S. 1980. "Ecology and Behavior of the Pileated Gibbon (*Hylobates pileatus*) in Khao Soi Dao Wildlife Sanctuary, Thailand." M.S. thesis, Mahidol University, Bangkok.

Srivardhana, R. 1986. "The Nam Pong Water Resources Project in Thailand." In J. A. Dixon and M. M. Hufschmidt (eds.), *Economic Valuation Techniques for the Environment*. Baltimore: Johns Hopkins University Press.

Tangtham, N. 1988. "A Review of Hydrological and Watershed Impacts of Khao Yai National Park." Unpublished manuscript, Kasetsart University, Bangkok.

Tansakul, P. 1983a. *Biomass in Thale Noi*. Songkhla: Prince of Songkhla University.

————. 1983b. *Utilization of Aquatic Plants in Thale Noi (Lake Songkhla)*. Songkhla: Prince of Songkhla University.

TDRI. 1987. *Thailand Natural Resources Profile*. Bangkok: Thailand Development Research Institute.

Thorsell, J. W., ed. 1985. *Conserving Asia's Natural Heritage*. Gland, Switzerland: IUCN.

Thresher, P. 1981. "The Economics of a Lion." *UNASYLVA* 33(134):34–35.

TISTR. 1982. *Ecological Studies for Conservation of Shore Birds in Songkhla Lake*. Vol. 2: *Conservation Plan*. Bangkok: Thailand Institute of Scientific and Technological Research, Ecological Research Division.

Touche Ross. 1984. *Kangaroo Island National Parks Cost-Benefit Study.* Adelaide: Touche Ross Services.

United Nations. 1974. Resolution 3281 (XXIX). Sixth Special Session of the United Nations General Assembly. New York: United Nations.

United States Agency for International Development (U.S.A.I.D.). 1987. *Manual for Project Economic Analysis.* Washington, D.C.: U.S.A.I.D., Bureau for Program and Policy Coordination.

van't Hof, T. 1985. "The Economic Benefits of Marine Parks and Protected Areas in the Caribbean Region." In *Proceedings of the Fifth International Coral Reef Congress,* 27 May–1 June, Tahiti.

————. 1989. "Making Marine Parks Self-Sufficient: The Case of Saba." Paper presented at the Conference on Economics and the Environment, November 6–8, Barbados.

Vickland, K. 1989. " 'New' Tourists Want 'New' Destinations." *Travel and Tourism Executive Report* 9 (October):1–4.

Wells, M. P. 1989. *Can Indonesia's Biological Diversity Be Protected by Linking Economic Development with National Park Management? Three Case Studies from the Outer Islands.* Washington, D.C.: World Bank, Environment Department.

Western, D. 1984. "Amboseli National Park: Human Values and the Conservation of a Savanna Ecosystem." In J. A. McNeely and K. R. Miller (eds.), *National Parks, Conservation and Development.* Washington, D.C.: Smithsonian Institution Press.

Western, D., and W. Henry. 1979. "Economics and Conservation in Third World National Parks." *Bioscience* 29(7):414–418.

Western, D., and P. Thresher. 1973. *Development Plans for Amboseli.* Nairobi: World Bank.

Wildlife Conservation Division. Various years. *Statistics.* Bangkok: Royal Forest Department.

Wilkes, H. G. 1987. "Plant Genetic Resources: Why Privatize a Public Good?" *Bioscience* 37(3):215–218.

Wilson, E. O., ed. 1988. *Biodiversity.* Washington, D.C.: National Academy Press.

World Resources Institute. 1989. *Natural Endowments: Financing Resource Conservation for Development.* Washington, D.C.: World Resources Institute.

World Wide Fund for Nature (WWF). 1987. *The Korup Project, Cameroon.* Gland, Switzerland: WWF.

World Wildlife Fund. 1989a. "A Program to Save the African Elephant." *World Wildlife Fund Letter* 2:1–12.

————. 1989b. "WWF and Madagascar Swap Debt for Nature." *Focus* 11(5):1–3.

Index

ABOUT THE AUTHORS

JOHN DIXON was a research associate at the East-West Center's Environment and Policy Institute from 1981 to 1990. As leader of the applied economics research activity, he was involved in both methodological studies on the process of economic valuation and applied work on various resources including ground and surface water, drylands, mangroves, protected areas, and watersheds. Co-author or co-editor of eight books on these topics, Dr. Dixon has taught and consulted widely for various national and international organizations. His undergraduate degrees are from the University of California at Berkeley (economics and Chinese) and his doctorate in economics is from Harvard University.

Although he has lived or worked in Asia over most of the past 25 years, Dr. Dixon spent his middle-school years in Puerto Rico. In mid-1990 he joined the World Bank as environmental economist, Latin America and Caribbean Region.

PAUL SHERMAN is a resource economist with advanced degrees in both environmental management (Duke University School of Forestry and Environmental Studies) and economics (Ph.D., University of Hawaii). From 1981 to 1983, he was a research assistant at Resources for the Future in Washington, D.C. In 1983 he joined the Economic Analysis of Nature Resources Program at the East-West Center's Environment and Policy Institute in Honolulu, where he remained until mid-1990. He has also worked as a consultant to U.S.A.I.D. on protected-area issues in Thailand and Indonesia. Currently, Dr. Sherman lives in Honolulu and works as an economist for the Hawaiian state government, focusing primarily on issues of growth and economic development.

ALSO AVAILABLE FROM ISLAND PRESS

Ancient Forests of the Pacific Northwest
By Elliott A. Norse

The Challenge of Global Warming
Edited by Dean Edwin Abrahamson

The Complete Guide to Environmental Careers
The CEIP Fund

Creating Successful Communities: A Guidebook for Growth Management Strategies
By Michael A. Mantell, Stephen F. Harper, and Luther Propst

Crossroads: Environmental Priorities for the Future
Edited by Peter Borrelli

Environmental Agenda for the Future
Edited by Robert Cahn

Environmental Restoration: Science and Strategies for Restoring the Earth
Edited by John J. Berger

The Forest and the Trees: A Guide to Excellent Forestry
By Gordon Robinson

Forests and Forestry in China: Changing Patterns of Resource Development
By S. D. Richardson

From The Land
Edited and compiled by Nancy P. Pittman

Hazardous Waste Management: Reducing the Risk
By Benjamin A. Goldman, James A. Hulme, and Cameron Johnson
for Council on Economic Priorities

Land and Resource Planning in the National Forests
By Charles F. Wilkinson and H. Michael Anderson

Last Stand of the Red Spruce
By Robert A. Mello

Natural Resources for the 21st Century
Edited by R. Neil Sampson and Dwight Hair

The New York Environment Book
By Eric Goldstein and Marc Izeman

Overtapped Oasis: Reform or Revolution for Western Water
By Marc Reisner and Sarah Bates

Permaculture
By Bill Mollison

The Poisoned Well: New Strategies for Groundwater Protection
Edited by Eric Jorgensen

Race to Save the Tropics: Ecology and Economics for a Sustainable Future
Edited by Robert Goodland

Reforming the Forest Service
By Randal O'Toole

Reopening the Western Frontier
From *High Country News*

Research Priorities for Conservation Biology
Edited by Michael E. Soule and Kathryn Kohm

Resource Guide for Creating Successful Communities
By Michael A. Mantell, Stephen F. Harper, and Luther Propst

Rivers at Risk: The Concerned Citizen's Guide to Hydropower
By John D. Echeverria, Pope Barrow, and Richard Roos-Collins

Rush to Burn: Solving America's Garbage Crisis?
From *Newsday*

Saving the Tropical Forests
By Judith Gradwohl and Russell Greenberg

Shading Our Cities: A Resource Guide for Urban and Community Forests
Edited by Gary Moll and Sara Ebenreck

War on Waste: Can America Win Its Battle with Garbage?
By Louis Blumberg and Robert Gottlieb

Western Water Made Simple
From *High Country News*

Wildlife of the Florida Keys: A Natural History
By James D. Lazell, Jr.

For further information about Island Press, our titles, or ordering information, please call our toll-free number, 1-800-828-1302.